TONIGHT WE DIE AS MEN

The untold story of Third Battalion 506 Parachute
Infantry Regiment from Toccoa to D-Day

OSPREY
PUBLISHING

TONIGHT WE DIE AS MEN

The untold story of Third Battalion 506 Parachute
Infantry Regiment from Toccoa to D-Day

IAN GARDNER & ROGER DAY
FOREWORD BY ED SHAMES

First published in Great Britain in 2009 by Osprey Publishing,
Midland House, West Way, Botley, Oxford OX2 0PH, United Kingdom.
443 Park Avenue South, New York, NY 10016, USA.
Email: info@ospreypublishing.com

A CIP catalog record for this book is available from the British Library.

ISBN 978 1 84603 322 3

Page layout by Myriam Bell Design, France
Index by Alan Thatcher
Typeset in Bembo and Myriad Pro
Originated by PPS Grasmere Ltd., Leeds, UK
Printed in China through Worldprint

09 10 11 12 13   10 9 8 7 6 5 4 3

For a catalog of all books published by Osprey please contact:

NORTH AMERICA
Osprey Direct, c/o Random House Distribution Center
400 Hahn Road, Westminster, MD 21157, USA
E-mail: uscustomerservice@ospreypublishing.com

ALL OTHER REGIONS
Osprey Direct, The Book Service Ltd, Distribution Centre, Colchester Road,
Frating Green, Colchester, Essex, CO7 7DW
E-mail: customerservice@ospreypublishing.com

www.ospreypublishing.com

Photographs not otherwise credited in the text are from the authors' collections
or the Currahee Scrapbook.
Front cover image Signal Corps courtesy Michel de Trez Collection
Back cover and flaps image courtesy John Reeder via Roger Day Collection

Contents

3426

Foreword

Please allow me to introduce you to the most detailed history ever written about the battles that began the drive to free the European continent of the German armies. If you are a student of history, especially World War II history, and the battle for Normandy is of interest to you, then prepare yourself for an experience very few readers have yet known.

Many books and accounts have been written about the invasion of Normandy, but never have you read one that has been more accurate about the facts and events of this period of warfare. What makes me qualified to know what happened during the battle and the involvement of the 506th Parachute Infantry Regiment of the 101st Airborne Division? I was there from the birth of the 506th at Toccoa, Georgia, in early September 1942, and participated in every battle from the jump into Normandy to the capture of Berchtesgaden in May 1945.

As the operations sergeant of the 3rd Battalion 506th, it was my responsibility to construct "sand tables" for the purposes of briefing the entire battalion as to where they would land and assemble. I also had to point out each company's battle objectives once they had regrouped on the ground into fighting units.

Many times since the war years, I have walked over the grounds and hedgerows of Normandy, and have been privileged on several such occasions to do so with the authors of this book.

My dear friends Ian Gardner and Roger Day have meticulously researched Ramsbury and the battle for Normandy to such a fine degree that no other historical record can be anywhere near the accuracy of truth and events. As part of this historical masterpiece, there are remarkably detailed maps and charts that allow the reader to retrace the steps and movements of the paratroopers as they fought to secure

Normandy and its place in history. When I read their manuscript I felt that I was again in my parachute and beginning my odyssey of World War II that started with my touchdown in Carentan, Normandy, France. This book is truly a work of historical art.

Edward D. Shames – June 2008
Virginia Beach, Virginia, USA

Introduction

Six years ago, an English history fan named Ian Gardner read my first book, *The 101st Airborne at Normandy*. Ian himself is a former paratrooper in the post-World War II British Army and for some reason he became fixated on the subject matter of Chapter 22 of my book, which deals with 3rd Battalion 506th Parachute Infantry Regiment, and their D-Day objective, the wooden bridges near Brévands, France.

This launched Ian on a lengthy research project, driven by an obsession to learn as much detail as possible about this event, by contacting every available survivor of 3rd Bn and hearing their testimony. Ian also searched out obscure, detailed maps, studied vintage aerial photos, walked the ground many times, and did a good deal of detective work. What you will read between these covers is the result of Ian's research, the fulfillment of an original and valuable research project.

Ian's colleague Roger Day, a consummate historian of the wartime history of Ramsbury, England (and the author of a book and website on that subject), has been on board with Ian since the start of his 3rd Bn 506th research. For five years, they walked the ground together, puzzled over new evidence, and collected facts and stories, and Roger's writing skills made presentation of the final manuscript possible. So this book is very much a joint product of their teamwork.

This is not just another anthology of World War II stories, resulting from the labors of many other historians and disguised as an original presentation. As an avid reader (as well as producer) of World War II books, I enthusiastically endorse this book as a product of original research and an important contribution to the literature. In its pages, many new stories and facts will be revealed. Also, any work encompassing many years of investigation, fueled by obsession and produced as a labor of love, has got to be worthwhile.

Two bridges, installed by the occupying German forces in Normandy, crossed the Douve river east of Carentan, France, about 1 mile apart. These became a significant objective in Allied D-Day planning. The Germans had installed these bridges in 1943–44 for tactical purposes; they allowed the German defenders (in the event of Allied landings) to rush replacements to defend the strip of east Cotentin coastline that Allied planners had designated as "Utah Beach." The mission of LtCol Robert L. Wolverton's battalion was simply to seize control of these bridges as soon as possible after parachuting in to Drop Zone D, and prevent German reinforcements from crossing toward the coast by any means necessary. The series of events that resulted when this plan was put into action is the subject of this work.

The assigned battalion suffered grievous losses on the drop zone, and only a small percentage of it found their way to the objective. The decimation of Wolverton's battalion (both he and his executive officer were among those killed) is described in this book in terms of personal human loss. Despite their casualties, the small percentage of 3rd Bn 506th paratroopers who survived were able to accomplish their mission of controlling the bridges and preventing the enemy from crossing them in order to reinforce the Nazi coastal defenders.

After the war moved on toward Germany, the French required the removal of the bridges, because their presence prevented seaborne commerce from entering the small port in Carentan from the Channel. So after Allied planes bombed the center out of each bridge, the French continued the removal job, doing it so thoroughly that only small remnants of the original bridge footings remain. By walking the north bank of the Douve river for miles in 2003, Ian Gardner and Roger Day located those crucial pieces of evidence, which had eluded me and other researchers for half a century. The significance of the physical evidence they discovered was important, proving that previous published references to the placement of the foot and road bridge respectively were in error. In my previous books they are transposed, because I followed the information marked on the map of the 506th regimental S3 officer, Maj H.W. Hannah, which showed the road bridge closer to the Channel, when in fact it was the one nearer to Carentan. One reason for this is that Maj Hannah himself never physically visited the 3rd Bn objective, nor did he stand in view of either bridge during the Normandy campaign. Here is an example of ostensibly reliable information proving to be inaccurate.

I had learned while researching the La Barquette lock battle that the devil is indeed in the detail. The deeper one delves into any historical event, the more questions arise and the more contradictory evidence surfaces. No two participants in any battle seem to agree on all of the details that transpired. While researching this work, Ian and Roger have also discovered that certain disputed details will never be fully resolved.

We should regard this work as an amazingly detailed glimpse into the tragic experiences of this heroic parachute battalion. I am pleased that reading my earlier work served as the impetus that launched Ian on his mission to discover so much more about the saga of LtCol Wolverton's 3rd Bn 506th and the wooden bridges of D-Day. Had he not embarked on his investigation when he did, the mortality rate of our World War II veterans would have ensured that much of this information would have been lost forever. This slice of history, collected and preserved by Ian Gardner and Roger Day, can now be added to the complex mosaic that was the battle of Normandy.

The chaos and complexity of those times is still being gradually sorted out, but, sadly, the time is rapidly approaching when we will be unable to consult World War II survivors for this kind of firsthand testimony. I applaud both Ian and Roger for their dedicated achievement, and I would urge all who are students of the Normandy invasion to read this important historical compendium of fact and personal experience.

Mark Bando – June 2008
Detroit, Michigan, USA

Preface

As a former British paratrooper, I have always been interested in the history of airborne warfare. In early 2001, whilst visiting my local bookshop, I picked up a publication entitled *101st Airborne at Normandy* by Mark A. Bando. This seminal work was the start of a journey that changed my life forever. I have no idea what made me purchase the book, and never in my wildest dreams ever imagined that its respected author would become a personal friend.

I read it again and again until the pages were ragged and worn, but kept coming back to Chapter 22, "The Wooden Bridges at Brévands." Something in Mark's writing captured my imagination. I wanted to learn more, and began reading other books about the 101st Airborne Division. I soon discovered that little had been written about the actions of 3rd Bn, 506th Parachute Infantry Regiment, the unit responsible for the capture of the bridges. It became apparent that their entire Normandy campaign had been largely overlooked, due to a complete lack of historical comprehension and battlefield appreciation. It seemed almost inconceivable that previous historians had failed to grasp the significance of, and recognize, the accomplishments of these incredibly brave men – they were truly D-Day's forgotten battalion.

In March 2002 I went to Normandy for the first time, accompanied by my wife Karen. We visited many sites described in Mark's book but failed to locate the remains of the two bridges at Brévands, which merely served to fuel my growing interest. After returning home, two important things happened – meeting Roger Day and finding out about the World War II Aerial Photographic Archive at Keele University in Staffordshire.

I became aware of Roger after he appeared in an "After The Battle" publication sporting a helmet worn in Normandy by Sgt "Gil" Morton, a member of 3rd Bn, who had been billeted with Roger's relatives in Ramsbury. On a hunch I went to the village and eventually found his brother, who kindly passed on my details. Roger rang me a few days later and told me that he had written a wartime history of the village called *Ramsbury at War,* and that it was a refreshing change to talk about something other than "Band of Brothers." The BBC had recently broadcast the TV miniseries, and he had been inundated with emails and telephone calls from people trying to tap into his knowledge of the 506th in England. As a result of the global success of "Band of Brothers," E Co had taken the lion's share of the limelight, and I wanted to redress the balance and bring more of the 506th story, notably 3rd Bn's contribution, to the public's attention.

The second defining moment was the day I visited the Air Photo Archive at Keele University. There, to my amazement, I discovered that all previous 101st Airborne Division histories had recorded the locations of the foot and road bridges at Brévands the wrong way round! The photographic evidence was compelling, and I knew that I was on to something – shortly afterwards I approached Roger with the idea of writing this book.

Our research took four years to complete, and during that time we forged many good friendships with people in the United States, France and Britain. In April 2003 Roger, his son Christopher, Joe Beyrle II (son of a 3rd Bn veteran), and I visited Normandy. Our initial studies centered on the fields surrounding the village of St-Côme-du-Mont, and this brought us into contact with Michel Léonard. Michel was interested in what we were doing and invited us into his home, where he and his wife Martine plied us with Calvados. We learnt that his family were residents of St-Côme-du-Mont at the time of the invasion, and it soon became obvious that Michel was in a great position to help us with our research. However, there was one big problem – the language barrier!

Several months later I attended a family party at which my English-born cousin Susan Rochat was present, and fate played its hand. Susy has lived in Switzerland with her Swiss-born husband and two children for nearly 30 years and speaks fluent French. After some tough negotiating she agreed to act as our translator, and so the "French connection" was established.

Acknowledgments

This section has been one of the hardest parts of the book to compile, as we were anxious not to forget any of our many contributors. If anyone's name has been overlooked we hope that they will accept our sincere apologies.

Individual thanks are extended by country to the following. **United States of America:** Miles Allen (G Co), Alex Andros (H Co), Fred Bahlau (H Co), Manny Barrios (I Co), Joe Beyrle (I Co), Ralph Bennett (H Co), Kathy Bennett, Dave Berry, Lurie Berteau (G Co), Dr James Bigley, Judith Grant-Botter, Tom Bucher (HQ Co Machine Gun Ptn), Sharon Bunker, Roy Burger (HQ Co 81mm Mortar Ptn), Ray Calandrella (Co HQ), Mario "Hank" DiCarlo (H Co), Joe Doughty (G Co), Bob Dunning (HQ Co 81mm Mortar Ptn), George Dwyer (HQ Co Machine Gun Ptn), Bette Dziepak, Teddy Dziepak (I Co), Arthur "Bud" Estes (H Co), Bill Galbraith (I Co), Johnny Gibson (Medical Detachment), Lenny Goodgal (I Co), George Grant Jr, Clark Heggeness (H Co), Randy Hils, Ben Hiner (Co HQ S1), Ken Johnson (H Co), Tom Kennedy (G Co), John Klein, Laurie Kotsch, John Kutz (C Co 326th Airborne Engineers), Alfred Lowe (207th Combat Engineers), Walt Lukasavage (I Co), Mary Madden, Pete Madden (H Co), Chris Malterre, Jimmy Martin (G Co), Clair Mathiason (G Co), Sid McCallum (I Co), Jim McCann (H Co), Pat McCann, George McMillan (I Co), John Merkt, Tim Moore, David Morgan (I Co), Neil and Dai Morgan, "Gil" Morton (HQ Co 81mm Mortar Ptn), Mary Lou Neally, Don Orcutt (440th Troop Carrier Group), Marykay Perez, John Reeder (Regimental Communications Ptn), Bobbie Rommel (HQ Co Machine Gun Ptn), George Rosie (HQ Co 81mm Mortar Ptn), Don Ross (Co HQ S3), Barney Ryan (assistant 3rd Bn surgeon), Harold Stedman (I Co), Jay Stone (321st Glider Field Artillery), Bob Webb (Co HQ S4 Supply), Bob Webb Jr, Lou Vecchi (H Co), and Don Zahn (H Co). **France:** Msr and

Mme Brohier, Charles Carel, André Descamps, Charles Destrès, Michel DeTrez, Thérèse Dieudonné, Msr and Mme Drouin, Msr Dumoncel, Eugéne Enot, Thierry Ferey, Maurice de Folleville, Philippe Frigot, William Hébert, Nicole Laurence, Amand Laurent, Léon Lehay, Jean Pierre Lemesnil, Michel and Martine Léonard, Louis Letourneur, Paulette Menilgrente, Jean Mignon, Msr and Mme Poisson, Msr La Rue, Jean Savary and Henry Villand. **United Kingdom:** Rosemary Connor, Elsie Douglas, Robert Dudley (our literary agent), Patricia Howard, John Mundy, Doreen Ramsden, Monica Tovey, and Graeme Trim.

Sadly, during the course of our research ten of our veteran contributors have passed away: Joe Beyrle, Ray Calandrella, Clark Heggeness, Ben Hiner, Jim McCann, Dave Morgan, Gil Morton, George Rosie, Don Ross, and Barney Ryan – God bless you boys. We hope that in some small way our book helps keep alive your memories for future historians who follow in our tracks.

We would also like to thank News International Syndication, London for permission to use Ward Smith's article "I Saw Them Jump to Destiny," and John Shank, editor of *Military Magazine*, for permission to use quotations from Charles Santarsiero's article "My Most Memorable Meeting with General McAuliffe" – December 1985.

Particular mention must be made of the assistance given by Mark Bando: for his encouragement, for his unrivalled knowledge of the 101st Airborne Division and for writing the introduction to this book, plus Susy Rochat, our French translator, and Joe Beyrle II, who, in addition to being the son of a veteran, read the manuscript several times and made many important changes and recommendations.

Finally, very special thanks are extended to Eddy Shames (Co HQ S3 operations sergeant), who helped us above and beyond the call of duty and who has become a sort of unofficial "public relations" officer for our work.

To conclude, we ask any reader who may have additional contributions, no matter how small, to write to us so that the information may be included in any further editions of this book.

∽ 1 ∾

"Hit it – 13 weeks of pain"
Creation of the 506th PIR

Toccoa

The 506th Parachute Infantry Regiment was activated at Camp Toombs (later renamed Camp Toccoa), Georgia, on July 20, 1942, and was commanded by Col Robert Frederick Sink. Sink was born in 1905 at Lexington, North Carolina. His interest in the military began as a teenager after spending hours listening to relatives and friends recount their World War I experiences. In 1923 Sink entered the military academy at West Point and graduated four years later. He served in the infantry until 1940, when he heard about the formation of a parachute test platoon. The platoon made its first jump on August 14, and in the middle of September the War Department authorized the establishment of the 501st Parachute Battalion. Sink immediately volunteered, and served as a captain under Maj William M. Miley. He was then given the task of activating the 506th Parachute Infantry Regiment (PIR) and became its first commanding officer, a position he held throughout the entire war.

It was rumored at the time that senior members of the War Department's civil service had the unprecedented idea of creating a "super unit" recruited directly from the civilian population. The civil servants did not believe that the regular army could supply the quality of soldier required to fill the ranks of such a regiment. It was correctly assumed that the principle of civilian volunteers would raise the country's morale after the recent Japanese humiliations like the attack on Pearl Harbor and the invasion of the Philippines. The 506th became the first such organization, and with great energy and determination Col Sink put into effect one of the most rigorous training schedules any World War II American military unit had been required to undergo.

The regiment was divided into three battalions. The 1st was commanded by LtCol William Turner, the 2nd by LtCol Robert Strayer, and the 3rd, whose wartime exploits are the subject of this book, by LtCol Robert Wolverton. Wolverton was universally loved by his men because he put them first, even before any officer in the battalion. He was born on October 5, 1914, came from Elkins, West Virginia, and like Sink was West Point trained. He graduated from Command and General Staff School, Ft Leavenworth, Kansas, in 1942, shortly before taking command of the 3rd Bn.

Each battalion had four companies, and the 3rd's were designated HQ, G, H, and I. The regiment spent its first few months at Camp Toccoa, where 7,000 raw recruits were subjected to the grueling training regime. This was known as A Stage; it lasted 13 weeks and was designed to eliminate all but the very strongest. By the final week nearly 5,000 men had fallen by the wayside.

Cpl Martin "Marty" Clark (HQ Co) recalls his enlistment as a paratrooper:

> Shortly after arriving at an army reception center, a young officer spoke to me and about 400 other recently sworn-in soldiers about the wonders of joining the paratroopers. I was the only one who volunteered!
>
> After arriving at Camp Toccoa we were put into W Co. [This was a motley array of tents where all new recruits were sent prior to their initial physical examination. It was also where those who had failed the tests were kept prior to leaving the paratroopers for non-airborne units.] Here we were subjected to extremely rigid examinations. A history of broken bones was enough to cause exclusion, as was color-blindness. Mental requirements were also considered very important, and to pass one had to have a qualifying score equal to, or surpassing, those for officer training school. We were all very young but the youngest I knew was Charlie Price from Philadelphia, who was just 15!

Our time in W Co was blessedly short and was followed by selection to the line companies. This was a rather haphazard process. Those with prior military training, including high school Reserve Officer Training Corps and even the boy scouts, went to the 1st Bn. After the 1st Bn had all the people it needed, the 2nd Bn filled its ranks. Those of us that arrived at Toccoa in September made up 3rd Bn.

Ben Hiner (HQ Co) was 21 years old when he arrived at Toccoa. He came from Morgantown, West Virginia, had just finished a two-year college course, and was newly married. His first day at the camp was very memorable:

> I was in the orderly room when 1st Sgt James "J. P." Shirley said that the "old man" wanted to see me. I asked who the "old man" was. He told me it was Col Sink and I should get straight up to his office! When I arrived he ordered me in and said, "Hiner, can you shine brass?" I replied, slightly bemused, "Yes, sir." He then proceeded to take off his belt; for a moment I thought he was going to give me a whipping, but he simply removed the buckle and said, "Hiner, go clean it up and make it look good, son!"

When Hiner got back to his tent he told Shirley what had happened. Shirley found some brass cleaner and showed him how to polish the buckle the "army way." When they had finished it was gleaming like a new pin. Shirley wrapped it in tissue paper and jokingly told him to return it before the colonel's trousers fell down! Sink was very impressed with the results and sent Hiner on his way. Later the same day Hiner was called back to Sink's office: "I stood to attention and the colonel said, 'Soldier, we do not encourage married recruits in this unit.' Suddenly the penny began to drop, and I realized it was make or break time for me." Fortunately, Sink had been reading Hiner's file and noticed that he had some previous military experience – this, together with the way he conducted himself over the buckle, kept him in the regiment.

However, there appears to have been a degree of inconsistency interpreting this strange ruling, as Pvt Teddy Dziepak (I Co) recollects that "Chaplain John Maloney married Bette and myself in the recreation hall on Wednesday October 28, 1942. 1 Ptn paraded with rifles and crossed bayonets, and Col Sink lent us his car and driver. We were driven into town and stayed at the Hotel Albemarle on a three-day pass."

Near the camp at Toccoa stands a mountain known by its American Indian name of "Currahee," which means "Stand Alone." Pvt Ed Shames (I Co) remembers his first encounter with the mighty rock: "During the first few days we were told by our instructors that our fitness was going to be tested on the mountain, and as long as we didn't stop we would be OK – it was quite a wake-up call and a lot of recruits washed out." Several times a week the men would run the 7-mile round trip up and down the mountain, and "Currahee" became the battle cry of the 506th. Marty Clark recalls: "It was about 3½ miles up and the same down. On several occasions, following regimental reviews, we would run up and down that stupid mountain and past the reviewing stand again. I can still hear Capt 'Shifty' Feiler (regimental dentist) yelling, 'who's setting the pace?' He was in the rear with the medics of course!" Toward the end of A Stage the companies were running the mountain in under 50 minutes.

All Non-Commissioned Officers (NCOs) down to squad leader level came from the regular army and formed the initial nucleus of the regiment, known as the cadre. Pvt Hank DiCarlo (H Co) recalls:

The cadre NCOs trained us in the arts and sciences of all aspects of military life, including close-order drill, physical training, weapons instruction, and field maneuvers. Most of them were airborne volunteers and remained with us when we moved on to our airborne training phase. However, a few stayed behind as cadre for the next intake. Our 1 Ptn commander was a certain Lt Ulm, who, even to my untutored rookie perception, was a bastard in spades. As supercilious and arrogant as any Nazi officer I ever met, he would have been a big hit in Hitler's army! We were thrilled when he washed out and Lt Mehosky replaced him.

At the camp was an obstacle course that included a 20ft-high jump tower. One day Ben Hiner was waiting his turn to drop. Each man lowered himself from the platform and hung from a bar waiting for the command "Go." Hiner remembers:

It was like a production line. As soon as the guy in front hit the deck the next guy followed. Providing he rolled forward everything was fine. However when I let go and began to drop the man in front fell backward. I desperately tried to avoid him and landed very badly, smashing my feet against the toughened leather toecaps of my boots.

The directing staff on the ground saw what happened and ordered me to sort myself out. After removing my boots I could see that my toes were swollen, bleeding, and in very bad shape. I put my boots back on and finished the assault course with blood seeping through the seams. Lt Meehan pulled me to one side to take a look. One of the nails had come away and I pulled another off with my fingers. Meehan nearly passed out and immediately ordered me to the Medical Center. The big march to Fort Benning was only a week or so away, and I knew that if the medics saw my feet I would not be allowed to take part and would have to leave the regiment. I went to the latrine, washed all the blood off, and cleaned them up as best I could. My feet were so swollen that I decided the best thing to do was to go to the clothing store and exchange my boots for a larger pair. I was walking toward the store, with boots in hand, when Sink passed by in his car. He stopped, got out, and asked me what the hell was going on? Somehow I managed to throw him off the scent and carried on to the clothing store. There they exchanged my boots for a much larger pair, and these got me through the march to Benning!

Another of the new recruits was Don Ross, who eventually became the battalion's bugler. Don recalls:

Somebody in our barrack had a trumpet and was trying to blow bugle calls on it. I grabbed it and said that I could blow it better than anyone. The guys in the barrack wanted to hear what I could do and Ed Shames told me to blow Reveille, which I did together with a couple of other tunes. It was about midnight, and Shames dared me to step outside and blow taps. People started falling in as if for a morning formation. We ran back inside laughing and watched as they all looked around, wondering what was going on.

After this Don sharpened up his playing skills and got into the habit of following the camp's public address system announcements with blasts of mail, chow, and officers' calls. Because Wolverton was billeted some distance from the enlisted men's quarters, he was totally unaware of what was going on.

Some months later, whilst at Camp Mackall, Col Wolverton decided that the battalion needed a bugler. Ed Shames was now a sergeant on Wolverton's staff and told the colonel, "We've got one, sir, Pvt Ross from I Co." Wolverton sent a runner to fetch Ross. Don remembers:

I was told to report to Col Wolverton at the battalion command post in full uniform; I thought I had done something wrong. I knocked on the office door and was told to enter. On the desk was a brand new bugle and the colonel wanted to hear me blow it. I nervously asked what he wanted me to play and he named a few calls. Suddenly someone spotted Col Sink heading in our direction and I was hidden, along with the bugle, in a locker. Wolverton was worried that if Sink found out what was going on he would transfer me over to Regimental HQ. Sink came in and looked around, said a few words and left the office. Shortly after this I moved to HQ Co.

Toward the end of November the battalion marched to the Clemson Rifle Ranges, 48 miles from Toccoa. Here their marksmanship skills were honed to perfection. The visit culminated in a Skill at Arms competition, and a three-day pass was on offer to the highest scorer. On the very first day Pvt Ben Hiner, using a .30cal machine gun, hit 98 out of 100, which was HQ Co's top score. On the second day Col Sink watched as a nervous Hiner hit the bull's eye 99 times and became the battalion's best shot! Sink walked away smiling and Ben got his three-day pass. Hiner had been using guns since childhood, which explained his dexterity in this discipline. He later qualified for the

Expert Infantryman's Badge by training on several additional weapons (60mm mortar, M1 rifle, carbine and pistol).

After the competition Hiner, together with the rest of the battalion, marched back to Toccoa. Waiting to greet him was his wife, Ruth Anna, and mother-in-law. The pair had driven to Toccoa to be with Ben for Thanksgiving and had booked themselves into a local hotel for the weekend. It was a wonderful surprise for Hiner, and came as a welcome break from all the training.

Fort Benning

In December, following basic training, the regiment moved to Fort Benning, Georgia, and the journey was turned into an endurance test that became 3rd Bn's crowning glory. Marty Clark describes the move:

> The 1st Bn went by train from Toccoa to Benning. The 2nd took three days to walk to Atlanta, a distance of 102 miles, and then traveled the rest of the way by train. The 3rd took the train to Atlanta before marching through the streets of the city to Fort McPherson. Then, for the next four days, we did nothing but put one foot in front of the other, setting a marching record of 136 miles! The worst part of the journey for me was from the gates of Fort Benning out to the "frying pan" area – my knees almost locked. During the march Col Wolverton's feet became very swollen and he couldn't wear his boots. He marched for part of the time wearing just three or four pairs of socks! After the trek we were offered a weekend pass.

The officers and NCOs had to complete the entire distance or risk being thrown out of the unit. The minimum requirement for enlisted men was 100 miles – everyone made it. This amazing achievement smashed the previous record held by the Imperial Japanese Army, and the propaganda value in raising the profile of the US airborne soldier was incalculable.

During their time at Benning the students were always expected to run between assignments. This became known as the "Fort Benning shuffle." "The instructors couldn't match our running fitness," recalls

Hiner, "but soon discovered we were weaker in other areas like push ups and pull ups. It was the push ups that really caught us out, and somebody calculated that on one training day alone the machine-gun platoon completed over three thousand!"

All jump training took place at Benning. Here the soldiers learnt how to pack parachutes, and then made several descents from specially built 250ft-high training towers before graduating to real aircraft. Ed Shames has vivid memories of this period:

> I Co was the last class (no. 49) from the regiment to go through jump school. Because of our strenuous training at Toccoa we were in superb physical condition and were showing our instructors up – they didn't like that! For the first two qualifying jumps we packed our own parachutes, but for the following three jumps they were packed by teams drawn from our ranks, under the supervision of qualified riggers. All five jumps were made without carrying additional equipment.

After five successful drops each man was fully qualified, and to mark this achievement the men were awarded small silver jump wings. This was a very proud moment because they could now truly call themselves paratroopers. Ed continues: "After two weeks' leave we went to the Alabama frying pan area, where we made two equipment descents and our very first night drop."

Near the camp is an airstrip known as Lawson Field where most of the drops took place. Sgt Ralph Bennett (H Co) was worried about the prospect of jumping at night:

> The Chattahoochie River ran close to the perimeter road at Lawson Field and would have been bad news for anybody landing in it as it was very fast-flowing. During one night drop one of our platoon leaders mistook the perimeter road for the river. As he descended he threw away his reserve 'chute, unbuckled his harness, crossed his arms and let go when he thought he was about to hit the water. He fell some 25ft on to the road and broke both hips! Each day the battalion was expected to run 9 miles

around the same perimeter road and I remember 1st Lt Christianson pushing the platoon to its limits. I was quite small and in order to keep up had to run more quickly than the rest. The lieutenant knew I was struggling and realized that it would look bad if I dropped out in front of my men. When he thought that I'd reached my limit he ordered me to drop back and pick up stragglers – there weren't any of course! He didn't have to help me in this way but I am pleased he did. I don't think I would have been allowed to stay in the battalion on just my skills alone.

Whilst at Benning, and without Col Sink's knowledge, a notice was distributed inviting those who felt they might be officer material to attend a recruitment lecture. About 50 men from the battalion turned up to hear what was on offer, and it soon became clear that successful applicants would have to leave the 506th. Ed Shames was in attendance and recalls, "Sink came in and broke up the meeting. He was furious and told us he didn't want the team split up in this way. He said that maybe after we'd got into combat there might be opportunities for promotion, but not here and not now!"

Camp Mackall and the Tennessee maneuvers

In March 1943 the regiment moved to Camp Mackall, North Carolina. The camp was named after the first US paratrooper killed in action during World War II, Pfc John T. Mackall, who died in North Africa whilst serving with the 82nd Airborne Division. Camp Mackall was the complete opposite of both Toccoa and Benning, being a purpose-built site complete with every modern convenience including a hospital, several cinemas, and an airfield. Here training became far more realistic, and the men were taught to jump with all manner of equipment, including bazookas, light machine guns, and 60mm mortars.

It was at this time that Col Wolverton noticed Ed Shames's map reading skills, as Ed recalls:

One Friday afternoon, during the battalion's first exercise at Mackall, I was in the field with my machine-gun team. Col Wolverton was wandering around looking at the positions. He came over to me with Capt Shettle and 3 Ptn leader Fred Anderson, and started talking to the platoon. It was at this moment that he noticed my map overlays. "Can you read a map?" he asked. I replied, "Yes, sir, it's one of my hobbies." Wolverton continued, "I need men like you. How would you like to be my operations sergeant? See me on Monday morning in my office." Afterwards I said to Shettle, "Did he really mean that, sir?" Shettle replied, "If he told you to go, then go."

I walked into Wolverton's office on that Monday morning but couldn't get past 1st Sgt Shirley (the most senior NCO in HQ Co), who didn't realize that my request to see the colonel was serious. 1st Lt Alex Bobuck, the battalion adjutant, came out of another office and started giving me a hard time. Eventually Wolverton heard what was going on and called out "Bobuck, my office now." After everything was cleared up I was immediately promoted to sergeant, and a couple of days later was out of I Co and on Col Wolverton's staff.

If the men were not on training exercises, they were normally given other duties to occupy their time. Ben Hiner recounts:

On one occasion I was helping Sgt Bob Webb. Capt McKnight, our new company commander, had ordered him to work a weekend as duty sergeant. Nothing much was going on, and Webb asked me to keep an eye out while he got his head down. For some reason McKnight was looking for Webb, who was by now fast asleep on the floor under one of the bunks. McKnight had been all over the camp raising hell trying to locate him, and ended up near where Bob was sleeping. I had almost convinced him that Bob was not there when he heard snoring coming from under one of the beds. He stormed over and proceeded to kick Webb furiously until he crawled out and stood to attention. Capt McKnight really went to town on him and he was lucky to keep his stripes.

Whilst at Mackall, the 506th started producing a magazine called *Para-dice*. It was edited and published by the Special Service Office and cost 25 cents. Men from all ranks of the regiment were encouraged to contribute articles, and each monthly issue carried a couple of pages of jokes, which were often a reflection of the men's feelings about army life. For example: "A small boy was leading a donkey past an army camp. A couple of soldiers wanted to have a laugh at the lad's expense. 'Why are you holding your brother so tightly?' they asked. 'So he won't join the army,' the youngster replied without blinking an eye."

On April 7, 1943, the battalion made a jump near the small town of Hoffman, North Carolina. The weather was bad and crosswinds were gusting up to 30 knots, way beyond acceptable safety tolerances, but the jump still went ahead. Soldiers from H Co and Machine-Gun Ptn were the worst affected and men were blown all over the place. Cpl Tom Bucher remembers the incident where Pvt Earl McGrath struck the chimney of a building in the town:

> Earl had lied about his age and was only 16½ when we jumped at Hoffman – he took the chimney clean off just like a scythe would cut through wheat. When I got to him he was in a great deal of pain and was trying to remove his boot. As I cut the boot off his ankle popped just like a balloon being inflated. Although nothing was broken the only cure was rest, so they sent him home with orders to report to the nearest army hospital for periodic examinations. We pleaded with him to take this opportunity to contact Regimental HQ and tell them the truth about his age, but he ignored us and returned to duty several weeks later.

The owner of the property damaged by McGrath eventually received compensation from the US government, and many questions were asked as to why the men had been put at so much risk. McGrath subsequently became the butt of many jokes including a spoof entry in the May issue of *Para-dice*! Fortunately, although there were many casualties, nobody was killed. Pfc Teddy Dziepak from I Co also has good reason to remember the drop: "After my 'chute opened Pvt Lonnie Gavrock, who had a split panel in his 'chute, came through my risers. I was certain we would break something on landing but amazingly we both walked away unharmed."

Toward the end of May, the 3rd Bn, together with the rest of the regiment, moved westward to Camp Breckenridge to take part in what became known as the Tennessee maneuvers. The exercises started on June 5, lasted for nearly six weeks, and were the nearest thing to combat the battalion had thus far experienced. On June 10 the 506th PIR officially became part of the 101st Airborne Division.

The entire division took part in the maneuvers, and Ben Hiner spent much of his time umpiring for Capt Cole with the 502nd PIR:

We were jumping about twice a week, and on one flight I remember standing behind Cole in the aircraft's door looking at the terrain below. The area was known as Tennessee hill country, but some of those "hills" seemed like small rocky mountains to me. The drop went in with little thought to the rising and falling ground that was strewn with boulders. Tanks had driven onto the DZ [drop zone] by mistake, and it was a wonder nobody was killed. However, there were several serious injuries. One guy's 'chute only just opened as he landed; he broke both legs and was stranded on top of a rocky outcrop. A medic eventually found and looked after him for almost a week until the pair were brought down. The medic was awarded the Soldier's Medal for his actions.

Teddy Dziepak remembers dropping in the same area: "We made the lowest jump ever, at 380ft. By the time the last man exited he was close to the mountainside; one oscillation of the 'chute and you were on the ground."

During this time the weather was extremely hot, and the men learnt the importance of water conservation – some the hard way! A number of men became so thirsty that they drank from stagnant water holes and streams, forcing Col Sink to declare these places out of bounds on health grounds.

By July 1943 it was becoming clear that the regiment was desperately short of parachute-trained personnel in the 81mm mortar, machine-gun, and communication sections. Consequently men already trained in these areas were brought in from other airborne units, which did not go down too well with the original Toccoa men. Surnames starting with either R or S made up the bulk of this intake, including privates George Rosie, Francis Ronzani, Henry Ritter, and John Robbins. Another new arrival was Pvt Bobbie Rommel, who recalls his first day with the machine-gun platoon: "I was fresh out of jump training, so they put me in the ring to box with Sgt Garland 'Tex' Collier. I was good with my left jab and kept him at bay by constantly picking away at his nose. 'Tex' was considered the best in the platoon, and after that fight I had no more problems about not being trained at Toccoa!"

Preparing for shipment overseas

With the maneuvers over, the entire 506th Regiment traveled by train to Fort Bragg, North Carolina. Whilst at the camp the men were issued new weapons and uniforms, and many realized that the next move would be shipment overseas. The only question on most people's minds was the destination – would it be the Far East, North Africa, or Europe?

At about this time Ben Hiner was working in supply, when the battalion received a consignment of brand new M1A1 folding stock carbines:

When they were checked into the armory two rifles were unaccounted for. Obviously a bit of a fuss was made about the missing weapons but it soon blew over. I don't think Col Wolverton ever knew about it as Capt McKnight kept it all very quiet. Later, I found out why. It was McKnight who'd taken them! A short while later he approached me with a proposition, and offered me one of the carbines in return for my help. I couldn't believe what I was hearing! I reluctantly agreed, as he would have made my life hell if I had refused to do it. As officer in command of HQ Co he could not run the risk of being caught with a stolen weapon, and asked me to deliver one to his home in Columbus, Georgia, when I next had a weekend pass. The task went without a hitch, and shortly afterwards I did the same thing with my carbine. When I came home after the war I found that my parents had "sold" it to their next-door neighbor, who never paid them and had moved away by the time I got home.

On Saturday August 28, the 3rd Bn left Fort Bragg by train for Camp Shanks, arriving almost 24 hours later. The camp was about 30 miles up the Hudson River from New York City, and was their final staging area before embarkation. George Rosie (HQ Co) remembers, "There was no leave, lots of inspections, inoculations, and repacking. It was a frustrating time and we drank day and night." Seven days later the battalion moved out to New York harbor where it boarded His Majesty's Troop Ship (HMTS) *Samaria*. The *Samaria* was an old British Cunard liner built to carry 1,000 passengers and was now crammed with over 5,000 US troops, most leaving America for the very first time. On board, in addition to the 506th PIR, was the 327th Glider Infantry Regiment (GIR), 81st Airborne Anti-Aircraft Bn (AAA), 321st Glider Field Artillery (GFA) Battalion, and the 326th Airborne Medical Company.

Atlantic crossing

On September 5 the *Samaria* set sail, and as it left New York the men lined the ship's rails. They waved to the people on the passing ferries and watched the Statue of Liberty slip by. For some, this was the last time they would see America's shores. George Rosie remembers the crossing to England:

Troopships are the pits. You're jammed in like sardines, sleeping in triple bunks with your clothes on, getting only two meals a day, if you could call them meals! We were allowed fresh water twice daily between 7.15 and 8am, and from 6.45 to 7.30pm, which we used for shaving. Showers were salt water – better than nothing, but not much! On clear days we'd walk around the deck checking out the convoy, which was very interesting. To the right and back of us was a battleship that gave you a feeling of security. There were small cruisers scooting around between the ships checking for German U-Boats.

Sgt George "Doc" Dwyer (HQ Co) recalls one very alarming incident:

> There were 115 ships in the convoy, and they were all zigzagging to confuse the German submarines. One foggy day a few of us were standing at the stern when another ship came out of the fog heading right toward us. Bells started clanging, whistles blowing, sirens screaming, men yelling, and it looked from where we were standing that there was no way a collision could be avoided, but somehow it was. The other ship only missed us by about 40ft, and we all thought that we were going to start our war experiences by being dumped in the north Atlantic!

Pvt James McCann (H Co) has vivid memories of his Atlantic crossing: "The ship was overcrowded so we only got to sleep below deck every third day. I remember being seasick for the whole ten days it took to cross the Atlantic. At 6am the deckhands would yell out 'Out the way, Yanks, or we'll wash you overboard.' They were hosing down the decks because so many of us had been sick."

One of those who suffered was Pvt Elmer Goff (HQ Co), according to Ben Hiner: "He was so seasick on the journey over that he spent most of the voyage in a lifeboat barely able to move. He was always last man on parade during the crossing." On September 15, the *Samaria* docked at Liverpool, and as soon as the men had disembarked 1st Sgt Shirley made a roll call. "Once again Goff was not present," remembers Hiner. "Shirley called his name again and a little voice shouted from the direction of the gangway 'Present, First Sergeant.' He'd overslept and was running down the jetty burdened with his kit bag and guitar!"

As soon as they arrived at Liverpool's railway station, the soldiers boarded trains that carried them south through Britain's wartorn industrial Midlands to the rolling downland of Wiltshire. George Rosie recalls his first impressions of an English train: "They really fascinated us with their individual compartments. All had doors to the outside where you could get straight out on to the station platform."

Pfc James "Pee Wee" Martin (G Co) arrived at Hungerford station, together with the rest of the battalion, during the dark morning hours of September 16. "We were met by a sergeant from the advance party whose job it was to get us to our assigned billets. Someone asked 'Where are we?' and the sergeant said 'This is Hungerford,' with the emphasis on 'hunger.' There followed a short truck ride to Ramsbury."

2

"Time, gentlemen, please"
The 506th at Ramsbury, UK

Three weeks earlier, an advance party from the 101st Airborne Division had arrived at Liverpool aboard the SS *Louis Pasteur*. The group comprised 34 officers, three warrant officers, and 39 enlisted men, and it was their job to take over and open up a number of camps in Wiltshire and Berkshire in preparation for the division's arrival. Most of the camps were in the Kennet valley between Reading in the east and Ramsbury in the west, a distance of about 30 miles. 101st Divisional HQ was midway between these two points at Greenham Lodge near Newbury. The 506th Regiment established its command post at Littlecote House together with Regimental HQ Co and HQ Co 1st Bn. The entire 2nd Bn went to the village of Aldbourne, about 3 miles north of Ramsbury, and was joined by companies A and B. C Co found itself in the comfortable surroundings of Ramsbury Manor, and 3rd Bn was installed in huts at Camp Ramsbury. Service Co, which was in charge of the regiment's motor pool, went to Manor Farm, Froxfield, and the riggers were given quarters near the parachute packing sheds at Chilton Foliat.

The picturesque old village of Ramsbury lies beside the river Kennet, which flows eastward through water meadows bordering its southern fringe. Its population at the outbreak of war was about 1,500. Until as recently as 1986 the main focal point was an old elm tree, which had reputedly stood in the square for nearly 300 years. A mile or so to the west is Ramsbury Manor, an imposing mansion completed in 1676. A similar distance to the east is Littlecote, one of the finest examples of an early 16th-century Tudor manor house in England.

The nearest large town is Swindon, 15 miles to the north, which once boasted the largest railway locomotive manufacturing works in the world. London is 68 miles due east and the nearest railway station, Hungerford, is just an hour's train journey from the capital.

During the first half of the 20th century, the majority of Ramsbury's male population worked on the land or had occupations that were in some way linked to agriculture. Few were lucky enough to own their own homes, and many lived in ancient thatched cottages that were tied to their jobs, owned by their employers, and in many cases desperately in need of renovation.

Because of its location, far from Britain's major industrial areas, the village had received little attention from the enemy, and apart from the local civil defense organizations (for example the Home Guard, Air Raid Precautions, and Air Cadets) and the occasional army exercise, the war had, to a large extent, passed it by. However, during the spring of 1941 this rural idyll was brought to an abrupt halt when work started on the construction of Ramsbury airfield. At about the same time a camp, consisting of 17 plasterboard-type buildings and a Nissen hut, was built in a field on the northern edge of the village beside Love's Lane. On September 16, 1943, this camp became 3rd Bn's new home, and remained so throughout its entire period in England. Soon after the battalion's arrival, Col Wolverton noticed that the camp had no flagpole and nowhere to raise the "Stars and Stripes." As a matter of urgency he detailed Cpl Tom Bucher and Pfc Andy Bryan (both HQ Co) to cut down a suitable tree and erect it next to battalion headquarters.

As soon as the battalion had settled in, the men were put through a period of indoctrination. They were told about the British and their customs, with special emphasis placed upon the importance of good conduct, especially when off duty in Ramsbury. Rationing was explained, as was the complicated British money system of pounds, shillings, and pence. Until this indoctrination period had been completed, the men were confined to barracks. However, by September 18, Col Wolverton was satisfied that the men understood their limitations and allowed them off camp to explore the delights of their new English home.

Ramsbury, 1944

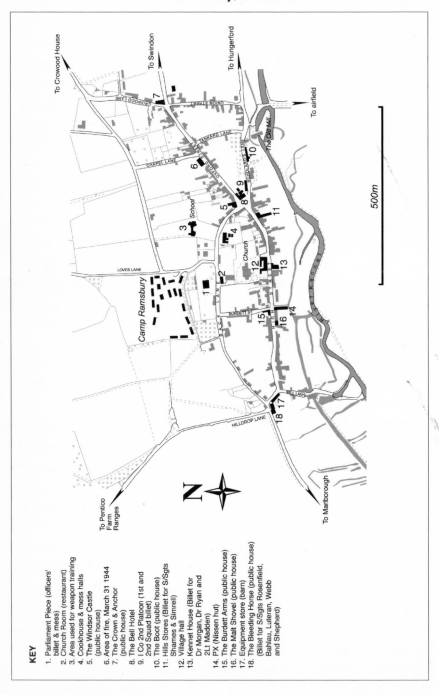

KEY

1. Parliament Piece (officers' billet & mess)
2. Church Room (restaurant)
3. Area used for weapon training
4. Cookhouse & mess halls
5. The Windsor Castle (public house)
6. Area of fire, March 31 1944
7. The Crown & Anchor (public house)
8. The Bell Hotel
9. I Co 2nd Platoon (1st and 2nd Squad billet)
10. The Boot (public house)
11. Hills Stores (Billet for S/Sgts Shames & Simrell)
12. Village hall
13. Kennet House (Billet for Dr Morgan, Dr Ryan and 2Lt Madden)
14. PX (Nissen hut)
15. The Burdett Arms (public house)
16. The Malt Shovel (public house)
17. Equipment store (barn)
18. The Bleeding Horse (public house) (Billet for S/Sgts Rosenfield, Bahlau, Luteran, Webb and Shepherd)

George Rosie remembers the first few days:

> We were quartered in barrack huts with double-tier bunks along either side of the room. The mattresses were made of canvas stuffed with straw, and until you got the straw spread out a little you had to be careful not to fall out of bed! There were four electric bulbs in each hut of very low wattage that produced insufficient light to read by, and two stoves which just about generated enough heat to prevent water from freezing.

The straw for the mattresses came from a local farmer's rick that was in a field near the camp, as Ralph Bennett recalls:

> The US Army had paid the farmer a considerable sum of money for the straw. A few days after our arrival, men returned to the rick to replenish their mattresses. When the farmer found out he demanded more money from the battalion – we couldn't believe his audacity! Late one night, while the payment issue was still under negotiation, somebody torched the entire rick. This act caused us untold problems, as nobody owned up. To pay for the damage, a fine of $10 a month was imposed on every man in the battalion for a period of six months.

Jim "Pee Wee" Martin remembers how sparsely equipped the huts were: "There was no furniture of any kind in our barracks, we each kept our clothes and other possessions in barrack bags stored between our cots." George "Doc" Dwyer remembers how radios were installed to help liven up the place: "We had brought some personal short wave radios from the States and wasted no time in getting them on air." The first station they tuned into was the German propaganda channel presented by "Axis Sally," who within days of the 506th's arrival had "warmly" welcomed them to England. The American troops enjoyed listening to the big band music "Axis Sally" played, but ignored her pathetic propaganda efforts. Jim "Pee Wee" Martin remembers the pot-bellied stoves: "Often if someone returned to the barrack hut late at night they would drop a handful of blank cartridges into the fire. Needless to say, it caused quite a stir." Each hut could accommodate one platoon comprised of three 12-man squads. In overall charge of each squad was a sergeant and his assistant.

Shortly after their arrival 1st Sgt Shirley had a very unpleasant experience, as described by Ben Hiner:

> Some of HQ Co were accommodated in one hut with Sgt Shirley sleeping nearest the door. When the battalion got its first furlough into the village every pub was drunk dry, and most returned to the camp a little worse for wear. One of the guys got up in the night and staggered bleary-eyed to where he thought the hut's toilet was located. The following morning Shirley woke to find his bed soaked in urine. Of course nobody owned up, and he had little choice but to let the incident go.

One of the huts became 3rd Bn's HQ, and was divided into a number of rooms that were used as offices. LtCol Wolverton had an office all to himself, as did his executive officer (XO – second-in-command), Maj Carl Buechner. Other members of his staff, mostly from the S3 operations section, occupied the remainder of the building. Maj Buechner was a West Point graduate and had seen military service in Panama. He considered himself a more experienced officer than Wolverton and the pair rarely saw eye to eye. Wolverton was a good organizer and quickly had everything at Ramsbury running smoothly. However, he was soon ordered away for a few days to attend a conference at Regimental HQ. Before leaving he told Buechner that on no account was he to mess with any of his systems. Ben Hiner, now a mail clerk in battalion HQ, was working in the office and recalls:

> The major nodded and told the colonel not to worry about a thing! Over the next few days Buechner totally rearranged everything, and issued the most ridiculous orders that confused all the company commanders. When the colonel returned he was as mad as hell, got straight on the phone to Col Sink, and told him that he couldn't work with Maj Buechner any longer. After a brief exchange of words, Sink agreed to replace him and transferred Maj George Grant to become 3rd Bn's new XO. Nobody in

3rd Bn knew at the time what kind of man Grant was. I think that Col Sink was playing a little game with Wolverton as the major turned out to be more of a handful than Buechner had ever been, and now we were stuck with him! Before Buechner left the battalion, I saw the colonel make a note in his personal file. He wrote, amongst other things, "This man is unfit to command troops," and I'm certain he meant every word of it.

Both 1st Lt Alex Bobuck (battalion adjutant) and 2nd Lt Jack Esco (mess officer) were also in the same office as the S3 section, as was S/Sgt Paul Simrell. Simrell was the personnel section's chief clerk, and helping him with his duties was T/5 Ray Calandrella, who was a very good typist. Calandrella enjoyed his job and had been on Wolverton's staff for more than 12 months, but things were about to change. When Grant arrived he brought with him Pfc Bill Atlee, whom he appointed the new assistant clerk. This move left Calandrella without a job: "Paul Simrell was livid, as Atlee couldn't even type," he recalls. "I was busted back to private and had to leave the staff. As I left the battalion office Col Wolverton followed me outside saying, 'Calandrella, I just want you to know that I'm not happy with this either, but it wouldn't look good if I overruled a decision from the XO at this point. Don't worry, we'll sort something out.' "

Calandrella was a sensitive and deeply religious man, and took the demotion hard. Many thought he was too nice to be a paratrooper, and he became the butt of numerous jokes, the worst being that he was a German spy! Col Wolverton was good to his word and soon found Calandrella a new job working in the assault/reconnaissance section. He recalls:

By April I had moved into the platoon billet, which was located in rooms at the back of the Windsor Castle pub. We were pretty much left to get on with things in our own way. One particular night, Pvt Ken Beard, who helped run the section, had a girl in the room and wanted to be alone with her. He gave me a ten-shilling note and told me to go and see a movie. I took his money and let him get on with it.

The S3 section was responsible for planning operations and exercises, preparing maps and overlays, and making sand tables. It was always a very busy place, and for this reason the section's NCOs and enlisted men were relieved of some of their normal day-to-day responsibilities, such as kitchen police and guard duty – a fact that did not go down too well with the rest of the men in the battalion!

When the S3 first arrived at Ramsbury, Capt Charles Carmen was in charge. However, in February 1944 he was given command of HQ Co (following Capt McKnight's transfer to I Co) and Capt Charles Shettle took his place. The men in the section never really understood how Shettle got the job, as he had no obvious map reading or navigation skills and seemed to have no idea what the S3 section did. They nicknamed him "the red death" because of his permanently flushed complexion. Shettle was surprised, and one must imagine somewhat relieved, by the amount of knowledge within the group, and let S/Sgt Ed Shames get on with running the department. He even sent Shames, in place of himself, to battalion or regimental briefings because Ed was so much better at extracting the relevant information.

Most of the battalion's enlisted men were billeted in huts at the camp. However, the officers lived in some of Ramsbury's larger houses, sharing the properties with the resident civilian families. Col Wolverton and his staff were at Crowood House, a large property built in 1686 and located a mile or so northeast of the village along the Swindon road.

Parliament Piece, which lies 50 yards or so south of the battalion's camp, was another house pressed into service. The officers living there quickly discovered a short cut to the camp through a gate in the garden fence. The house was built during the reign of Charles I, and is so named because Oliver Cromwell held a meeting of his parliament in a field nearby. The building is three storeys high and the rooms on the top floor are built into the roof or attic space. It was in this part of the house that most of G Co's officers were accommodated. For example, 1st Lt Turner Chambliss shared a room with 2nd Lt Tom Kennedy, 1st Lt Joe Doughty was with 2nd Lt Linton Barling, 1st Lt Durwood Cann and 2nd Lt Frank Rowe lived in another room, whilst G Co's commander, Capt Harold

Van Antwerp, shared the central bedroom with his executive officer 1st Lt James Morton. As a result of living and working together for the best part of nine months, a strong bond of camaraderie developed between them. During the cold winter nights several of the officers would gather in Capt Van Antwerp's room, where they would brew coffee on an old electric stove and make toast spread with jam stolen from the kitchen. Below, on the center floor, a large room was converted into an officers' club. The officers' mess and kitchen were on the ground floor where Violet Wyndham, who owned the property, had her private living rooms.

When 1st Lt Bernard "Barney" Ryan arrived in England, he was an assistant surgeon with the 2nd Bn's medical detachment based in Aldbourne. During November 1943 he was promoted to captain and in December was transferred to the 3rd Bn. He was unhappy about the move because he had made many friends in Aldbourne and was reluctant to leave them. His mood did not improve upon arrival at Ramsbury, as he recalls:

> I was billeted in Parliament Piece with four other officers. In the house was a room that served as our officers' club and bar – most of the time it was bedlam. You could not read and you certainly could not sleep with officers coming in drunk from the club at all hours of the night. After a while I told Capt Morgan (3rd Bn's chief surgeon) that I could not take this any longer, and he kindly moved me across the village to his billet in the local doctor's house. Dr Mills lived there with his wife and two children and they were absolutely wonderful to the pair of us. In return I gave Mrs Mills my cigarette ration of one carton per week, as she adored American cigarettes.

As already mentioned, the huts at Camp Ramsbury housed the majority of 3rd Bn's enlisted men, but there was not enough room for everyone. For example, sergeants Gil Morton, James Shirley, and John Taormina lived with Mr and Mrs Winchcombe at 27 High Street, and staff sergeants Paul Simrell and Ed Shames stayed with the Blain family, owners of Hill's Grocery Store. Ed has fond memories of his time there:

I shared an upstairs bedroom with Paul Simrell. The billeting officer who showed us to our room told us in no uncertain terms that the remainder of the house was strictly "out of bounds." Whenever we had a meal, or needed a shower, we had to go to the Memorial Hall or back to the battalion's camp in Love's Lane. For the first three weeks or so Mr and Mrs Blain kept their distance. Then one Saturday, while on leave, I went to Stonehenge [Stonehenge was a surprisingly easy place to visit during the war because there was always a steady flow of military traffic between the camps around Swindon and those on Salisbury Plain]. I returned to the village during the early afternoon and found Mr Blain busy working in his shop, which was inundated with customers. I asked him if he needed any assistance, adding that back home in Virginia I helped my mother run a small grocery store. My offer was cautiously accepted, and at the end of the day Mr Blain asked how much he owed me. I said that no reimbursement was necessary as "Uncle Sam" was paying my wage, and that I would be delighted to help in the shop at any time in the future, providing of course I was not on duty. From that day on I could do no wrong. The following morning Mrs Blain brought me breakfast in bed, which included the rare luxury of a real egg. I was then allowed to use the Blains' personal bathroom facilities whenever I wished.

As the weeks passed so their friendship grew, and Ed kept in contact with Tommy Blain and his family for many years after the war.

Two squads from I Co's 2 Ptn were quartered in a stable block belonging to the Bell Hotel. Bill Galbraith was a member of that unit and recalls, "The platoon's 1st and 2nd squads were in the stable, and our NCOs, sergeants Mann and McCallum and corporals McCarty and Zebrosky, were in a temporary building opposite, which was just large enough to accommodate the four of them. Not far away was another temporary hut that became our latrine and housed the infamous 'honey buckets' [these were galvanized steel containers fitted with a wooden seat]."

Wartime Ramsbury boasted eight public houses: the Bleeding Horse, the Malt Shovel, the Burdett Arms, the Windsor Castle, the Bell, the Boot, the Crown and Anchor, and the Halfway. George Rosie says, "We spent a lot of time in the pubs because it was great fun. I often played darts with some of the elderly English gentlemen, but they'd been playing the game all of their lives and always beat me – it was just no contest!" When Ralph Bennett was off duty he used to drink in the Boot, which was about 100 yards east of the Bell:

> The Boot backed onto the river Kennet and a mill stream ran through the pub garden and under an old watermill next door. It was only a foot or so deep, but the publican, in order to cool the beer and satisfy American tastes, always kept a small barrel in the stream. The locals, who all seemed to be farmers, had their own individual pint pots and jugs that were hung on hooks behind the bar.

Pvt Len Goodgal's (I Co) favorite pub in the village was the Malt Shovel: "When the bartender said 'Time, please' you learned to finish your drink quickly. At first we complained, but there was nothing we could ever do about it and that was that." Pfc Hank DiCarlo (H Co) has fond memories of the barmaid who worked in the Burdett Arms:

> At the end of the month, when nobody had any money, Nellie Liddiard would give us free beer. She was in her mid-forties, and, I kid you not, could have had her pick of any one of us. What made her even more memorable was the easy manner with which she handled the boisterous lads who were obviously on the make for her. Despite this she was always pleasant and humorous, what we used to call a class act.

Pvt Bob Dunning (HQ Co) has memories of another incident that took place in the Bell:

> At night the toilet, which was at the back of the pub, was always in total darkness. One evening Pvt Walter Ross (HQ Co) went out the back to relieve himself and accidentally urinated all over one of our officers. The officer was wearing his Class A uniform and all hell broke loose. Ross came running through the pub, wished us all goodbye, and ran outside.

The officer came running in, mad as a wet hen and said, "Who the hell did this?" Of course nobody knew a thing about it.

Bill Galbraith visited most of Ramsbury's pubs except the Bell, as he never felt accepted there, and the following story may explain why. Sometime during the late autumn of 1943 a full "honey bucket" was stolen from 2 Ptn's latrine. After closing time its entire contents were deposited on the hotel's doorstep, and a smoke grenade thrown through one of the building's front windows. The landlord, Mr Smith, ran through the slippery mess as he rushed outside to see who had thrown the grenade. He was not a happy man, and assumed that as 2 Ptn were the nearest soldiers to the pub they must have been responsible. The men protested their innocence but their platoon commander, 1st Lt Nye, would have none of it and ordered Bill Galbraith, Jim Brown, and Joe Madona to clean up the mess. Nye placed Cpl Stan Zebrosky in charge of the detail. Some of the battalion had their suspicions as to the real culprit. Earlier that same week Pvt Secundino Alvarez (H Co) had been refused a drink at the Bell. This was more than his ego could stand, as he was a bit of a smart dresser and thought himself better than the average GI. As he left the pub several people heard him say, "Payback time won't be long in coming!"

This was not the only time that Bill Galbraith found himself in trouble:

I remember going on leave to Reading and was late getting back. 1st Lt John Kiley [I Co's executive officer] was in charge of discipline, and my punishment was to wake 1st Lt Nye for reveille every morning. Nye was billeted at Crowood House, which is a good mile from the Bell Inn, and I had to get up an hour earlier than everybody else to get there in time. I Co's 3 Ptn was also billeted at Crowood, and one of its men was away on leave so I slept in his bunk – this gave me an extra hour in bed. Unfortunately, Nye got wind of my caper and told me he now wanted a morning report each day. In order to get the report I had to attend reveille, so I didn't bother to go and raise him. At reveille Lt Kiley asked where Nye was. I said I'd not woken him because he wanted me to bring him a morning report. Kiley said, "Take a jeep and fetch him!" On reaching Crowood, I derived great pleasure from telling Nye that he was late for parade and in trouble with Lt Kiley!

Occasionally anti-Semitic sentiment reared its ugly head within the ranks of the regiment, as Ed Shames recalls:

> Just prior to Easter 1944, 3rd Bn HQ received an invitation from a synagogue in a nearby town inviting Jewish soldiers to join their Passover service. I was given the task of organizing the trip. Thirteen men expressed an interest in attending, and I approached LtCol Wolverton for permission to use a vehicle. The colonel said, "Absolutely, go to Service Co and tell them I said you can have a vehicle, any vehicle you want." I hopped in the colonel's jeep and together with his driver went over to Froxfield. I called at the company office and explained that I needed a truck, only to be told by the officer on duty that "there are too many Jews in this regiment." I ignored his comments, picked up a vehicle and went on my way.

Due to a shortage of personnel in certain areas of the battalion, a steady trickle of new recruits began joining its ranks. Toward the end of 1943 two non-Toccoa trained men, privates Morgan and Stedman, arrived at Ramsbury. Eighteen-year-old David Morgan had crossed the Atlantic aboard the liner *Queen Elizabeth*. He was assigned to I Co, where he was made very welcome. This came as a pleasant surprise – he had thought he would get a hard time for being the new boy, but everything worked out well.

Harold Stedman's arrival proved to be very memorable. He was also assigned to I Co, and was waiting in the cold outside one of the huts at the camp. It was so cold that he decided to step inside, and could not believe his eyes when he saw Pvt Bobbie Rommel, his neighbor and old school friend from Modesto, California, lying on a bunk reading a book. Rommel looked up and said, "What the hell are you doing here?" Harold was nearly speechless, but replied, "I can't believe it's your damn hut – I only came in to get warm."

The movement and disposition of military units in Britain during World War II was guarded with great secrecy. Therefore, 3rd Bn's arrival in Ramsbury during mid-September 1943 caught the local population by surprise. Doreen Ramsden (née Gaskin) remembers the day very clearly:

> The American soldiers arrived unexpectedly and we were anxious to discover what was going on. My father was a part-time policeman and he soon found out who they were! Initially the soldiers had difficulty sorting out our money, and pub landlords would often give them incorrect change. My father didn't like seeing them being ripped off and made a point of telling the publicans to get it right or they would be in deep trouble!

Doreen lived with her parents and brother Edwin in the High Street, not too far from the Bleeding Horse public house. The pub was owned by the Morland brewery and run by Florence Saunders and Jack Potter. The pub became home to the battalion's four supply sergeants: Fred Bahlau, Zol Rosenfield, Bob Webb, and John Luteran, plus S/Sgt Othis Shepherd from Service Co. Bob Webb had a bedroom all to himself upstairs, whilst the others shared a room on the ground floor. To the rear of the Bleeding Horse is a timber barn that during the war belonged to Westfield Farm. The Americans sub-divided this building and used the portion nearest the pub as a cookhouse. The remainder became a store for clothing, rifles, ammunition, and food. Often Fred Bahlau would surreptitiously supply the Gaskin family with items from the store such as ham, butter, and sugar – food that was strictly rationed in wartime Britain. Doreen's brother would act as a runner, taking the items of food back to his parents' house. Later, by way of exchange, he would return with fresh meals cooked by Mrs Gaskin. She was always worried about the best way of explaining the large stocks of US Army food in her pantry, should the authorities ever search her home!

Compared with their British hosts, the Americans had ample food supplies, but a few soldiers wanted more. Tom Bucher recalls:

Poaching became very popular during the first few months that we were in England. Eight of us from 4th Squad were billeted with the 81mm mortar platoon, which had the best poachers in the battalion! Often the smell of their barbeques would waft across the entire camp. Col Wolverton thought that he had eradicated the problem by ensuring that all live ammunition used on the ranges was accounted for. However, the situation did not improve, and the next step, at least for HQ Co, was for all weapons to be locked in an old glider crate, but that still didn't stop the most determined, who turned to local people for help.

In Back Lane, near the battalion's kitchen and mess hall, was another glider crate that had been internally divided into two rooms. One room was used by Zol Rosenfield as an office, whilst the other became a store occupied by elements of the battalion's communications platoon. Zol enjoyed listening to the radio, and it was always on whilst he was working. One day, without his knowledge, Archie Tingle from the communications platoon rigged up an extra speaker inside the radio and connected it to a microphone. Archie and some colleagues then waited in the storeroom for Zol to start work. He entered his office as normal, sat down behind his desk, switched on the radio and began sifting through paperwork. As Zol settled down, Archie made an announcement stating that the war in Europe was over and the Germans had surrendered! Rosenfield leapt up from his chair shouting and screaming for joy. He ran out of the office, still clutching a load of paperwork, and met Archie and his friends, who were ecstatic that the joke was going so well. They played along, encouraging him to tell the colonel, and could not believe their luck when he actually ran off in the direction of the camp, whooping and wailing at everybody he passed! When Zol arrived at Wolverton's office, he drop-kicked the latch on the door, crashed inside, and threw his paperwork in the air, shouting that the war was over and they could all go home! Wolverton looked across his desk and said, "Rosenfield, pick up those papers, get back to your office and stop wasting my time," before demoting him from sergeant to private. As a very embarrassed Rosenfield made his way back to his office, he passed

Archie Tingle and his gang, who were rolling around on the ground in hysterics. Back in the battalion office Wolverton looked at Hiner, who was working nearby, smiled, shook his head from side to side and went back to work!

Not too far from Rosenfield's office was a large hall owned by the church. During the early part of the war it became Ramsbury's "British Restaurant." These restaurants were run by local authorities and subsidized by central government. By September 1943 over 2,000 had been established across Britain. This self-service chain provided, for soldier and civilian alike, good, cheap, and plentiful meals without the need for food ration coupons. Ray Calandrella often visited the place:

> When off-duty I would go to the Church Room British Restaurant. From the High Street there was a short cut to it through the churchyard. A big heavyset woman who was maybe 50 or 60 years old ran the place. I was cheerful and always whistling, and she called me her "little blackbird." I guess I went there because I liked the French toast, beans on toast and other English snacks she served up.
>
> Our army meals were eaten at set times in two Quonset huts that were just behind the cookhouse. I remember playing cards with Sgt Tony Zeoli, one of the cooks. He was a chubby, typical Italian kind of guy with a bad temper whom we nicknamed "Blackass." He didn't like being cheated and occasionally placed a .45cal automatic on the card table as a warning to others!

T/5 John Gibson (Medical Detachment) has slightly different memories of Zeoli: "He was a fine person and we all liked him, but he could not cook, some said he couldn't even boil water! He always seemed to overcook the powdered eggs, which you could pick up in chunks and eat like bread or pizza."

John Gibson was an amateur weightlifter and bodybuilder. He owned a complete set of weights that he'd bought in London from his sporting hero and ex-champion weightlifter, Bill Pullum. In his spare time he organized and ran a gymnasium at the camp. George Rosie and Pvt

Charles Lee often used its facilities. Gibson recalls: "George was the biggest and best built man in the mortars, but his colleague Charles Lee was no weakling. Lee could stick his arms inside the 81mm mortar tubes and support them in a crucifix shape, holding the position longer than anybody else in the platoon."

Boxing was not the only sport in which 3rd Bn excelled. Football was a big attraction and actively encouraged. Capt McKnight trained and captained an 11-man regimental team named "Skytrain," and Col Wolverton, who had played football at West Point, decided to join. Ben Hiner was watching one of the early practice sessions and recalls: "Col Wolverton took the position of quarterback. The team played rough and he ended up with a huge black eye." The star of the team was Joe Madona from I Co, who was small, fast, and powerful. Other talented 3rd Bn players were Dean Winner, Sammy Pettinella (both HQ Co), 1st Lt Jim Walker, and Stan Stasica (both H Co). The men from Jim Walker's 3 Ptn often felt that he spent far too much time on the football field and not enough time with them on military training.

About midway along Ramsbury's High Street, just opposite the Burdett Arms public house, the American Red Cross set up a recreation club and post exchange (PX). The club was for enlisted men only and was housed within a very large Nissen hut. Here the men could always get a cup of coffee or a donut, and play games such as ping-pong or chess. The club, unofficially called the "Wolverton Donut Dugout," was run by a Miss Helen Briggs, known affectionately as "Briggsey." She would organize quiz nights, bingo sessions, card games, and sometimes outings by bus to local places of interest. She ate her meals in the officers' mess at Parliament Piece, and it was here that she got to know H Co's commander, Capt Robert Harwick.

"Briggsey" wanted to get a newsletter off the ground called the "Poop Sheet," and during the spring of 1944 Harwick, who was a married man, helped her with the project. Shortly afterwards a relationship developed and they started going steady. Hank DiCarlo confirms this: "It's quite true that Helen Briggs was Capt Harwick's girlfriend during our time in Ramsbury. They made little attempt to conceal their attraction, and it must have been one of the worst-kept secrets of the war! Harwick returned to his wife afterwards, but I know for a fact that Helen never got over her infatuation with him."

Ben Hiner recalls: "Our battalion cooks would make donuts and give them to 'Briggsey,' who would sell them back to us to raise funds for the Red Cross. She and the Donut Dolly from 2nd Bn were always waiting when we came back from an exercise with coffee and the donuts. We were only allowed one each, which always struck me as odd since they were trying to raise as much money as possible."

James McCann did not drink or smoke, and spent many of his off-duty hours at a roller-skating rink in Swindon.

> When we went to Swindon it was every man for himself. We would walk, hitch-hike or hire a taxi driven by a local gentleman ("Pop" Reeves) who had a touring car. Because petrol was rationed, he would wait for eight of us to fill the car before he'd set off. He would drop us off near the outskirts of Swindon and pick us up again at 2am. The drop-off point was still a couple of miles from the roller rink, so I bought a bicycle for £10 and stored it at a nearby garage. The manager of the rink was a cigar smoker, and I used my ration to keep him supplied. In return he kept a nice pair of skates ready for my many trips to the rink.

The garage was near the present-day Common Head roundabout, and the bicycle was abandoned there following McCann's departure for Normandy in June 1944.

Ramsbury's village hall stands in the High Street not too far from the church. It was built just after World War I as a memorial to the 65 men from the village who lost their lives during that terrible conflict. Doreen Ramsden remembers attending a Christmas dance at the hall in 1943:

> No tickets were issued but each person had the back of their hand marked in ink with a rubber stamp. We went in and sat down. However, with so many American soldiers present you didn't watch for long before you were up on the dance floor having a great time. I can

FROM TOP TO BOTTOM:

Robert Wolverton pictured with his wife Kathleen in 1939. (Mark Bando)

It did not take long for the 506th to become acquainted with Mount Currahee. The recruits ran up and down the mountain once every other day (or more frequently as a form of punishment) and the distance had to be completed within a specified time. (Jim Martin)

The 506th sign that stood beside Col Sink's office at Camp Toccoa. (Jim Martin)

At the beginning of the obstacle course was a 12ft-high log wall that was followed by a sharp climb uphill. (Jim Martin)

Members of 1 Ptn H Co practicing rifle drill. L to R: Lou Vecchi, Mario "Hank" DiCarlo and Fred Neill. "Hank" was 17 years old when this picture was taken and came from the small coastal resort of Wildwood-by-the-Sea, New Jersey. (Hank DiCarlo)

Battalion mail clerk Cpl Ben Hiner. (Bob Webb Jr)

FROM TOP TO BOTTOM:

3rd Bn Staff pictured at Fort Bragg during 1943. L to R: Sgt Bill Pauli (Communications Ptn), S/Sgt Bob Webb (S4 Supply), S/Sgt Ed Shames (S3 Planning and Operations), S/Sgt Paul Simrell (S1 Personnel), and 1st Sgt Jim Shirley (HQ Co). (Bob Webb Jr)

A "Prop Blast Party" was held in November in the officers' mess. One ritual required that a concoction of spirits be consumed within 30 seconds. 2nd Lt Ed Harrell is here cheered on by, amongst others, Bob Wolverton (partially obscured behind Harrell), Salve Matheson (regimental personnel officer – cigarette in hand), and next right George Grant. (Mark Bando)

2nd Lt Ken Christianson, who was in command of 2 Ptn H Co, talking to his men. Christianson was half Cherokee Indian. He could be "gung-ho" at times but nevertheless was a superbly gifted and natural leader. (Hank DiCarlo)

FROM TOP TO BOTTOM:

Day one of 3rd Bn's record-breaking 136-mile march from Atlanta to the parachute school at Fort Benning. (Jim Martin)

The Long March — men from H Co during a break. Fourth from the left is Sonny Sundquist, the company's bad boy extraordinaire, who missed the Normandy jump because he was "detained" in the stockade! On the left is Pvt George Montilio, who became the first man in the battalion to win a DSC. The medic in the background is Pvt James Baker. (John Gibson)

Men from G Co taking part in a battalion skill at arms competition. L to R: Lt Harold Van Antwerp, Sgt Wilbur Croteau, Pfc Don Austin and, in the background, Capt John Graham. Graham was G Co's first commander and a talented musician. He wrote "Song for the Paratroops" whose chorus, "We're the parachute infantry," was sung continuously by the company during the Long March.

The Victory Belle

Who is the girl the boys all like?
Makes them laugh, inspires to fight?
She's the girl the boys know well
For she is the Charlotte Vict'ry Belle

Attending parties here and there,
To be with servicemen everywhere.
No dull moments when she's around,
'Cause she's the tops that can be found.

The marines, soldiers, and saliors, too,
Will tell you that the fact is true
That by her actions and her deeds
She treats alike all races and creeds.

When maneuvers come, the soldier knows
Where there's fun, so it's there he goes.
He'll have a swell time; she'll see to that.
She'll make him feel he wants to come back.

She's got the situation well in hand
When Marines land with many a man.
A friendly smile, a wink or two
Is all they need to pursue.

The airman, chutist, and soldier shy
At beauty, he can just stare and sigh.
These little traits our Vict'ry Bell sees
But she knows how to give a soldier "At Ease!"

She'll wish us luck when we go away,
Give us spirit to win the fray.
We couldn't help but be enthused—
Fighting for her, we couldn't lose.

Some will come back, and some will not.
But when we do, she'll be on the dock.
She'll welcome us home, she's sweet that way.
It certainly will be one happy day.

Three cheers to her, God bless her soul.
Now all her deeds should be told.
We, the living, and those in Hell
All join in thanks to the Vict'ry Belle.

Ray. Calandrella
Hq. Co., 3rd Bn.
506th Parachute Inf.
Camp Mackall, N. C.

26

LEFT:

While at Camp Mackall Ray Calandrella had a poem published in the *Para-Dice* magazine. It was entitled "The Victory Belle" and was named after a local women's organization in Greensboro. At the end of the war the editor Alan Westphal and Hank DiCarlo co-wrote the *Currahee Scrapbook*, given to every 506th veteran. (Bob Webb Jr)

BELOW:

Prior to the regiment's main parachute training at Fort Benning, the Regimental Training Staff (known as the cadre), together with 21 other officers, become qualified military parachutists at a special one-day series of jumps near Camp Toccoa on October 29, 1942. After each descent (which was watched by the entire regiment) the candidates were trucked back to Le Tourneau airfield to draw and fit fresh parachutes ready for the next jump.

Camp Mackall — members of the battalion relax before a training jump. (John Gibson)

Pvt Don Artimez (H Co) poses with his newly issued jump suit and Griswold bag. On D-Day, during his parachute descent, Artimez was shot 23 times in the lower half of his body. (John Gibson)

Pvt Bobbie Rommel was 19 years old when he joined 3rd Bn at Camp Mackall as a machine gunner. Incredibly, he was related to Field Marshal Erwin Rommel, who commanded the German forces in Normandy at the time of the invasion. (Bobbie Rommel)

ABOVE:

The 81mm Mortar Ptn, Fort Bragg, North Carolina, summer 1943. All ranks listed as at D-Day.

Front row L to R: 2nd Lt Pete Madden* (SWA Jun 7, 1944), S/Sgt Roy Burger* (POW Jun 6, 1944 – escaped).

2nd row L to R: Sgt Joe Hunter*, Cpl Ivan Glancy* (SWA), Pvt William Adams, Pfc Dennis Lunsford*, Pfc George Rosie* (POW Jun 6, 1944), Pfc Ed Renock*, Cpl John Allison* (POW June 6, 1944 – escaped SWA), Sgt Danny Hayes.

3rd row L to R: Cpl John Montgomery* (POW), Pfc Allister Towne Jr*, Cpl John Stegmeier*, Pvt Del Ripple* (transferred to pathfinder platoon), Pvt Eigil Rasmussen* (POW), Pvt Ernest Raxtor, Pvt James Smith, Pfc John Facer*.

4th row L to R: Cpl Jim Bradley* (POW Jun 6, 1944), Pfc Emanuel Scherer*, Pfc Leo Krebs* (POW Jun 6, 1944), Pvt Francis Ronzani* (KIA Jun 6, 1944), Pfc Henry Ritter* (POW Jun 6, 1944 – escaped), Pvt Hubert Reasor* (LIA), Pvt Robert Stevens, Pvt Marshall Clark* (POW?).

5th row L to R: Sgt Gil Morton*, Cpl Charles "Chick" Stewart* (SWA), Pvt Luther Turner, Pfc Paul Cathcart Jr* (POW?), Pvt Charles Lee* (KIA Jun 6, 1944), Pfc Joseph Scurlock*, Pvt Winford Hopper, Pfc Lyle Rowcliffe* (SWA), Pvt Walter Ross* (SWA), Cpl Jewell Beck.

*denotes jumped in Normandy.
KIA – killed in action, SWA – seriously wounded in action, LIA – lightly injured in action. (Bob Webb Jr)

BELOW:

H Co 3 Ptn mortar sergeant Ralph Bennett at Camp Mackall, 1943. (Ralph Bennett)

The Machine Gun Ptn, Fort Bragg, North Carolina, summer 1943. All ranks listed as per D-Day.

Front row L to R: Sgt George "Doc" Dwyer* (POW Jun 8, 1944 – escaped), 1st Lt Robert Machen* (KIA Jun 6, 1944), S/Sgt Tom Simms*, Sgt Charles Easter*.

2nd row L to R: Cpl Martin Clark* (POW Jun 6, 1944 – escaped), Cpl Clarence Kelley* (POW Jun 6, 1944), Cpl Fayez Handy* (LIA Jun 6, 1944), Pfc Audrey Lewallen*, Pvt Al Fabec, Pfc Dean "Joe" Winner* (KIA Jun 6, 1944), Cpl Tom Bucher* (SWA Jun 6, 1944), Pfc Earl McGrath* (KIA Jun 7, 1944).

3rd row L to R: Cpl Ralph Fischer* (KIA Jun 6, 1944), Pfc Charles Cartwright* (POW), Cpl Don "Dog" Gallaugher*, Pfc John Pinchot* (KIA Jun 6, 1944), Pfc John Hermansky* (SWA Jun 13, 1944), Pfc Richard "Swede" Stockhouse*, Pfc Eugene Darby*, Pvt Robert Boehm* (KIA Jun 6, 1944).

4th row L to R: Cpl Garland Collier*, Pvt Phil Germer* (KIA Jun 6, 1944), Pvt George Cowden, T/5 John Milhako*, Pvt Joseph Mielcarek* (POW Jun 6, 1944 – escaped), Cpl Neal Lewis (transferred), Pfc Andy Bryan*, Pvt Bobbie Rommel*.

5th row L to R: Pvt Lloyd Wierbach, Cpl Nathan Bullock*, Pvt Steve Radovich* (KIA Jun 6, 1944), Pvt John Robbins* (KIA Jun 6, 1944), Pvt Dewey Rex, Pvt Darvin Lee* (LIA Jun 13, 1944).

*denotes jumped in Normandy
KIA – killed in action, SWA – seriously wounded in action, LIA – lightly injured in action

Not pictured: Pvt Elmer Goff*, Pvt Soini "Hawk" Hall* (KIA Jun 6, 1944), and Pvt Charles Price*. On May 13 during Exercise *Eagle* Fabec and Wierbach received severe injuries, which precluded them from taking part in the invasion. (Bob Webb Jr)

Littlecote House – home to 506th Regimental HQ throughout its entire period in England. (John Reeder photo via Michel De Trez Collection)

Members of second section 81mm Mortar Ptn at Camp Ramsbury. L to R: Pfc George Rosie, Pvt Phil Abbey, and Pfc Leo Krebs. On D-Day the three men were caught in a German ambush, which resulted in the death of Abbey and the capture of Rosie and Krebs. During his 11 months of captivity Rosie's weight plummeted from 196 to 140lb. (George Rosie)

TOP:

Camp Ramsbury – astride the bicycle is Pfc Jim "Pee Wee" Martin (2 Ptn G Co). Jim must have sent this photograph home to his parents in the US as his Screaming Eagle shoulder patch has been removed from the picture by the Army censor. (Jim Martin)

BOTTOM:

Sixty-five years later and nothing remains of the wartime camp.

Pre-war picture of Parliament Piece. This building quartered officers from 3/506 throughout their time in England. (Francis Wyndham)

Maj George Grant, 3rd Bn's executive officer. Grant was killed on June 6 after landing in the grounds of Rampan Manor near St-Côme-du-Mont. Grant came from Batesville, Arkansas, and was 22 years old when this 1938 photograph was taken. He was related to Civil War Union hero Gen Ulysses S. Grant. (George Grant Jr)

Dr Bernard "Barney" Ryan took over from Jackson Neavles as assistant battalion surgeon in December 1943. (Barney Ryan)

A wartime photograph of the Square, Ramsbury. At its center was an old elm tree that was reputedly over 300 years old, and behind it the Bell Hotel. On the right are the stables where the 1st and 2nd squads from I Co were billeted. (Mark Bando)

Father John Maloney, the Catholic chaplain, is sitting in his appropriately named jeep "Jumping Jesus" in Ramsbury High Street. Naively, Maloney often loaned the vehicle to colleagues for "sightseeing trips." This practice came to an abrupt end when the vehicle was found parked outside a house of ill repute in Swindon! (Mark Bando)

Bill Galbraith enlisted into the US Army at Long Beach, California on September 9, 1942 – he was 19 years old. Later he became a member of 2 Ptn I Co's machine-gun squad together with Pvt Jim Brown and Pvt Bob "Young 'un" Young. (Bill Galbraith)

Pvt David Morgan (2 Ptn I Co). (Neil Morgan)

Pvt Harold Stedman (3 Ptn I Co). (Harold Stedman)

Fred Bahlau (H Co supply sergeant) pictured near the Bleeding Horse. He is wearing an Air Corps flying overall possibly obtained via a contact at Ramsbury Airfield. (Fred Bahlau)

Medic John Gibson using his barber skills on Cpl Jim Bradley (81mm Mortar Ptn). This picture was taken at Ramsbury in April 1944 near the camp's infirmary and aid station. Following the D-Day drop Gibson and Bradley were both captured by the Germans. (John Gibson)

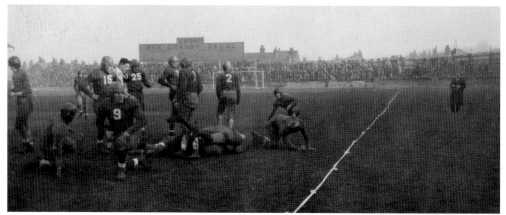

FROM TOP TO BOTTOM:

Skytrain regimental football team, Camp Ramsbury, winter 1943/44. Rear standing L to R: 1st Lt Jim Walker (H Co), Pvt Stan Stasica (H Co), 1st Lt Howard Littell (Service Co). Front row L to R: 1st Sgt Bruno Schroeder (Regiment), ? Newton (?), Pfc Joe Madona (I Co), Pfc Dean Winner (Machine Gun Ptn), Capt John T. McKnight (I Co), Pvt Sammy Pettinella (H Co), Pvt Martin Majewsky (Regiment), ? Peternel (?).

This football match, played at Reading on October 31, 1943, was a 40–0 victory for the "Skytrain" team. H Co's Stan Stasica (1) played a pivotal role in the game against the "Red Tornados" who were representing a US armored division. (John Reeder photo via Michel De Trez Collection)

Miss Helen Briggs, known affectionately as "Briggsey," ran Ramsbury's American Red Cross Club and PX . In this postwar photograph "Briggsey" is with her husband Roy Ramsey. (Hank DiCarlo)

Ramsbury High Street pictured in 1944, looking east. The building in the background with writing on the wall is the Burdett Arms public house. The officer on the left is Father John Maloney. (Mark Bando)

Capt Robert Harwick was H Co's commander from the early days at Toccoa. At 5ft10in he was well built and had been a chemical engineer before joining the army. Harwick hardly ever raised his voice but was not in the habit of repeating orders. He gained the respect of his men for his cool leadership.

Christmas Party organized by the battalion for local children, Christmas 1943. (John Klein)

During Britain's invasion scare of 1940 all sign posts and name boards were removed in order to confuse the enemy. In 1943 the signs were still missing and causing problems for the newly arrived American troops. In areas away from the coasts, many of the signs were replaced, as in this picture of airborne troops approaching Knighton crossroads near Ramsbury. (John Reeder via the Roger Day Collection)

When Pfc Martin Collins arrived at camp Ramsbury in September 1943 he was just 19 years old. He met 16-year-old Monica Trim at a roller-skating rink in Swindon and it was not long before they were engaged. A member of 2 Ptn H Co, Martin was perceived as an intelligent, kind, and knowledgeable man who thought deeply about his role in the forthcoming conflict. Left: Camp Mackall, North Carolina 1943. Right: Monica and brother Graeme in 1947 at Burnham-on-Sea, Somerset. (Anna Black and Graeme Trim)

particularly remember one big American who was a very good dancer. He could jitterbug like nobody else! The Air Corps (stationed on the hill) and the paratroopers were never allowed to attend dances together. There was always a certain amount of friction whenever the two groups met socially.

It was at about this time that the battalion decided to organize a Christmas party for the local children. Hank DiCarlo recounts:

I don't remember who first broached the idea of having a Christmas party. We started writing home, asking for candy, fruit, and trinkets to be sent to us. Even the officers got into treat procurement mode, which helped immeasurably. The party was a smashing success, and the hit of the day, outstripping sweets and toys, was unquestionably the fresh oranges. The look on the children's faces, as they bit into a citrus fruit for the first time, was worth all the effort. The cooks outdid themselves with cookies and cakes and every child present had a day to remember – an ant would have starved on the crumbs they left behind.

On another occasion Col Wolverton asked Ed Shames to organize a dance in the hall. The colonel had heard that a band was touring bases in the area and that they made no charge for their services. He had no idea what music they played but told Ed to book the band because "the boys will love them." The night came, the whisky flowed, but the band was a chamber orchestra and the "boys" were not impressed. They soon went looking for Ed who, sensing trouble, was nowhere to be found.

On Friday, March 31, 1944 the village experienced its worst fire for more than 50 years. It started at 1.30pm in a barn at Ramsbury Farm, Oxford Street, where a lorry had recently been parked. The fire quickly spread to other barns and cart sheds before engulfing four cottages in Oxford Street and Chapel Lane. Ramsbury's National Fire Service appliance was quickly on the scene, followed by two American fire tenders from the airfield. These were later joined by appliances from

Hungerford, Swindon, Marlborough, Bulford, and Trowbridge. So great was the need for water to quench the flames that pumps and hoses were laid down to the river over 200 yards away.

At the time of the incident, the battalion had just left Ramsbury to take part in a command post exercise. However, Ben Hiner and several other members of HQ Co had been left behind to guard a number of men who, for various reasons, were serving detention in the stockade. The officer of the guard had gone off on an errand and no one could find him. Hiner had to make a quick decision, and decided to release his prisoners. After collecting fire buckets from the camp he marched them to the inferno. As soon as they arrived, Pvt Don Howenstine (HQ Co) and Pvt Macrae Barnson (G Co) helped rescue an elderly lady by carrying her downstairs from her burning house. When the officer of the guard returned and discovered what Hiner had done, he went ballistic and reported him to Col Wolverton. The colonel checked all the facts and told Hiner that he had acted correctly. He then nullified the punishments of some of the men who helped with the rescue, including those of Howenstine and Barnson.

In April 1944, the 112th Infantry Regiment, part of the 28th Infantry Division, moved into a tented encampment near Ramsbury. The camp was in woodland about a mile west of the village beside the Ramsbury–Marlborough road. Relations between the units were uneasy at the best of times, and deteriorated further when the 112th invented a measles epidemic that confined the 3rd Bn to its barracks. Hank DiCarlo recalls:

> The 28th was finding it difficult to get a toe-hold in any Ramsbury social activity, especially dances. To cut down the odds their medics spread a rumor that they were having a measles epidemic, so that we were confined to our area and forbidden to enter the village hall. It did not take us long to realize that we'd been tricked, and a few well-placed smoke grenades soon cleared the hall. The local girls were a little testy about it at first, but they eventually forgave us, and life went on pretty much as before.

Just prior to the 3rd Bn's departure for Normandy, they managed to extract a little more revenge, as Hank recounts: "We made several stealthy forays into the camps of the 28th Infantry Division, either to supplement our ration, carry off their crew-served weapons, or just raise some hell."

To encourage closer links with British families, local children were often invited to spend a day at the camp. Graeme Trim, then a seven-year-old Swindon schoolboy, had a much older sister, Monica, who was engaged to Pfc Martin Collins (H Co). Martin invited Graeme to Ramsbury and these are his memories of that day:

> One Saturday in the spring of 1944 I was taken in a US Army lorry from Swindon to the camp at Ramsbury. I was made very welcome by the soldiers who spoilt me with chocolate and candy. I was kitted out with a metal canteen set and queued up with the soldiers for dinner. I recall being given an extra ladle of custard and a piece of tart. After this Martin took me back to a large bell tent, which he shared with four other paratroopers. I rested on his camp bed whilst he carried out some duties. It felt great to be called "Buddy" by his comrades. Then it was time to leave and I was driven back to Swindon in a jeep. I was wearing short trousers, and by the time I reached Swindon my knees were frozen and I had difficulty getting out, but it was a wonderful adventure for a young child in wartime! On June 6, 1944 Martin and his buddies parachuted into Normandy. He landed safely, but later in the day was shot by a sniper and died instantly. He was just 19 years old.

For soldiers on leave, Marlborough and Swindon were popular destinations, but London was the Mecca, and 48-hour passes to the capital were always the most sought after and hardest to get. One weekend Bob Dunning and Jack Manley (both HQ Co) each had passes to London, but because both were short of money they decided to go to Swindon instead. Bob Dunning takes up the story:

> We ended up in a pub near the railroad station, I think it was called the Great Western Hotel. We'd been drinking gin and some sort of lemon

mixer. After about four or five of these we could feel no pain and were just about ready for anything. Just as we were walking away from the pub we suddenly needed to find a place to relieve ourselves. We were beside a tall building that looked like a gym. It had large swinging doors that easily opened if you leaned against them. Inside there were a number of big street buses – keys and all! We had found ourselves a free ride back to Ramsbury. Within about 10 minutes we were in the transportation business; the only trouble was we had to remember to drive on the left.

As we made our way out of Swindon, every GI who saw the bus wanted a ride and they all piled on. Just after you leave the town there's a steep hill with a long winding road, and this proved to be quite a problem. Imagine the scene; two drunks in charge of about 20 other drunks all trying to double clutch this damn big bus and keep it moving up the hill. After about four attempts we made it – never mind which side of the road we were on, just aim! I bet if any English people heard us that night they must have thought the Germans had landed. We dropped some of our passengers off in Aldbourne, but when we arrived in Ramsbury we had to find a place to hide the bus. We knew if caught we'd probably be cleaning "honey buckets" for the rest of the war. We eventually left it in a wooded area somewhere between Ramsbury and Marlborough. Next day police were everywhere and Col Sink was madder than hell. He called a formation to check who'd been on pass in Swindon. To his surprise, he discovered that Jack and I had passes to London, so that let us off the hook! No one moved the bus for quite some time, and Col Sink said that if somebody didn't hurry up and claim it he'd paint it pink and keep it.

A lot of Ed Shames's time as battalion operations sergeant involved working with and understanding maps, and he purchased many of these from Stanford's Hiking and Map Shop near London's Covent Garden. During the time Capt Carmen was in charge of the S3 section Ed could travel to London and buy maps whenever he needed them. However, as soon as Capt Shettle took control, Ed's traveling arrangements were curtailed. When off duty Ed and his assistant Sgt Joe Gorenc used their spare time to teach the principles of map reading to the men. The lessons took place in Ramsbury's Memorial Hall, were strictly voluntary, and open to everyone within the battalion – enlisted men and officers alike.

Next to the Memorial Hall was a vehicle garage and workshop. Ed was friendly with the owner, who told him about a reliable source of good quality whisky. The price for each bottle was £10, and periodically Ed would travel around the village and collect orders from the men. However, there was one major problem. The whisky had to be fetched from the Hop Blossom public house in Farnham, Surrey, over 30 miles from Ramsbury. Never one to be beaten, Ed always managed to find some excuse to borrow Col Wolverton's jeep for his clandestine journeys!

Only Wolverton and the company commanders had regular transport, and jeeps were almost impossible to get hold of unless, like Ed, you had good connections. The wartime law dictated that all unattended vehicles, both military and civilian, had to be immobilized. The quickest and easiest way of doing this was to remove the rotor arm. However, necessity is the mother of invention, and when the paratroopers visited London someone always carried a spare. Jeeps could be found on most streets in the city, just ripe for the picking, as Ralph Bennett recalls: "We would replace the missing rotor arm, drive around until the jeep ran out of gas and then steal another one."

Word quickly spread that American soldiers with plenty of money to throw around had moved into the Ramsbury area. This news soon reached the many prostitutes who plied their trade on the streets of London and other large British cities, and they were soon regular weekend visitors to the 506th's camps in Wiltshire. Soldiers and civilians alike euphemistically referred to these women as "Piccadilly commandos."

Located in a field in Back Lane, not too far from the camp, were a number of chicken coops owned by Mr Talmage. Prostitutes often used these huts during their visits to the village, and Mr Jack Gaskin, one of Ramsbury's special police constables, often found them sleeping there during the day and quickly moved them on.

George Rosie recalls how LtCol Wolverton came across one of these women at work:

> One evening the colonel drove his jeep up to the main gate at the camp and found its sentry post deserted. He walked around to the side of the small guard hut and found the sentry having sex with an English girl. He arrested the guard but instead of putting him in the guardhouse he had him dig a hole 6ft deep into which he made him bury a dinner spoon. The colonel told him that if he was caught deserting his post again he'd have to dig the spoon out with a dinner fork!

However, it was not always the prostitutes that made money. Hank DiCarlo recalls the bizarre behavior of one man from H Co: "He was a sleazy kind of man in every way imaginable, and not very popular with the men. One of his little tricks was to rob prostitutes while on furlough in London. He took some perverse pride in coming back to Ramsbury with more money than when he'd left."

3

"Here's to your dog tags"
Preparations for D-Day

Training

No sooner had the 506th Regiment's three battalions settled into their new homes than there began a long period of intensified training. Col Sink immediately called meetings with his battalion and company commanders and on September 20, 1943, Gen Lee, 101st divisional commander, visited the unit and gave a talk entitled "The responsibility ahead of us."

The first field exercise undertaken by the regiment in England took place on October 7. Parts of the 506th were "tail gate jumped" onto a field designated DZ-3 that was just west of Crowood House. The term "tail gate jump" is used to describe an exercise where paratroopers are delivered to the drop zone from the back of trucks. The 327th Glider Infantry Regiment and the 321st Glider Field Artillery also took part. The aim of the exercise, which lasted two days, was to drive enemy forces (in reality other 101st units) from Ramsbury and then defend and hold the village against a possible counterattack. Gen Lee watched the exercise and was reported to be very unhappy with its progress. One reason for his lack of enthusiasm may have been the following incident recounted by Hank DiCarlo:

We were tasked to take control of the village and approached via the fields and hedgerows below Ramsbury airfield. The final objective was the huge elm tree that grew in the square opposite the Bell public house. S/Sgt "Mac" McCullough and his small team were in charge of defense.

"Mac" had illicitly procured three Amatol concussion grenades that he thought might inject a bit of realism into the last phase of the exercise. As the rest of the platoon was closing in on the tree, "Mac" decided it was time to set the grenades off. The Bell and every shop in the square had their windows blown in and people came rushing out of their homes, wondering what had happened. The damage and the noise of explosions ultimately led to an enquiry. However, 1 Ptn closed ranks and nobody was charged. Subsequently the armorers were asked to account for every single Amatol grenade they had issued.

The countryside around Ramsbury consisted mainly of small fields and hedgerows and was an ideal area for regimental maneuvers, as it was not too dissimilar to northern France. The 506th trained day and night in every location imaginable, and street-fighting exercises sometimes took place in the village. Local people were often surprised to find soldiers running through their gardens and hiding in sheds and outbuildings. Early one dark winter morning Doreen Ramsden, who worked as a land girl at Hilldrop Farm, was walking to work with a friend to fetch the cows in for milking. She recalls: "About midway between Ramsbury and the farm, Hilldrop Lane passes through an area of woodland. As we reached this point a dozen soldiers suddenly came out of the woods and squatted beside the road. It was a very frightening experience."

One night, soon after the battalion's arrival in England, some silver spoons disappeared from a YMCA hostel. The hostel had been used as a command post throughout a battalion exercise, and it was during this period that the cutlery went missing. Suspicion fell upon H Co's 1 Ptn, commanded by 1st Lt Edward Mehosky. Hank DiCarlo has vivid memories of the events that followed:

Col Wolverton came over to our platoon area with Capt Harwick. He found "Moose" (our pet name for 1st Lt Mehosky) and demanded. "OK, Ali Baba, let's run your 40 thieves out here and get the score on this thing." A bemused Mehosky ordered us outside as Wolverton and Harwick began questioning everybody in turn. The platoon had no choice but to play dumb and denied ever being in the building, let alone seeing the spoons. "Moose" looked on and said nothing as we were questioned. Afterwards Wolverton told us, "If the silver is returned nothing more will be said." But it was already too late as the spoons had been sold to a silversmith in Swindon, helping to pay for one of the best nights out we ever had.

An area of about 5 square miles, just north of Ramsbury and centered on Pentico Farm, was used extensively for live firing exercises. The farm had been unoccupied for several years but its outbuildings were still in a reasonable state of repair. G Co's 1st Lt Joe Doughty recalls the demise of one particular building. "A barn that lay in a valley belonging to Sir Francis Burdett was destroyed, I believe, due to multiple live firing exercises and overzealous demolition trainees. As to the culprits involved in the deed, I guess I would have to say it was us!" Col Sink received communication from Lady Burdett about the matter. The Burdetts lived in Ramsbury Manor and owned much of the land surrounding the village and many of the houses within it. Sink sent Maj Hannah (regimental operations officer) over to Ramsbury Manor to sort things out. He was told, much to his and Col Sink's relief, that compensation was unnecessary because if the building's destruction in any way hastened Hitler's downfall then it was worth the loss. However, during subsequent training exercises at Pentico, the entire farm was totally destroyed and after the war the Burdett family had the US government pay for the damages. Ironically, when the battalion started using the ranges, the farmhouse was in disrepair and would, in all probability, have fallen down on its own without any help from bazookas, grenades, and pole charges!

Pfc Johnny Houk (I Co) was involved in a grenade-training incident on the Pentico ranges. Bill Galbraith and the rest of 2 Ptn were waiting their turn:

We were passing the time by watching Johnny's squad put in a live attack on the farmhouse. During the exercise Johnny bounced a grenade off a window frame and we all stood up in horror as the grenade rolled back and stopped at his feet. Houk threw himself to the ground as the grenade exploded and much to everyone's surprise, and relief, walked away from the whole thing. Word went round the battalion about the episode and we all reckoned that Houk had a charmed life – after a while I think he began to believe it himself.

One of Capt Harwick's favorite field problems was to send men out on camouflage and concealment exercises. A squad would make and hide a position and the rest of the company would act as a hunter force and attempt to locate it whilst, at the same time, practicing their patrolling skills. Ralph Bennett recalls one particular exercise. "My 3rd Squad found a hazelnut copse and prepared a luxurious dugout. We removed all the spoil and put the grass back on top of the position! By the time we finished we had several pheasants roosting on top of it. Of course nobody found us and after a week we decided to give ourselves up and end the exercise."

Whilst taking part in any exercise, the regiment was expected to live off the land and actively discouraged from purchasing local produce. Tom Bucher recalls:

During one particular exercise we had been chasing a chow truck without success. We had been in the field for three days when I decided to buy my guys some bread from a nearby store. Back in the USA this would have been OK but here it was totally against regulations, but I took a chance. As I was leaving I ran straight into an umpire who promptly took down my details before sending me on my way. During the post-exercise debrief Col Sink made some comment about the incident and bellowed, "Who owns Cpl Bucher?" Lt Machen, who was not amused by all this, put his hand up and said "I do, sir." The colonel replied "Well, he's a buck private now and he knows why!" I didn't remain a private for long but during that time I became eligible for "soldier of the month" [the battalion ran a monthly scheme whereby the enlisted men could win merits for smart dress, good soldiering and exemplary behavior] and won a three-day pass to London, so it wasn't such a bad thing after all!

Sometimes during training things would go wrong. On January 13, 1944, G Co made a demonstration jump for the Duke of Gloucester. Sgt Homer Sarver was killed when his parachute failed to open. His death was the first suffered by the battalion as a direct result of jumping. "Pee Wee" Martin remembers the day very clearly: "The weather was wet and windy and we flew around for quite a while to see if it would settle. It didn't, but we still jumped! Some of us had broken down our rifles and put them in Griswold bags while others, including Homer, held theirs across their reserve 'chute." The company jumped from a height of 700ft and Sgt Sarver was the last trooper of a 15-man stick to leave the aircraft. The probable reason for the main parachute's malfunction was that Sarver's rifle got caught up in the 'chute's suspension lines. Lt Joe Doughty was G Co's 3 Ptn leader on that day and Sgt Sarver was under his command. He recalls: "On landing I must have been dragged 100 yards or more before I could collapse my 'chute. When I eventually stopped I was about 50ft from Sarver's body." One officer and seven enlisted men were also injured on the same jump and required hospitalization. Sgt Sarver was buried on January 26 at Brookwood American Military Cemetery near Woking, Surrey.

During October/November 1943, planning began for a small-scale forces exchange between British and American airborne enlisted personnel. The principal aim of the seven-day exercise was to exchange ideas and test each other's equipment. "Col Wolverton sent me along to Bulford Camp near Salisbury Plain to assess the potential program," recalls Ed Shames. "I stayed for three days and was billeted nearby in the sergeants' mess at Tidworth Garrison. During this time I accepted an invitation from the British to make a descent from a barrage balloon, which, time permitting, they were hoping to make part of the program."

With only a few places available, it was not easy to get on the course. Sgt Ralph Bennett and Pvt Dud Hefner put their names down to go. "Out of the six people selected from the battalion we were the only two from H Co," recalls Bennett. "The course coincided with a handful of British guys coming to Ramsbury. I loved the parachute that the British were using, as it opened more smoothly than ours. However, when it came to the balloon jumps I thought that jumping through a hole in the floor of a cage was going a bit too far!"

One day Ed Shames and Paul Simrell decided to play a practical joke on the battalion. They posted a realistic-looking request on the notice board asking for volunteers to jump at low level into water without a parachute! "We offered each man a three-day pass and were amazed at the response," remembers Ed. "Over 30 dumb sons of bitches put their names down, including Paul Garrison, who was I Co's first sergeant!"

Dress rehearsals for D-Day

Gen Bill Lee had been in charge of the 101st Airborne Division since its formation. However, during February 1944 the general suffered a severe heart attack that ended his active service and resulted in his evacuation to the United States. The man chosen to replace him was Gen Maxwell D. Taylor, who had recently arrived in England following active service with the 82nd Airborne Division in Italy. He took command on March 14, and nine days later, together with Gen Eisenhower and Prime Minister Winston Churchill, watched a demonstration parachute drop by the 2nd and 3rd battalions of the 506th. The 1st Bn stayed on the ground and was inspected by the visiting dignitaries. The landing zone was located on farmland just east of Welford Airfield that belonged to a Mr Jack Baylis, owner of nearby Court Oak Farm. Pvt Walter "Luke" Lukasavage (I Co) recalls: "Directly after the jump we paraded and I was standing a couple of hundred feet away from Winston Churchill. He lit up one of his big cigars and as a joke I did the same with one of mine, much to the anger of 1st Sgt Paul Garrison."

In the days following the demonstration drop, Gen Taylor got to know his regimental and battalion commanders and soon started preparations for the division's final D-Day training phase.

So that the Allies could test, under fairly realistic conditions, their plans for assaulting Hitler's "Fortress Europe," a number of training areas were established along England's southern coast. It was essential that these stretches of coastline had similar features to the actual Normandy landing beaches. Slapton Sands, in a part of Devon known as the South

Hams (literally meaning southern hamlets), was chosen to represent "Utah" Beach. "Utah" was the codename given to the area at the base of the Cotentin Peninsula where "U" Force was to land on D-Day.

Bounded by the river Dart to the north, the English Channel to the east and south, and the Kingsbridge Estuary in the west, the South Hams region had seen little in the way of change to its rural existence for hundreds of years. Toward the end of 1943, this idyllic situation altered dramatically.

The first landing exercise took place on August 16, 1943, when US soldiers from the 175th Infantry Regiment were put ashore from Royal Navy landing craft. However, future exercises would need to be much bigger and more realistic, and involve the use of live ammunition – including bombardment of the shore by naval gunfire. It was therefore decided, from both a safety and security point of view, that civilians would have to be evacuated. Within a period of five weeks between November 16 and December 20, the area was requisitioned under the 1939 Defence Regulations and Compensation Act and over 3,000 local people were forced to leave their homes.

In total there were seven major exercises conducted within the Slapton Battle Training Area between December 31, 1943 and May 6, 1944. The 101st Airborne Division took part in two of these: Exercise *Beaver* (March 29–31) and Exercise *Tiger* (April 26–29).

The 3rd Bn took no part in Exercise *Beaver*, which proved to be poorly conceived. Many units performed badly and confusion reigned; men became separated from each other and were unable to fully complete their missions. In the days immediately following the exercise meetings involving all participating parties were held in an attempt to sort out the many problems. One further exercise, "U" Force's dress rehearsal for D-Day, was scheduled for the end of April, when it was hoped that all the difficulties experienced during *Beaver* could be ironed out. This operation was codenamed *Tiger*.

Exercise *Tiger*

All units of the 101st Airborne Division participated in *Tiger*. Its overall commander was Gen Collins from VII Corps and the 4th Division was to lead the amphibious assault. Just like the real thing, the 101st had three participating echelons – parachute, glider, and seaborne.

Between April 20 and 25, the 101st left its bases in Wiltshire and Berkshire and headed for the hotels of Torbay. Company B of the 327th Glider Infantry Regiment, which was to land at Slapton Sands by sea, was one of the first participating units to arrive in the area. Following their train journey from Reading to Ivybridge, the company marched 2 miles northwest to a marshaling area near the village of Cornwood. Unfortunately their arrival was not anticipated and this resulted in a great deal of confusion. The problems did not end there. On April 26 the seaborne elements began loading onto 16 different vessels, a mixture of LSTs (Landing Ship Tanks) and LSIs (Landing Ship Infantry) at two ports of embarkation, Dartmouth and Plympton. Unfortunately the loading was badly handled and several units were split up – for example, the division's 37mm artillery pieces were placed on one vessel whilst their gun crews were put aboard another!

Security on Exercise *Tiger* was taken very seriously and strictly enforced. Whilst en route to the exercise area, all personnel from the 101st were ordered to wear field uniform F and change into fatigues for the actual exercise. Jumpsuits were not to be worn! It was vitally important that the Germans were kept in the dark regarding the purpose of *Tiger*, and to further confuse the enemy the 101st Airborne Division was renamed the 1st Tank Destroyer Group. All other regiments, battalions, companies etc within the division had their titles altered in a similar way. The 506th was redesignated the 801st Tank Destroyer Battalion (Towed) and 3rd Bn became Company C.

The 1st and 3rd battalions of the 506th PIR left Ramsbury and Aldbourne for Torquay on April 24, with the 2nd Bn following the next day. James McCann remembers his arrival: "We were transported to Torquay and billeted in the Grand Hotel overlooking the harbor. Sergeants and corporals got to sleep in the beds and the rest of us were in sleeping bags on the floor."

Col Wolverton, together with his small advance party, left Ramsbury for the exercise area by jeep. Ed Shames was one of the group and recalls:

"The weather was beautiful, and we felt like tourists and even stopped at Paignton Zoo to take a look at the animals. There was this big old tiger pacing up and down in its cage, and in a moment of dumb stupidity I called out to the animal. I had my hand on one of the bars of its cage. The tiger suddenly turned and lashed out, I jumped back in surprise and found the cat had ripped the top of my thumb with its claw."

Some of the regiment's assistant platoon leaders had recently arrived in England from the States, and *Tiger* was their first major exercise with the 506th. Most were keen but very inexperienced and lacked credibility with the men. They became known as "90-day wonders" because of their accelerated three-month training program.

The exercise was to closely follow the plans that had been laid down for the forthcoming assault on Utah Beach. After a naval bombardment by two cruisers and seven destroyers, the 4th Division would secure a bridgehead and then move inland. The 101st was scheduled to land northwest of Slapton Sands before dawn on D-Day before moving southeast in order to meet up with the 4th Division. The 82nd Airborne Division was given the task of securing the land to the east of the bridgehead. Imaginary "enemy" forces occupied the area inland from the beach, from Plymouth in the west to Exmouth in the east. Exercise umpires were left to decide how successful the attacking forces had been in overcoming the "enemy."

The following units of the 101st participated in *Tiger*: 501st, 502nd, and 506th Parachute Infantry regiments, 377th Parachute Field Artillery Battalion, Company C of the 326th Airborne Engineers, Division HQ, Division Signal Company, and the 326th Medical Company. All of these were parachute units that were "tail gate jumped" onto the drop zones. Simulated glider landings also took place involving the 321st and 907th Glider Field Artillery battalions, 326th Medical Company, Divisional Signal Company, 426th Airborne Quartermaster Company, and elements of Divisional HQ. Arriving by sea were the 327th, and 1st Battalion of the 401st, Glider Infantry regiments.

All units of the 101st Airborne Division were briefed about *Tiger* before leaving their staging areas. At 0230hrs on the morning of April 27,

5 hours before the first seaborne landings, the paratroopers started making their "tail gate jumps" in the general area of Kingsbridge, East Allington, Loddiswell, and Churchstow. Within 1½ hours the troops had assembled and were moving off toward their objectives. "Jay" Stone (Battery B, 321st Glider Field Artillery), who was on detached service to the 506th as a forward observer, takes up the story:

> The airborne activity was simulated. Parachute elements were formed up into sticks just as we would be if we were loaded into C-47s. At about 3am the sticks began walking across the simulated drop zone area. Every 50ft or so the last man in the stick would drop off. This continued until all sticks had jumped. Upon a signal we assembled and moved out on our missions. Glider elements, including the 321st, started their simulated landings at 6.30am and then moved into position. During the exercise the 321st fired their howitzers in support of the 506th, but did not use live ammunition. The firing was just straight service practice.

The 502nd, together with the 377th, moved east from the drop zone and captured a strongpoint at Merrifield before attacking the beach exits at Slapton Sands. The 506th, minus its 3rd Bn, secured the high ground around Stokeham. Meanwhile 3rd Bn, who had joined up with part of C Co from the 326th Airborne Engineers, took the coastline between Salcombe and Thurlestone. James McCann recalls:

> We marched up a hill near a British AA [antiaircraft] gun position and were told to dig in. We could see the amphibious forces practicing storming the beach below. We had been issued with every item of equipment that we would be expected to carry with us into Normandy on June 6, including three days' worth of K-rations. Even the medical battalion received realistic training. They came up the hill stopping at about every fifth foxhole informing the occupant that he was designated "wounded." The soldier was then treated and tagged with a label stating "leg wounded" or some other injury. The stretcher-bearers then carried

Littlecote, March 18, 1944. The entire regiment turned out to honor T/5 Francis Fleming from 1st Bn, awarded a bravery medal for saving Cpl Robert Brochard during a training jump, who is seen (far right on podium) receiving the salute from 3rd Bn staff. L to R: Maj George Grant (executive officer), 1st Lt James Holstun (S2 intelligence officer), Capt Charles Shettle (S3 operations officer), Capt Stanley Morgan (battalion surgeon), and 1st Lt John King (S4 supply officer). (John Reeder photo, courtesy Michel De Trez Collection)

1st Lt Edward "Moose" Mehosky (left) and S/Sgt Gerald "Mac" McCullough, both H Co.

A misty morning in a Wiltshire farmyard. Pfc Jim "Pee Wee" Martin makes full use of the "outdoor facilities"! (Jim Martin)

A training drop in England typical of many that took place during the build up to D-Day. (John Reeder via Roger Day Collection)

1st Lt Joe Doughty, 3 Ptn leader G Co, pictured in Austria during 1945. (Joe Doughty)

Bad exit! An I Co training jump, somewhere in England. This very unusual picture shows the wrong way to leave a C-47 in flight. (Harold Stedman)

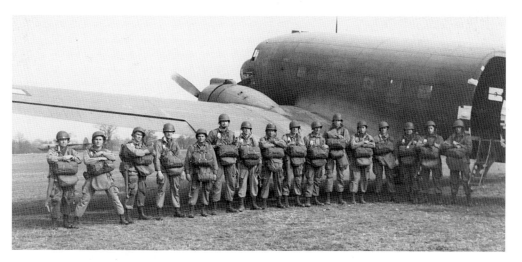

FROM TOP TO BOTTOM:

Men from Regimental HQ Co about to board a C-47 at Ramsbury airfield on yet another training exercise. Note the tape stuck around the aircraft's door. Before a drop the jumpmaster would tape over items that might snag equipment or hinder a trooper's exit. (John Reeder via the Roger Day Collection)

A close-up view of another jumpmaster's handiwork – safety was always paramount. (John Gibson)

As part of their training program, men of the 101st learned British communications procedure and handled British radio equipment. They also swapped stories and traded Airborne insignia with their British counterparts. (John Klein)

3rd Bn supply crew and technicians at Welford Airfield on March 23, 1944, when the battalion made a demonstration jump in front of Churchill and Eisenhower. Rear standing L to R: S/Sgt Bob Webb (S4 supply), 1st Lt John King (S4 supply), T/5 Leslie Riley (I Co armorer, KIA Normandy), T/5 Warren Nelson (G Co armorer, KIA Normandy), Pfc Bruce Paxton (H Co). Front kneeling L to R: S/Sgt Fred Bahlau (H Co supply), S/Sgt Zolman Rosenfield (G Co supply), S/Sgt John Luteran (I Co supply), Pfc Eugene Darby (HQ Co), T/5 John Mihalko (HQ Co armorer). (Bob Webb Jr)

In the days just before Exercise *Tiger* men from 506th Regimental HQ were billeted in the Hotel Regina, which enjoys fine views over Torquay's harbor area. (John Reeder photo via Michel De Trez Collection)

Following Exercise *Tiger* some lucky members of the 506th were given time off to explore Torquay. S/Sgt Leonard Hornbeck and M/Sgt Robert Plants from Regimental HQ pose beside the town's clock tower in the Strand (John Reeder photo via Michel De Trez Collection)

HQ Co supply sergeant Bob Webb on exercise near Ramsbury. (Bob Webb Jr)

2nd Lt Tom Kennedy. Prior to his joining the 506th Kennedy had spent a year with the US 1st Infantry Division before being sent to Officer Candidate School (OCS) at Fort Knox. Just days before the invasion, Kennedy took command of G Co's 1 Ptn after Lt Derwood Cann was hospitalized with yellow fever. (Mark Bando)

Personnel from 506th Regimental HQ waiting at Hungerford railway station for a train to take them to their D-Day marshaling area at Upottery Airfield in May 1944. The officer in the center wearing a steel helmet is Col Chase, regimental executive officer, and the regiment's commander, Col Robert Sink, is seated on the bench. The man standing between them is regimental adjutant Capt Max Petroff. (John Reeder via the Roger Day Collection)

The Brown twins from 2 Ptn I Co. Pvt Jim Brown (left) and Pfc Jack Brown (right) were born and raised in Alaska. Despite pressure from both their family and the Army they chose to serve in the same unit. (Bill Galbraith)

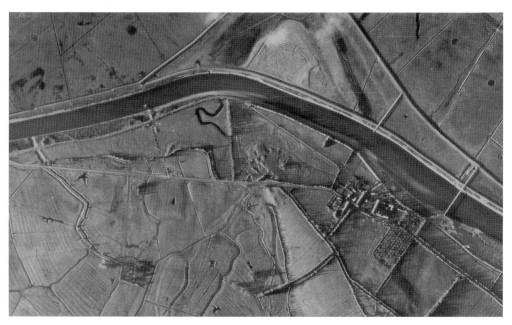

An Allied aerial reconnaissance photograph of the river Douve near the village of Brévands, dated December 24, 1943. On the left the road bridge is being constructed, one of 3rd Bn's objectives on D-Day. A wooden prefabricated support truss can be seen on the river being moved into position from the southern bank. Also visible, running diagonally from top center right to bottom right, is the berm carrying the path to the passenger ferry and the footbridge, 3rd Bn's other D-Day objective. (Crown Copyright 1944/MOD, reproduced with permission of the Controller of Her Majesty's Stationery Office – with special thanks to the Air Photo Archive at Keele University, Staffordshire)

3/506 TABLE OF ORGANIZATION – JUNE 6TH 1944

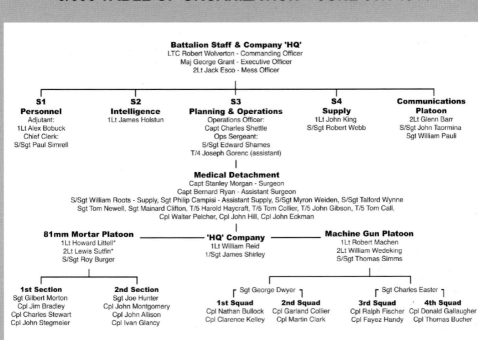

Battalion Staff & Company 'HQ'
LTC Robert Wolverton - Commanding Officer
Maj George Grant - Executive Officer
2Lt Jack Esco - Mess Officer

S1
Personnel
Adjutant:
1Lt Alex Bobuck
Chief Clerk:
S/Sgt Paul Simrell

S2
Intelligence
1Lt James Holstun

S3
Planning & Operations
Operations Officer:
Capt Charles Shettle
Ops Sergeant:
S/Sgt Edward Shames
T/4 Joseph Gorenc (assistant)

S4
Supply
1Lt John King
S/Sgt Robert Webb

Communications Platoon
2Lt Glenn Barr
S/Sgt John Taormina
Sgt William Pauli

Medical Detachment
Capt Stanley Morgan - Surgeon
Capt Bernard Ryan - Assistant Surgeon
S/Sgt William Roots - Supply, Sgt Philip Campisi - Assistant Supply, S/Sgt Myron Weiden, S/Sgt Talford Wynne
Sgt Tom Newell, Sgt Mainard Clifton, T/5 Harold Haycraft, T/5 Tom Collier, T/5 John Gibson, T/5 Tom Call,
Cpl Walter Pelcher, Cpl John Hill, Cpl John Eckman

81mm Mortar Platoon
1Lt Howard Littell*
2Lt Lewis Sutfin*
S/Sgt Roy Burger

'HQ' Company
1Lt William Reid
1/Sgt James Shirley

Machine Gun Platoon
1Lt Robert Machen
2Lt William Wedeking
S/Sgt Thomas Simms

1st Section
Sgt Gilbert Morton
Cpl Jim Bradley
Cpl Charles Stewart
Cpl John Stegmeier

2nd Section
Sgt Joe Hunter
Cpl John Montgomery
Cpl John Allison
Cpl Ivan Glancy

Sgt George Dwyer

1st Squad
Cpl Nathan Bullock
Cpl Clarence Kelley

2nd Squad
Cpl Garland Collier
Cpl Martin Clark

Sgt Charles Easter

3rd Squad
Cpl Ralph Fischer
Cpl Fayez Handy

4th Squad
Cpl Donald Gallaugher
Cpl Thomas Bucher

'G' Company
Capt Harold Van Antwerp
1Lt James Morton - Executive Officer
1/Sgt Woodrow Smith
S/Sgt Zolman Rosenfield - Supply
Sgt John Westeris - Commo
Pfc Andrew Sosnak - Medic

'H' Company
Capt Robert Harwick
1Lt Richard Meason - Executive Officer
1/Sgt Gordon Bolles
S/Sgt Frederick Bahlau - Supply
Sgt Gordon Yates - Commo
Pfc Lloyd Carpenter - Medic

'I' Company
Capt John McKnight
1Lt John Kiley - Executive Officer
1/Sgt Paul Garrison
S/Sgt John Luteran - Supply
Sgt Barron Dueber - Commo
Pfc Alvin Kidder - Medic

1st Platoon
2Lt Thomas Kennedy*
2Lt Frank Rowe
S/Sgt William Grantonic
1st Squad: Sgt Flintoff Brown
2nd Squad: Sgt Edwin Evans
3rd Squad: Sgt Harvey Jewett

1st Platoon
1Lt Edward Mehosky
2Lt Rudolph Bolte
S/Sgt Gerald McCullough
1st Squad: Sgt Frank Padisak
2nd Squad: Sgt William Reese
3rd Squad: Sgt Arthur Estes

1st Platoon
1Lt Gerry Howard
2Lt Floyd Johnston
S/Sgt James Japhet
1st Squad: Sgt John Turkovich
2nd Squad: Sgt Alexander Engelbrecht
3rd Squad: Sgt Beverly Manlove

2nd Platoon
1Lt Turner Chambliss
2Lt Eugene Dance*
S/Sgt Charles Skeen
1st Squad: Sgt Merville Grimes
2nd Squad: Sgt Carl Monson
3rd Squad: Sgt Donald Austin

2nd Platoon
1Lt Ken Christianson
2Lt Clark Heggeness
S/Sgt Alton Behringer
1st Squad: Sgt William Cumber
2nd Squad: Sgt Addison Marquardt
3rd Squad: Sgt Philip Parker

2nd Platoon
1Lt James Nye
2Lt John Windish
S/Sgt Jerry Beam
1st Squad: Sgt Earnie Mann
2nd Squad: Sgt Sidney McCallum
3rd Squad: Sgt Robert Nash

3rd Platoon
1Lt Joseph Doughty
2Lt Linton Barling
S/Sgt Marion Broussard
1st Squad: Sgt Roscoe Miner
2nd Squad: Sgt Hampton Scofield
3rd Squad: Sgt James West

3rd Platoon
2Lt Peter Madden*
2Lt John Williams
S/Sgt Harry Clawson
1st Squad: Sgt Frank Kleckner
2nd Squad: Sgt Charles Richards
3rd Squad: Sgt Ralph Bennett

3rd Platoon
1Lt Fred Anderson
2Lt Charles Santarsiero
S/Sgt George Retan
1st Squad: Sgt Frank Rick
2nd Squad: Sgt Albert Wall
3rd Squad: Sgt James Layfield

* Howard Littell and Lewis Sutfin joined the battalion just before the invasion. * Tom Kennedy moved from 2nd to 1st Platoon to replace Durwood Cann.
* Eugene Dance came in to take over from Tom Kennedy. * Pete Madden transferred to 'H' Company from the 81mm Mortar Platoon at Exeter.

NB: This Table of Organization is not an official document but has been created from first hand information supplied by the veterans.

3rd Bn 506th Table of Organization for Normandy.

As I Co was entering the S3 briefing tent at Exeter Ed Shames got some of them to sign a 100-franc note, which he kept as a souvenir. Two names, William Weber and Johnnie Edwards, stand out. According to the manifest they should have been at North Witham as part of I Co's pathfinder security team and not at Exeter! (Ed Shames)

OPPOSITE PAGE, FROM TOP TO BOTTOM:

Helmet recognition markings, Exeter – so that paratroopers could quickly identify themselves in battle the 101st Airborne Division ordered each regiment to paint identification symbols on every soldier's steel helmet. This photograph was taken on June 4 and shows Col Wolverton (left) with his adjutant, 1st Lt Alex Bobuck. Unfortunately mistakes were made during painting and the 3rd Bn went into battle with some of its dots in the 1st Bn position (i.e. to the right of the symbol). (SC photo via Michel De Trez Collection)

For the benefit of the camera Col Wolverton checks Alex Bobuck's equipment. In the background stands the 440th Troop Carrier Group C-47 aircraft 315087 "Lady Lillian," freshly painted in the black and white recognition stripes ordered on June 3. (SC)

L to R: Sgt Bill Pauli; S/Sgt John Taormina (POW Jun 6, 1944), both Communications Ptn, and T/5 Bill Atlee S1 (KIA Jun 6, 1944). Pauli broke his pelvis on landing in Normandy and could not get off the drop zone. By the afternoon of June 6, two German soldiers stumbled across him and took him to an aid station in St-Côme-du-Mont. There he remained until the town was liberated on June 8 and was then evacuated to a hospital in Wales. (SC)

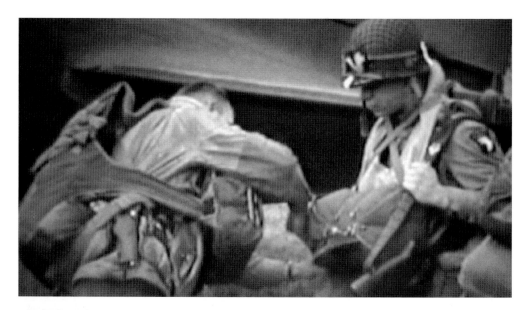

FROM TOP TO BOTTOM:

L to R: 1st Lt Alex Bobuck, (POW Jun 6, 1944) checks the reserve parachute of Pvt Ray Calandrella (Reconnaissance Ptn, POW Jun 7, 1944). (SC)

L to R: Bobuck and Pvt Jesse Cross (Reconnaissance Ptn, wounded Jun 6, 1944). (SC)

L to R: Pfc Harry Howard (Communications Ptn, POW Jun 6, 1944), T/5 Charles Riley (HQ Co armorer, POW Jun 6, 1944), S/Sgt John Taormina, T/5 Bill Atlee, and 1st Lt Alex Bobuck with hand on Howard's parachute. (SC)

Dr Stanley E. Morgan, battalion surgeon. Morgan was from New Orleans and a graduate of Louisiana State University School of Medicine. He sprained an ankle on the jump and was captured, but managed to establish an aid station in St-Côme-du-Mont. (SC)

1st Lt Howard Littell relaxing at his home in South Amboy, New Jersey, in 1943. Shortly before the invasion Littell was given command of 81mm Mortar Ptn following 2nd Lt Pete Madden's transfer to H Co. (Paul Bouchard Jr)

Adjutant 1st Lt Alex Bobuck checks a manifest on the morning of Sunday June 4 for the benefit of Signal Corps cameramen. In the background stands C-47 315087 "Lady Lillian." L to R: Pvt Anthony Wincensiak, Sgt Tom Newell, Pvt Ray Calandrella, Pvt Jesse Cross, Pvt John Rinehart, Sgt Bill Pauli, T/5 Jack Harrison, Pfc Harry Howard, T/5 Charles Riley, and S/Sgt John Taormina. (SC photo via Michel De Trez Collection)

This picture is one of the Signal Corps publicity photographs taken on June 4. Standing ready to jump is Pfc Don Ross from S3, the battalion's bugler. The instrument's mouthpiece can be seen sticking out from behind his reserve 'chute. (SC photo via Michel De Trez Collection)

Front to back, left hand group: Sgt Joe Gorenc, T/5 Charles Riley, Pfc Harry Howard, Sgt Bill Pauli, Pvt Jesse Cross, and Pvt Anthony Wincensiak. Front to back, right hand group: T/5 Bill Atlee (cigarette in mouth), S/Sgt John Taormina, T/5 Jack Harrison, Pvt John Rinehart (hidden behind Harrison), Pvt Ray Calandrella, and Sgt Tom Newell (without helmet). (SC photo via Michel De Trez Collection)

1st Lt Gerry Howard from 1 Ptn I Co. "The platoon was lucky to have Gerry as its commander," recalls Ed Shames. "He was a gentleman who cared about people." Tragically Howard was killed along with his men when his plane was shot down at Magneville. (Bill Galbraith)

Sgt Joe Gorenc, from Sheboygen, Wisconsin, the assistant S3, climbing aboard lead aircraft "Stoy Hora" on D-Night. Shortly before the battalion left Ramsbury for the marshaling area, Joe won $2,000 at cards and asked Ed Shames to hide the cash for him. Captured by the Germans, Joe managed to escape with Sgt George "Doc" Dwyer on July 20. (SC photo via Randy Hils)

Exeter on the evening of June 5, 1944. This picture shows a number of platoons from 3rd Bn who are marching out toward their waiting aircraft. On the extreme right is "Stoy Hora," the C-47 that was to carry Col Wolverton and his stick into Normandy (SC photo via Michel De Trez Collection)

Maj Grant (left) and the no. 2 stick marching out to "Lady Lillian." (SC photo via Michel De Trez Collection)

The majority of Col Wolverton's stick preparing to emplane. In the background behind the port wing is the Royal Aircraft Establishment hangar. L to R: unidentified, unidentified, Dr Stanley Morgan, 1st Lt Alex Bobuck, Pvt Jesse Cross, Col Bob Wolverton, T/5 Bill Atlee, Pfc Harry Howard, Pfc Don Ross, Sgt Tom Newell and Sgt Joe Gorenc. (SC photo via Michel De Trez Collection)

TOP:

T/5 Bill Atlee, a relative of British MP Clement Attlee (the American side of the family spelt the surname differently). Clement Attlee, known to Bill as "Uncle Kermit," was deputy prime minister in Winston Churchill's wartime coalition government. While in England Col Wolverton often gave Atlee additional leave passes so that he could visit his uncle. (SC photo via Michel De Trez Collection)

BOTTOM:

LtCol Bob Wolverton making last-minute adjustments to his parachute harness before emplaning. Less than 3 hours later he was dead. Wolverton had a premonition after arriving in England that he would not survive the war. As a result he wrote 21 letters to his infant son Lachlan (one for each year up until his 21st birthday). The letters were only to be opened in the event of the colonel's death. (SC photo via Randy Hils)

Col Krebs boarding his aircraft with Don Ross sitting in the plane. (SC photo via Randy Hils)

Pvt George McMillan from I Co was a member of 3rd Bn's pathfinder security team. (George McMillan)

A modern-day view from the tower of St-Côme-du-Mont's church looking south toward Carentan. Pathfinders Morgan and McMillan landed in the fields in the center of the picture.

them off down the hill and onto landing craft, where they were transported
out to the hospital ship and "treated." I was glad I wasn't tagged because
I had a chronic seasickness problem.

Pfc John Kutz (C Co 326th Airborne Engineers) remembers his part in
the exercise, "I was a runner for the engineers taking messages all over
the area. We were not allowed to use radios for fear that the Germans
might be listening. I remember getting very tired after continually
running across unfamiliar terrain in the dark of night."

The 501st PIR, minus its 3rd Bn which was securing the glider
landing zones north of Kingsbridge, moved northward from the drop
zone. They took the crossroads at Mounts, and the bridges across the
river Avon at New Bridge and Aveton Gifford. The remainder of C Co
326th Airborne Engineers and the 907th Glider Field Artillery Battalion
aided them. From an airborne point of view, Exercise *Tiger* went very
much according to plan. By 1400hrs the 502nd and 506th units that
had secured the beach exits had been relieved of their duties by elements
of the 4th Division. The paratroopers then moved westward to join up
with the rest of the 101st. Later that evening elements of the 327th
Glider Infantry Regiment landed by the sea, and the following day
joined up with the rest of the division. They then helped clear the
"enemy" from land sandwiched between the rivers Avon and Erme (an
area corresponding very roughly to the Carentan Estuary that divided
the Utah and Omaha beaches in Normandy). Thus ended the 101st
Airborne Division's part in Exercise *Tiger*.

Although the 101st had performed well, the same could not be said
about the exercise generally. Gen Collins, commander of VII Corps, was
unhappy with the many failures. Something had to be done urgently
about communications before the real landings, which were just five
short weeks away. All of the problems encountered during *Tiger* were
not helped by the loss of two landing ships following an attack by
German E-boats on one of the convoys heading for Slapton Sands.
Over 600 men lost their lives during this exercise, compared with about
20 fatalities at Utah Beach on D-Day.

With the mission completed, some men from the 101st were given the afternoon off. Jay Stone recalls:

> A few of us went into Torquay and found a delightful hotel bar which had a large curved window that gave a splendid view of the English Channel. We had the bar to ourselves as almost all civilians had been cleared from the area. The usual boisterous drinking was absent. It was hard to believe, but we were in a contemplative mood and the conversation was subdued. Some of us talked about our upcoming journey across the Channel, while others just looked out, lost in their own thoughts. Let's face it, we all knew that some of us were not going to return.

Exercise *Eagle*

Exercises *Beaver* and *Tiger* had been rehearsals for the role the 101st would undertake once it actually landed in France. However, Gen Taylor insisted upon a full-scale rehearsal of the entire division's movement, both parachute and glider, from its camps in the Kennet valley to its planned D-Day departure airfields. From these airfields the soldiers were transported in Troop Carrier Command C-47s and dropped near Welford (6 miles north of Hungerford) onto landing zones that simulated those the division would encounter on D-Day.

On May 9, 3rd Bn left Ramsbury and headed for Exeter airfield. Meanwhile elements of the 1st and 2nd battalions made for Upottery where they were joined the following day by Regimental HQ Co and elements of Service Co. The men spent most of May 11 sealed in their marshaling areas preparing for the exercise. By 2100hrs they had clambered aboard their designated aircraft and were waiting to go. After take-off, the planes followed routes that kept them in the air for the same duration as would apply on D-Day.

During the course of the previous night, a detail from the 28th Infantry Division, representing enemy forces, had moved into the exercise area. There was a full moon and for the very first time the various troop carrier groups participating were guided to their targets by lead aircraft fitted with "GEE" radar equipment. All of the groups, no matter which airfield they had departed from, eventually found themselves over the town of Devizes in Wiltshire, which was their final turning point (officially described as the initial point or IP). There were now over 400 aircraft in the sky, all heading east toward drop zones around Welford Airfield. The first paratroopers from the 506th jumped from their planes at 0055hrs on May 12. Once they had landed, the soldiers quickly assembled in the darkness and moved off toward objectives similar to those they would encounter in Normandy. Their mission was to assist an imaginary Z Corps in establishing a bridgehead north of Newbury by securing highways leading west, thus preventing the "enemy" from attacking Z Corps from the south, west, or northwest.

The exercise did not go entirely according to plan. As the huge airborne armada flew over Ramsbury, the lead pilot of a nine-plane formation from the 438th Troop Carrier Group, carrying H Co of the 502nd, told his radio operator to check the Aldis lamp. The remaining eight planes in the formation mistook this for the signal to drop their paratroopers, many of whom landed in Littlecote Park. Following the main drop each plane banked right, turned through 180 degrees and climbed to 4,000ft (to avoid incoming aircraft) before returning to its home base via a reversal of the route out. Four hours later it was the turn of the glider troops to make an appearance, and just as day was breaking about 80 gliders, a mixture of Waco CG4As and Horsas all loaded with jeeps, guns, and other equipment, touched down at Welford Airfield. The division as a whole suffered 436 hospital casualties (mainly broken bones), including 146 from the 506th, which was less than 7 percent of the total dropped and well within acceptable tolerances.

T/5 Joe Beyrle (I Co) missed out on *Tiger*, *Eagle*, and much of the immediate pre-D-Day training because he had been chosen for a special mission. Joe recalls:

During April I volunteered to take gold into occupied France. I was one of three picked from our regiment – I never found out who the other two men were. We went to Middle Wallop for training and from there to an airfield near Bournemouth where we were briefed and issued with bandoliers full of gold coins. I jumped at night and was met by the French underground. They looked after me for a week or so before I was picked up by plane and returned to England. In early May I did exactly the same thing again.

Moving out

For the next ten days the battalion took part in more intensified training culminating, on the night of May 22/23, in a jump, assembly, and attack problem. BrigGen Don Pratt, 101st assistant divisional commander, paid the unit a visit during this exercise. Sadly, Don Pratt would become the highest-ranking Allied officer to lose his life on D-Day.

Between May 24 and 27 the battalion started to prepare for movement to its D-Day marshaling area. This gave the men plenty of opportunities to think about what was to come. Soldiers about to go into battle for the very first time have different ways of dealing with their fears and anxieties. Bob Webb felt a need to reacquaint himself with his maker. Accompanied by a couple of his colleagues, he made his way to Ramsbury's church where the vicar talked for some time about the meaning of life. One thing that left a deep impression on the young Americans was the revelation that, 700 years earlier, local men leaving England for the Crusades had worshiped in the same church on the eve of their departure.

Soldiers going off to war like to take with them as many items of equipment as they possibly can, and men from the 506th were no exception. As a result, the US High Command looked into the possibility of using the British "leg bag." These bags were designed to carry a variety of items including radios, medical gear, machine gun tripods, and extra ammunition, and as the name suggests they were attached to the soldier's leg. A quick release strap was operated just after the parachute opened and the bag, which was attached to a 20ft coiled rope, dropped beneath the paratrooper and hit the ground first.

To evaluate these bags, a small number of paratroopers from the 3rd Bn were asked to perform a test jump. The group took off from Ramsbury Airfield in a C-47 aircraft that initially headed east before turning through 180 degrees and making its way back toward the village. As the plane flew low over the West End, the soldiers jumped, all landing safely in fields just west of the village. This was the first time the British "leg bag" had been used by US airborne forces. The trial was judged a success and the bags were employed by the 101st on D-Day.

On the morning of May 26, 3rd Bn was told to prepare for another exercise. In their heart of hearts the men felt that this was likely to be their last full day in Ramsbury prior to the invasion. Lt Tom Kennedy had been going out with an English girl called Sheila Thompson. She lived in London and he met her one Sunday afternoon at a tea dance held in the Piccadilly Hotel. Tom recalls:

> The hotel was first rate, with a large ballroom on the main floor. The bar was in the basement and sometimes, if you were very lucky, it would open briefly and serve Scotch, gin, or Pimms No.1. Back at Parliament Piece Lady Wyndham would often pass on messages for us via her own private telephone. On the morning before we left for the D-Day marshaling area, she telephoned Sheila and invited her to join me at Parliament Piece for a G Co party.

Tom has fond memories of that final evening in Ramsbury:

> We hadn't heard anything official but we all thought that this might be the big one. Capt Van Antwerp invited all of us to his room for a drink. We toasted each other and then Sheila toasted us, saying; "Here's to your dog tags and may they never part." Before we left the States for England every officer in the regiment had been given a bottle of Old Charter bourbon to save for an important occasion. Of course Barling and myself had finished ours months before, but somebody produced a few bottles and there was plenty to go round.

That same night a letter was pushed under the front door of Froxfield resident Elsie Gallagher. Elsie had a boyfriend in the 506th and an extract from the letter reads: " ... I would give anything in the world to see you tonight. Don't tell anyone but I'm sure that you will find out soon why I did not come to see you and why I will not be able to see you for a few days…" The soldier who wrote this note had done so at great risk. Had the authorities discovered this innocent act it would have been viewed as a serious breach of security. Sadly, the letter's author was killed in action during the Normandy campaign.

The following day at 0530hrs the battalion boarded buses in readiness for the short journey from Ramsbury to Hungerford railway station. George Dwyer recalls: "We were always being told not to talk to civilians about what we were doing. However, as we assembled and marched through Ramsbury all the townspeople seemed to be out lining the streets. There were shouts of 'Good hunting, boys,' some cheers and many tears. Somehow they knew that we were going to war." The rest of the 506th, less regimental staff, followed in stages throughout the remainder of the day.

Unusually for the month of May, the weather had been dominated by high pressure and was exceptionally hot. The men of the 3rd Bn, wearing woolen shirts, steel helmets, and jumpsuits (impregnated with a foul-smelling anti-gas solution), and carrying all manner of other equipment, sweated profusely as they waited at Hungerford for the train that would take them to Exeter's railway station.

After arriving at Hungerford, Sgt McCallum's squad from 2 Ptn (I Co) were told they had been volunteered for a special mission. However, only riflemen were required and Bill Galbraith, Jim Brown, and Bob Young, all machine gunners, were to stay with the rest of 2 Ptn. The remaining eight men transferred to another truck and prepared for a 135-mile journey that ended at North Witham Airfield near Nottingham.

The group comprised the following men: 2nd Lt John Windish, Sgt Sidney McCallum, Pfc Jack Brown (Jim Brown's twin brother), Pfc Johnnie Edwards, Pfc Bill Weber, Pfc George Kenfield, Pvt David Morgan, and Pvt George McMillan. After arrival at North Witham, the squad was told its mission was to act as a security group protecting 3rd Bn's pathfinders.

4

"Jump into the fight"
Operation *Overlord* begins

Twenty-four hours before the bulk of the battalion departed for Exeter, a small advance party consisting of Col Wolverton, 1st Lt John King (S4 supply officer), S/Sgt Ed Shames (operations sergeant), and Pfc Vernon Law (Wolverton's driver) left Ramsbury by jeep. Their mission was to check out 3rd Bn's marshaling area at Exeter Airfield and make preparations for the following day.

The airfield is about 120 miles southwest of Ramsbury and about 5 miles east of Exeter city center. In the summer of 1940, during a period now universally referred to as the Battle of Britain, the airfield was an important RAF Fighter Command station. Throughout the battle its squadrons of Spitfires and Hurricanes regularly engaged enemy bombers heading for Plymouth and the nearby naval dockyard at Devonport. On April 18, 1944, the RAF departed, and the US 440th Troop Carrier Group and its four C-47-equipped troop carrier squadrons began moving in. They immediately set about practicing night formation flying, glider towing, glider pick-up, and ground taxiing procedures. *Nunquam Non Paratus*, meaning "Never Unprepared," was the group's Latin motto.

May 26 dawned bright and sunny, and the English countryside, cloaked in its new coat of spring green, looked at its very best. It was difficult to imagine that there was a war going on as Wolverton's jeep headed west, passing through picturesque little villages with strange-sounding names such as Mere, Seavington St Michael, and Fenny Bridges. The journey took the best part of 4 hours, giving each man plenty of time to think. Ed Shames started wondering if this was the real thing or just another elaborate exercise.

Station 463 – Exeter airfield and marshaling area, June 1944

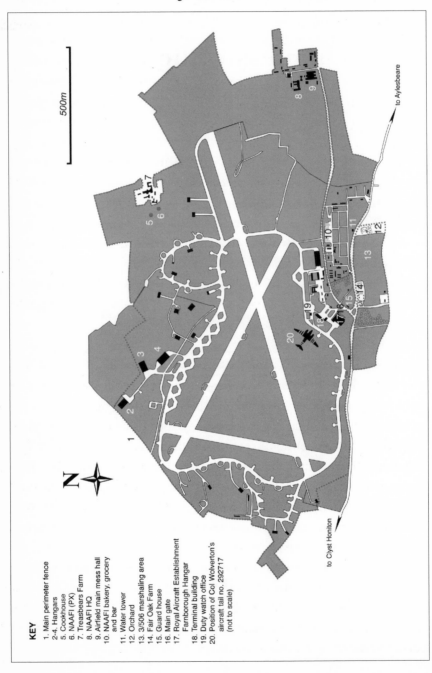

500m

to Aylesbeare

to Clyst Honiton

N

KEY

1. Main perimeter fence
2-4. Hangars
5. Cookhouse
6. NAAFI (PX)
7. Treasbears Farm
8. NAAFI HQ
9. Airfield main mess hall
10. NAAFI bakery, grocery
    and bar
11. Water tower
12. Orchard
13. 3/506 marshaling area
14. Fair Oak Farm
15. Guard house
16. Main gate
17. Royal Aircraft Establishment
    Farnborough Hangar
18. Terminal building
19. Duty watch office
20. Position of Col Wolverton's
    aircraft tail no. 292717
    (not to scale)

As they approached the airfield they could see camouflaged huts dotted around the perimeter and a large control tower in the southeast corner, not too far from the main gate. South of the airfield were the living areas, mess halls, and PX. These buildings were spread along a tiny road that gently climbed from the village of Clyst Honiton in the west toward the hamlet of Aylesbeare in the east. On the southern side of the road, just opposite the main gate, was a tented camp that was to become 3rd Bn's marshaling area.

After arriving at the airfield the group checked in with security, and once they had been admitted there was no way of leaving. The four men were shown to the battalion area which was made up of a number of pyramid tents. Each was just big enough to accommodate one squad and they were laid out around the much larger briefing tent, which for the next nine days would be home to the battalion's S3 team.

Col Wolverton walked around the area making sure that the engineers had assembled and built everything to his satisfaction. Ed recalls: "As we were walking around the compound, we were struck by an overwhelming feeling that this was it and we would actually be leaving here to begin the invasion of France – it was uncanny."

As the day drew to a close Wolverton, King, and Law retired to the Battalion HQ tent, leaving Ed alone to start preparing the S3 briefing area. The engineers had dumped a pile of fresh soil next to the tent, the perfect ingredient for sand table layouts.

Sunday May 27 was another warm and sunny day and after breakfast the advance party gathered in the HQ tent to await the battalion. Following their arrival Col Wolverton called a meeting of company commanders, executive officers, and platoon leaders. Here he explained where all the company locations were to be found and asked that each company assign five men to help the S3 team gather materials for the sand tables, such as twigs, rocks, and stones.

The rest of the men returned to their company areas. Cpl John Gibson from the medical detachment recalls, "We were housed in tents that were very close to the airfield and surrounded by barbed wire – it seemed like we were in prison. No one could leave, no one could enter and MPs [military police] patrolled the area constantly. Security and secrecy were demanded."

Despite these strict security measures, an unusual incident occurred involving Pfc Ken Johnson (H Co). During the journey to the marshaling area Johnson developed excruciating toothache. With no dental help available at Exeter, medic and amateur dentist Cpl Walter Pelcher was asked to help. Unfortunately he was unable to get at the tooth. It was clear that Johnson needed urgent outside medical assistance but the airfield was due to be sealed the following day – quick action was required. "Six burly MPs were summoned," recalls Ken, "I was put under close escort and forbidden to speak to anyone, as if I could, and taken to a nearby hospital where an English colonel successfully extracted my tooth. I was still drowsy from the anesthetic when the briefings began."

Following Wolverton's initial meeting, Capt Shettle, Sgt Gorenc, and privates first class Ross and Kendall joined S/Sgt Shames in the S3 area. There, Shettle and Shames got everybody occupied before returning to the HQ tent to attend a SHAEF (Supreme Headquarters Allied Expeditionary Force) briefing. SHAEF had dispatched representatives to all marshaling areas. These men brought along top-secret maps, photographs, and other information that identified the exact date, time, and place of the invasion. When Shettle and Shames arrived, the SHAEF officer had set up and was waiting for everybody to sit down. Ed recalls:

> There were about 30 people there. As I looked around I realized I was the only NCO present. The others were company commanders, executive officers, and platoon leaders, plus a couple of guys from C Co 326th Engineers. The tent fell silent as the SHAEF officer stood up in front of a flip chart mounted on a stand. The guy did the big showbiz thing, like a magician pulling a rabbit from a hat. He flipped open the cover of the chart to reveal a large heading that read "OPERATION OVERLORD – THE INVASION OF NORMANDY JUNE 4." Col Wolverton jumped out of his seat and said, "I had a hunch it was going to be there, boys, I knew it, I knew it!"

The officer began explaining the plan and gave out drop zone locations, mission targets, and important grid references. 3rd Bn's objectives were two wooden bridges and a passenger ferry crossing the Canal de Carentan near the village of Brévands. (Technically the canal is a continuation of the river Douve and for continuity's sake will be referred to as such on the following pages.) The bridges were about 6 miles inland from Le Grande Dune (Utah Beach) and nearly 2 miles east of St-Côme-du-Mont, providing an important link between the two American D-Day beaches. The ferry was operated by a chain link pulley system that had been in use for many years. However, this method of crossing the river did not suit the Germans, and during the latter part of 1942 they built a footbridge 275 yards east of the ferry. About a year later a second bridge, designed specifically for vehicular use, was built about half a mile upstream from the ferry. In August 1943 the dirt access road from Pénême was widened as were the track and dyke that led to the bridge. All roads were topped with crushed stone quarried from the Barantan area of St-Côme-du-Mont.

The discovery in 2002 of aerial photographs taken just before and after the invasion contradicts previous interpretations as to which bridge was used for road traffic and which for foot traffic. The pictures were found in the Air Photo Archive located at Keele University, Staffordshire (the current repository for World War II Allied reconnaissance photographs of western Europe) and were dated May 27 and June 12, 1944. They show that the bridge nearest Carentan was wide enough for vehicles whereas the bridge further downstream was only suitable for pedestrian traffic – a complete reversal of previous thinking! This error appears to have stemmed originally from a map incorrectly marked by Col Sink's operations officer, Maj Harold Hannah. Over the years this fundamental mistake has been repeated in every book and article written about the 101st in Normandy and has merely served to perpetuate the error.

The SHAEF officer then outlined each unit's role in the operation. HQ Co, supported by H Co, was to secure the road bridge, while G and I companies were to hold the footbridge, which was easy to find as a large white poplar tree grew nearby. The battalion was to hold these crossing points until relieved by the US 4th Division arriving from Utah Beach. Two platoons from C Co 326th Airborne Engineers were to assist 3rd Bn in holding the bridges and, if the need arose, prepare them for demolition. About 3 miles southwest of the bridges lies the town of Carentan, and SHAEF stressed that it was to be avoided at all costs. "Welcome" and "Thunder" were issued as the D-Night passwords and the briefing was concluded by a general question and answer session.

With the exception of Capt Shettle, all those leaving the tent were given aerial photographs, maps, and additional briefing notes. Shettle received a separate package containing more in-depth S3 information, which he immediately handed over to Shames. As the officers were leaving, Col Wolverton asked them to assemble the entire battalion, because he wanted to personally inform the men of their D-Day mission.

Afterwards Shames and his team returned to the S3 tent to begin putting the 20ft-square sand table together. The table was a large shallow wooden box full of sand and dirt with a 1:25,000 scale grid, made of string, strung across the top. It was orientated so that compass bearings matched the real location. Six farms ran along the road between the small hamlet of Pénême and the junction that led to the bridges. Each farm was lovingly recreated in miniature using materials collected specifically for the purpose. The farmhouse nearest the road junction was earmarked as the battalion aid station and supply store. Unfortunately, intelligence could not tell how many of these properties were occupied by the Germans, so all had to be viewed as potentially hostile. Where known the identity of enemy units and their respective strengths were marked, although the bridges were rather a gray area. Carentan on the other hand was known to be a German Corps HQ and Shames put a big note on the table saying, "Stay away."

Briefings, briefings, briefings

The following morning Ed Shames ordered Ross, Kendall, and Hiner (who had been temporarily attached to the S3) to fetch all the battalion's squads for their individual half-hour briefings, and one by one the units were ushered into the S3 tent. The tent was open 24 hours a day and Ed made it clear to everyone in attendance, whether officer or private, that they were all free to return at any time to talk to him or Gorenc about the operation. One man who took Ed up on his offer was H Squad leader Sgt Frank Padisak. Ed remembers:

Joe Gorenc passed a dumb comment about Padisak. Padisak had returned alone to our tent at least six times more than anyone else, only to go over the same information time and time again, all in infinite detail. Joe Gorenc smiled at me as he said, "What's wrong with this guy, is he stupid or something?" I began to put him straight about Padisak and Joe was visibly embarrassed. I said, "Can't you see what's driving this man?" Gorenc looked sheepishly at me. "Padisak's holding himself totally responsible for the lives of his squad and the extra work that he is putting in is giving him a confidence and understanding that I wish some of the other squad leaders had."

Col Wolverton and his staff were not exempt from these briefings and had to attend at their allotted times. "Wolverton had the same concerns and questions that everyone else was voicing during the week running up to the invasion," recollects Ed. "He told me at one of the briefings that the quality of the sand table was superb and that I wasn't to worry about attending the emplaning drills out on the airfield. He told me to stay in the tent and make sure everyone got the assistance they needed."

Not everyone showed Ed the same kindness, however:

1st Lt Holstun from HQ Co was attending one of my briefings in the S3 tent. During the proceedings he shouted in my face, "I would rather be fighting Limeys and Jews than the Krauts." The tent fell into an embarrassed silence and you could have heard a pin drop. Overcome with anger I called him a SOB and threatened, "If you ever come between me and a Kraut I'm going to blow your brains out!" After a short argument he backed down and I carried on with the briefing, but it was an awful moment for me and all the other people in the tent.

Pfc John Kutz, from 1 Ptn, C Co 326th Airborne Engineers, has vivid memories of the briefing period: "I was 25 years old, considerably older than most of the men I was serving with. We made quite a few trips to the sand table tent. The S3 men were very instructive and the aerial photos quite incredible. One picture showed a German soldier on guard duty. The photograph was so clear that if he'd been a buddy I would have recognized him instantly!"

Each platoon was assigned quarters surrounding the briefing tent, and from above the whole area resembled a large spider's web. Ralph Bennett describes the situation:

> It seemed to be raining a lot. Each day we attended lectures, had close order drill and unarmed combat, cleaned weapons and sharpened knives. We worked from 6am to about 5pm. A lot of the guys would spend their evenings watching movies. However, I was always busy and never had time to attend the film shows but I do remember getting my hair trimmed in a "butch cut," which was a kind of flat top. What I remember most were the briefings. The sand table tent was full of maps and aerial photographs and we attended at least two platoon-strength lectures there. Each would last about half an hour, then we would move on to the next thing. One day we were subjected to a gas drill. A couple of white smoke grenades were popped and somebody shouted, "Gas, Gas, Gas." This was supposed to test our response time and the serviceability and fit of our masks.

During this period Hank DiCarlo was unexpectedly promoted. "Cpl John Purdie decided to give up his stripes," recalls Hank. "He just didn't want the responsibility of making life and death decisions that could impact on his fellow squad mates. Someone had to do the job so our squad leader, Frank Padisak, chose me."

John Gibson remembers the waiting:

> When you are preparing for a very dangerous mission you think of family and good friends. You don't know if you'll ever see them again — life becomes precious and you appreciate everything. The medical detachment seemed to do a lot of waiting and sitting around. I remember, just to take my mind off things, playing blackjack for hours with Sgt Tom Newell — Tom cleaned me out real good. The amounts we betted were small and I didn't see any big money gambled in the marshaling area.

Jimmy "Pee Wee" Martin found a more humorous way of passing the time. His platoon leader, 1st Lt Turner Chambliss, was a West Point graduate, and although a fair man followed his training to the letter. As he was so "West Point" about everything the platoon did, "Pee Wee" decided to stencil "West Point" above the breast pocket of the unit's jump jackets. He recalls: "When we showed up in formation we were expecting an uproar but the lieutenant gave no indication, then or in the days that followed, that he'd ever noticed. This was a bit of a let down, but we all jumped into Normandy with our suits marked in this way."

Sunday June 4

As May gave way to June, the high pressure that had dominated the weather over the British Isles for the previous three weeks moved away, and was replaced by a deepening depression. On May 23 Gen Eisenhower had established the date for the invasion as June 5, but as the planners anxiously watched the weather charts it became clear that a postponement of 24 hours would be necessary.

Any nagging doubts about the operation being just another "dry run" were finally quashed when Gen Maxwell Taylor, the divisional commander, turned up to give a "get in there and fight" team talk. He made a point of telling the men that on no account should they allow themselves to be taken prisoner. Following his address many of the squad leaders used the same rhetoric when they gave their own last minute talks. Newly promoted Hank DiCarlo recalls: "Sgt 'Bud' Estes, who had only recently taken over as the 60mm mortar squad leader, made an impassioned speech to members of 1 Ptn. He vehemently declared that under no circumstances should any of us surrender to the enemy. The irony was that despite all his talk he became a prisoner on D-Day!"

On June 4 final briefings were given and live ammunition, passwords, recognition crickets, and sleeve detectors (for identifying the presence of gas) issued. Hank DiCarlo recalls three items he had to carry:

> We were given emergency medical kits, arm flags, and mimeographed
> maps of the jump area. I still have my copy and to this day have never

been able to decipher it! Our stay in the marshaling area built up to a fried chicken, steak, and strawberry ice cream finale, the first we'd had since coming to the UK. We were told we'd be taking off on the night of June 4, but this was later changed to June 5.

The parachutes and stores had been offloaded from trucks and placed beside the waiting aircraft, only for the jump to be postponed. The men and stores went back to their platoon areas and the 'chutes were placed aboard the planes. Ed Shames and his S3 team returned to the briefing tent and carried on with their work.

Earlier in the day a group of war correspondents had visited the airfield and interviewed men from the 3rd Bn, as well as personnel from the 440th Troop Carrier Group. 1st Lt Howard Littell (81mm Mortar Ptn leader) organized several demonstrations that included soldiers putting on their parachutes and clambering aboard aircraft. Cerfeda and Nehez from the Army Signal Corps filmed most of this activity. Ray Calandrella was taking part in the filming and recalls:

I'd forgotten to hand my goggles in, which is why I'm the only guy in the film wearing those stupid things on my helmet. Col Wolverton asked 1st Lt Littell to select a squad for the publicity pictures, but the battalion's officers suggested that Wolverton's stick should have the honor. I was privileged to be a member of that group. We were out at the aircraft and spent about 1½ hours making the film. The pictures taken that day have become some of the most iconic images of the invasion period. When my big moment came I didn't realize that the camera was actually rolling and continued fiddling with a parachute bag – I should have been looking straight at the lens. Later they caught me chewing gum while 1st Lt Bobuck checked my 'chute. Then they took some still shots inside of the aircraft. We didn't camouflage our faces for the filming but we did for the jump. My basic load for D-Day was: M1 rifle, 240 rounds of 30-06 ammunition (30 clips of eight rounds), five grenades, and one mine with two detonators – I kept these well apart in separate pockets! I wasn't issued a leg bag, only the support weapon troops were given those.

Monday June 5

During the morning of June 5, Father John Maloney conducted an open air Catholic mass in the middle of the bivouac area, and nearby Chaplain Tildon McGee held an Anglican service. Attending Father Maloney's mass was Ralph Bennett: "I'm not a Catholic, but many of my men were. So I thought it appropriate to pray alongside them despite being from a different religious denomination." One of the priests asked if anyone wanted to be baptized, and Pvt Bob Rommel answered the call: "I thought this was as good a time as any. When I told Cpl Bucher that I was going to attend the baptism he said, 'Rommel, you are never gonna make it home so why worry about it?' Bucher had a very weird sense of humor!"

That afternoon all the platoons held their final sand table critiques, as Teddy Dziepak recalls: "1st Lt Gerry Howard was my platoon leader. We had all kinds of critiques telling us where we were supposed to go, when we were going to jump, and what we were going to do. We were issued our ammunition at about 5pm. Then we started cleaning up our areas, sharpening knives, and blackening our faces."

Around 2000hrs Col Wolverton ordered everyone to gather on the parade ground as he wanted to talk candidly to every man. Standing on an earth bank, he started by suggesting that they should have a reunion after the war – everyone unanimously agreed. He then continued with an emotionally charged openness that took many people by surprise, as he said, "Men, I am not a religious man and I don't know your feelings in this matter, but I am going to ask you to pray with me for the success of the mission before us. I would like you to get down on your knees and pray and while you do this do not look down, but look up, with heads held high to the sky."

The colonel then began his special prayer:

God almighty! In a few short hours we will be in battle with the enemy. We do not join battle afraid. We do not ask favors or indulgence but ask that, if you will, use us as your instrument for the right and an aid in returning peace to the world. We do not know or seek what our fate will be. We only ask this, that if die we must, that we die as men would die, without complaining, without pleading and safe in the feeling that we have done our best for what we believed was right. Oh Lord! Protect our loved ones and be near us in the fire ahead, and with us now as we each pray to you.

Ralph Bennett was moved by what he heard:

Col Wolverton talked to us just like he was one of the guys and seemed genuinely concerned at the prospect of us not all getting back alive. No one spoke during the whole thing and you could have heard a pin drop. Afterwards he dismissed us and we returned to our own tents. I picked up my Thompson and all my gear and marched the squad out to join the battalion for the final parade. Then, loaded down like pack mules with all of our equipment, we made our way out to the planes.

The route to the airfield was lined with service buildings, barracks, and offices, and the men had to pass through several security checkpoints. As they made their way silently down the road people emerged from the buildings and watched them pass by – they must have sensed that this was the start of the invasion and were probably wondering how many of the soldiers would make it back.

The parachutes, which had been placed on the aircraft the previous evening, were offloaded by air force personnel and put under the wings. All aircraft had numbers chalked onto the fuselage near the cargo door. Every soldier was given a manifest detailing who was in each stick, which corresponded with one of the chalk numbers. As the men started boarding the aircraft, it became apparent that the jumpmasters were not checking names against the manifests. Some people took advantage of this lapse and switched planes so that they could jump with friends from other squads. However, medic Johnny Gibson was given permission by Dr Morgan to jump with any company or squad he desired. Morgan's policy was to place at least one medic on each of HQ Co's assigned aircraft. Gibson chose to join his friend George Rosie as there was space available on his plane (Rosie's stick was led by 2nd Lt Lewis Sutfin). Medics carried essential first aid supplies and were required by international law to wear at least one Red Cross armband. Some, like Gibson, wore one on each arm after being issued a second in the marshaling area. Unfortunately the new armband was made of a shiny material that caused Gibson problems on June 6.

Dr "Barney" Ryan was manifested on the no. 2 aircraft with Maj Grant and recalls:

I realized I'd left the airsickness tablets in my tent and rushed back to get them. I scooped some pills off the table and when I reached the aircraft gave them to the men. After putting them in their mouths they spluttered, "What the hell are you trying to do to us – these are salt pills!" Luckily nobody got airsick. Just before emplaning Maj Grant ordered me to the back of the stick. During training I'd always jumped directly behind him. However, a captain and two enlisted men from the navy were on our plane acting as forward observers to help direct naval gunfire. They were carrying bulky ship-to-shore radio equipment and Grant wanted them near him when he landed.

Hank DiCarlo suffered terribly from airsickness. His colleagues Donald Zahn and Frank Padisak had never been airsick and generously gave him their capsules. "I had no idea just how drowsy those things would make me feel," recalls Hank. "Because of my normal laid back demeanor many of my friends thought I was just being cool, but in actual fact I was fighting to keep my eyes open and stay awake!"

Whilst all this was going on Ed Shames was still working away in the S3 briefing tent:

It was early evening and most of my team had gone out to the airfield. Capt Shettle came in and I remember him setting his prismatic compass with a bearing for the road bridge. His arrival surprised me because it was the first time he had shown his face in over a week. What he'd actually been doing during that time God only knows, but he wasn't with me. Before the battalion departed I took down the maps and aerial photographs from the sides of the tent, crammed as much stuff as I could into my musette bag, grabbed my M1 and went out to Col Wolverton's aircraft. I didn't even have time to blacken my face.

As soon as Ed arrived, Wolverton told him to board another plane. A little surprised by this sudden change of plan he saluted, turned, and made his way toward the designated aircraft. Darkness had set in by the time he had fitted his parachute and clambered aboard. The jumpmaster directed him toward the back of the stick. The plane was bathed in a red glow from the interior lights and as Ed pushed past the men he was unable to recognize any of their faces.

A little earlier, Don Ross and Joe Gorenc had made their way out to the no. 1 aircraft. There they fitted their 'chutes and hung all the other equipment they were expected to carry about their person. On emplaning Ross sat next to Col Wolverton, who was smoking countless cigarettes to pass the time. The majority of the personnel on the plane were from the communications platoon, under the temporary command of 1st Lt Alex Bobuck.

Wolverton's plane had an unexpected guest. He was Frank Ward Smith, a 40-year-old British war correspondent working for the BBC and a Sunday newspaper. The following weekend his article entitled "I Saw Them Jump to Destiny" was published in the *News of the World*. An extract is reproduced here with the kind permission of News International Syndication, London:

The previous day I had flown to London and back on urgent business. Immediately on my return I was summoned to a squadron headquarters to sleep. But they didn't show me to my room. Instead they led me right out to the airfield, to the first of a line of waiting planes... The co-pilot, Major Cannon, was reading a historic message from General Eisenhower. It spoke of the "Great Crusade," and ended: "Let us beseech the blessing of Almighty God on this noble undertaking."

Almost before we realized it we were off... "Say," someone sang out suddenly, "What's the date? I'll feel kinda dumb down there if some guy asks me and I get it wrong." We all laughed uproariously at things like that – the littlest things, the silliest things. We exchanged cigarettes and we talked on, but somehow never about things that mattered.

Capt Don Orcutt was a pilot with the 440th Troop Carrier Group's 95th Troop Carrier Squadron. He recalls the hours leading up to take-off and the flight across the Channel to France.

We reported to our aircraft a full 2 hours before leaving and found time to talk with members of our stick. They all made light of what was facing them. During this period I had the great pleasure of being introduced to Col Wolverton by his pilot, and our group commander, Col Krebs, whose plane was parked behind mine on the field. He asked the usual things, "How are you feeling, how long have you been a pilot etc." He wasn't very tall and with blackened face and burdened with all his equipment he looked like a little gnome. I told him I'd been flying for a year and a half and saw a change in his expression. He must have felt some relief in the knowledge that complete novices were not flying his troops into action. I wished him God speed and a safe delivery. He showed no fear whatsoever.

Each squadron had its own location on the airfield. All the planes for the mission were numbered with large white chalk figures on the left side just in front of the main cabin exit door. Col Krebs taxied around the perimeter displaying his chalk number for all of us to see and we fell numerically into line behind him. At 11.50pm 45 aircraft were lined up ready for take-off. We had a signalman who flashed a green light at the end of the runway. If my memory serves me correctly, we took off at 10-second intervals and the entire group was airborne in roughly 8 minutes.

The colonel flew at a speed of 130mph and as each aircraft took off it went "balls out" playing catch the leader before eventually falling into position. Every plane had a series of dim blue lights, three on each upper wing surface and three on top of the cabin. After staring at those for a while your eyes began to cross. Krebs kept his landing lights on so that outbound planes could spot the head of the formation. This was always a bit hairy because there was little room for error, particularly at night.

The formation was divided into three columns (left, right, and center). Don was flying in the left hand column carrying chalk no. 16. This made him the lead aircraft of a three-ship element, known as a "V," and part of the formation's second nine-ship flight called a "V" of "Vs."

Once the group had fully assembled, it passed over Exeter and then headed out across the Channel to France via Portland Bill. Don continues: "We crossed the Channel at an altitude of 1,500ft, maintaining radio silence which we kept for the entire mission. As we passed the Channel Islands the Germans opened up with a stream of flak – pretty to see but ineffective."

The moon was reflecting silver on the Channel below and a brilliant pool of light shimmered on the surface of the sea. The sight was so beautiful it reminded medic John Gibson of the desert moon that shone so brightly over his home in Arizona. Sitting next to John in the aircraft was Pvt Charles Lee. Gibson recalls:

Talking over the roar of the engines was almost impossible but I yelled at my buddy, "How do you feel, Lee?" After two attempts at making him hear, Lee replied, "Better than expected, how about you?" I yelled back the same answer he gave me. Inside I was nervous, had butterflies in my stomach and my hands were damp and cold with sweat. The plane rocked and fell a few feet, only to quickly regain its position. As we approached the peninsula I could see our formation of aircraft stretching for what seemed like miles behind us.

Looking out from the open door of his aircraft, Pvt Galbraith could see the invasion fleet below:

It looked like you could move across them and not get your feet wet. When we came over the peninsula there was a lot of antiaircraft fire with tracers of every color imaginable. The plane didn't slow down for the jump and most of us lost our leg packs because of the exit speed. We were completely unaccustomed to parachuting with those things, as we'd never jumped with them before. The gun, ammunition, and everything my crew needed was lost when our leg bags broke free. Luckily I still had my carbine as I'd decided to carry it.

When full, the leg bags were large and heavy, and the paratroopers would have experienced greater than usual wind resistance as they jumped. This may explain why they thought the plane was flying faster than it actually was.

To help with navigation, Col Krebs's aircraft was fitted with "GEE." This was a British radio system based on triangulation. Two transmitters in England sent out signals that could be checked by the navigator against a special map covered with lattice lines. Where the signals crossed gave the aircraft's approximate position. In addition every plane in the formation carried a "Rebecca" receiver/transmitter. This was part of a radar beacon and responder system that had been designed by the British and manufactured by the Americans. Pathfinders carried man-portable "Eureka" sets to the drop zones. Once on the ground, the "Eureka" sets were placed in position and switched on 15 minutes before the main formation of aircraft was due to arrive. They could transmit on five different frequencies, so by careful allocation it was possible for every aircraft to correctly identify its drop zone. Only squadron leaders (one in every nine aircraft) were allowed to switch their "Rebecca" sets on, as it was believed that too many in use at the same time might cause signal saturation. The "Rebecca" sent out a pulse, and upon receiving the signal the "Eureka" replied automatically. The aircraft's navigator could then calculate his distance and compass bearing from the drop zone. Twenty minutes after the planes had passed the pathfinders switched off the "Eureka" sets.

Don Orcutt recalls:

Col Krebs had the only GEE installation in the group. I had constant visual contact with my squadron leader Col Anderson, who in turn had visual contact with Krebs. I did my very best to hold proper position on D-Night.

As we approached the coast of the Cotentin peninsula a layer of clouds became visible that looked like they rose to a height of at least 3,000ft. Continuing at our then present altitude would have meant flying into that cloudbank. The colonel chose to descend and fly under the overcast – a wise move as it turned out. He must have studied terrain maps of the peninsula and knew how low he could go without danger, as our new height of about 900ft above sea level was just right. Every plane in the group was able to maintain visual contact with each other. I recall flying through some cloud tendrils that hung down under the overcast, but had no problems maintaining contact with my squadron commander's plane.

The 440th's drop was the most successful and accurate on D-Night, mainly due to Col Krebs's decision to fly under the overcast and not through or over it, which was the undoing of several of the other groups. Once the formation reached the Initial Point or IP (25 miles from the drop zone) it flew directly to the target with no further turns. Don continues:

At 4 minutes prior to estimated time over the drop zone the group leader flashed a red beacon from the astrodome of his C-47, indicating that we should slow down to our drop speed of 120mph. In theory, every plane in the formation should have throttled back at the same instant. We were already at the correct height as I remember my altimeter registering 950ft above sea level.

At the same time as the group leader flashed his beacon a red light was switched on by the plane's exit door. This was the signal for the jumpmaster to start his safety checks. On the command "Stand up" the soldiers hauled themselves out of their seats and held the snap (a metal clip attached to the end of the static line) in front of their faces. (Most jumpmasters gave the commands "Stand up and hook up" as one order, although they should have been given separately). After the snap was clipped onto the cable, the command "Check equipment" was given, followed by "Sound off for equipment check." Every man in the stick responded by shouting in sequence from the rear, "Eighteen OK! Seventeen OK! Sixteen OK!..." The jumpmaster would then check that all the snaps were securely on the cable before returning to his designated position in the aircraft.

One aircraft, piloted by 1st Lt Ray Pullen, which was in the right-hand element of Don Orcutt's nine-ship flight, suddenly exploded in a brilliant flash of light. It veered off to the left and crashed in flames near the small village of Magneville (pronounced Manville). The plane was carrying men from I Co and everybody on board was killed. John Gibson witnessed the aircraft's final moments: "The flak had just started firing at the leading aircraft when I saw a huge red flash from a plane crashing off to our left. We all tried not to think about the explosion, but it wasn't a pleasant sight to witness. Shortly afterwards we came under heavy antiaircraft and machine gun fire."

Don Orcutt's plane was now over the target:

At 1.40am we received the green light from Col Krebs, and every aircraft in the formation began dropping its troops. I punched a stopwatch and at the same time flicked the switch for the green light. The men from the three planes in my "V" all jumped simultaneously. My crew chief was by the door observing the jump with headset and mike to advise me when the last man left the aircraft. I'm positive that I held the correct position relative to my squadron commander's plane and both my wingmen were right with me.

With the last man gone I stopped the watch and it showed 36 seconds had elapsed [more than twice as long as normal – someone must have stumbled and held the stick up] and applied the power as needed to maintain position in formation. I had no way of knowing at the time what was going on behind me. Afterwards I found out that two planes from the 96th Squadron had been hit and crashed into the Channel after the drop. The ride home was a bit of an anticlimax and we returned to Exeter in formation.

Pathfinders

Just like their colleagues at Exeter, the 506th security detachment, which had left Hungerford for North Witham ten days earlier, had been kept busy attending briefings and sand table orientation sessions – strangely, until they boarded their aircraft they never mixed fully with the men they had been sent to protect. David Morgan remembers being told that once on the ground they were not to open fire unless absolutely necessary.

About 2 hours before the 3rd Bn's departure from Exeter, the first of the pathfinder teams left North Witham. On board chalk no. 9, the 11th and last 101st plane to leave, were ten pathfinders and the 506th security detachment. They flew across the Channel in company with two other aircraft carrying the 501st PIR pathfinders and their security teams. All three planes were heading for Drop Zone D.

Once over open water the aircraft dropped to below 100ft, and the soldiers nearest the open door could feel spray on their faces blown in from the plane's prop blast. David Morgan was sitting near the front of the aircraft and recalls: "We were loaded before the pathfinders so that when we jumped they were first out of the door. It was dark when we took off and the flight over was uneventful until we crossed the coast."

Upon reaching the Cherbourg peninsula the pilot had difficulty finding the drop zone and made at least one pass over the area. This attracted German antiaircraft fire and multicolored tracer rounds lit up the sky. Pvt George McMillan was standing near the cockpit door and could see the plane's flight crew at work. He watched as the pilot put the aircraft into a tight left banking turn and pushed the throttles open before climbing. When the green light came on the aircraft was approaching the town of St-Côme-du-Mont from the north, along a line roughly parallel to the RN13, and still climbing. Most of the pathfinders landed north of the settlement where they decided to set up their "Eureka" beacon. Unfortunately this was over 1¼ miles west of the drop zone and the error had devastating consequences for the 3rd Bn's drop 45 minutes later. Of the nine-man pathfinder team, five were eventually killed, two wounded, and one captured.

The security detachment landed south of St-Côme-du-Mont. After exiting, George McMillan was in the air for less than 20 seconds before landing in a field of knee-high clover. Meanwhile David Morgan, who had barely enough time to orientate himself, landed in an orchard about 200 yards south of the town's girls' school and was caught in a tree. He hung in his harness for about 20 minutes before cutting himself free and dropping to the ground. Everything was very quiet and Morgan had no idea where his colleagues had gone, where the Germans were located or what he should do. Nearby was a tall dark hedgerow and he decided to hide there until daybreak.

~5~

"God, let me live 'til morning"
D-Night part 1

St-Côme-du-Mont lies on the Route Nationale 13 (RN13), the Cotentin peninsula's main communication road that links the port of Cherbourg with Carentan. Until recently, one of the region's outstanding attributes had been the centuries-old hedgerows that lined most roads and track ways and surrounded nearly every field. Some of the tracks were completely enclosed by the overhanging thick hedgerows, a feature the French called "double hedges." The Germans took full advantage of these barriers and used them for defensive purposes, as well as for camouflaging vehicles, equipment, and troops. A perfect example of this was a field kitchen that was hidden at the end of a "double hedge" behind houses near the Rue des Croix.

At the time of the invasion, St-Côme-du-Mont's civilian population numbered about 550. In addition approximately 1,000 German troops from the III.Bataillon/Infanterie-Regiment 1058 were billeted in and around the town. A Norman church, typical of many in the region, dominates the town center. The Germans installed a machine-gun position in the tower that gave commanding views of the surrounding area. Immediately to the east is a large square (Place de la République) that separates the church from the RN13 road.

The III.Bataillon/Infanterie-Regiment 1058 formed part of the 91.Luftlande Infanterie-Division, a part of the German mobile reserve, which had a total strength of 10,555 men. The division was sent to Normandy on May 14, 1944, to help reinforce the military presence in the central part of the peninsula, and set up its HQ at Château Picauville.

The center of St-Côme-du-Mont, June 6, 1944

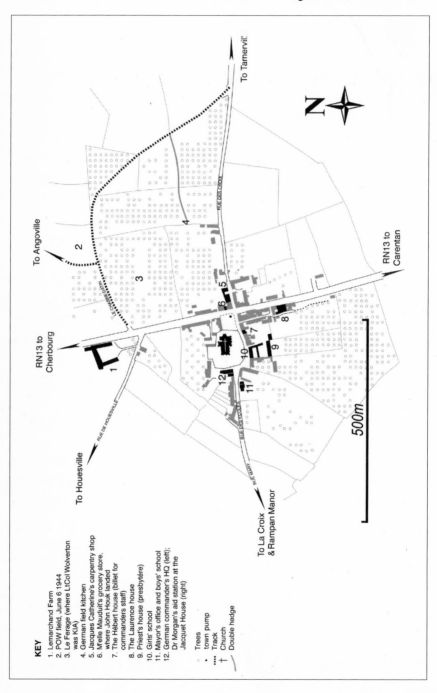

KEY

1. Lemarchand Farm
2. POW field, June 6 1944
3. Le Ferage (where LtCol Wolverton was KIA)
4. German field kitchen
5. Jacques Catherine's carpentry shop
6. Melle Mauduit's grocery store, where John Houk landed
7. The Hébert house (billet for commanders staff)
8. The Laurence house
9. Priest's house (presbytère)
10. Girls' school
11. Mayor's office and boys' school
12. German commander's HQ (left); Dr Morgan's aid station at the Jacquet House (right)

Trees
town pump
Track
Church
Double hedge

To Angoville

RN13 to Cherbourg

To Tarnervil!

RN13 to Carentan

To Housesville

To La Croix & Rampan Manor

RUE DES CROIX

LE CHASSE-LOUP

RUE DE HOUESVILLE

RUE DES ECOLES

RUE GARY

500m

N

Its appearance came as a shock to the Allied planners because it had established itself in an area chosen for the 82nd Airborne Division's landings. As a direct result the 82nd's drop zone and objectives were moved further east.

Located to the west of Carentan, just south of the Gorges marshes, was the German Fallschirmjäger Regiment 6 (6th Parachute Regiment), which was attached to the 91.Luftlande Infanterie-Division. This was an experienced and well-trained airborne unit that would play a significant part in forthcoming battles with the 506th. Also in the same area, and tactically part of the 91.Luftlande Infanterie-Division, was Panzer-Abteilung 100 (100th Replacement and Training Tank Battalion), mainly equipped with obsolete French tanks.

Protecting the entire eastern coastal sector of the peninsula was the 709.Infanterie-Division. It had arrived in Normandy during December 1943 and many of its personnel were older men; the average age was 36. During the middle of May 1944, Ost-Bataillon 795 was attached to the 709.Infanterie-Division and moved into the area surrounding the village of Turqueville. This location, midway between Ste-Marie-du-Mont and Ste-Mère-Église, placed the battalion right in the middle of the 82nd and 101st drop zones! Ost-Batallion 795 was made up of men from the Soviet republic of Georgia who had been recruited from POW camps. Many Georgians wished to see their country freed from the Soviet yoke and saw fighting for the Germans as a way of achieving this aim.

Gustave and Louise Laurence were the mayor and mayoress of St-Côme-du-Mont. Throughout the war the couple had administered the town's affairs from an office near the church. Several men from the town, including the mayor and Eugène Guilbaut (a schoolteacher) had been active members of the local Socialist Resistance group. On August 29, 1943, following a tip-off from Guilbaut's wife, the Gestapo paid the men a "visit." Nothing was found in the Laurences' house, but Guilbaut was not so fortunate. A pistol he had concealed in a toilet at the boys' school was discovered, and the men were arrested. Following a short spell in St-Lô prison, all were released with the exception of Guilbaut, who was sent to Dachau concentration camp. However, Gustave Laurence did not go unpunished and was stripped of his title as mayor and exiled to Isigny-sur-Mer for a period of six months. After a short while he secretly returned to his family and covertly continued his work as mayor from a room in their home. Unfortunately they no longer had any way of receiving outside news as the Germans had confiscated the town's official radio.

Louise was Gustave's second wife and these are her memories of the days leading up to the invasion:

> The family were preparing for my stepdaughter Jeannine's first communion on Sunday June 4. The fine weather caused a lot of apprehension amongst the locals. We hoped that nothing would happen during the night and that the Allies would wait until at least Monday 5th before launching their invasion. Sunday came and the communion went ahead as planned. We had 20 invited guests at the service including my brother Eugène [Jeannine's godfather] and his wife Marthe. That evening we had a celebration dinner at our house. After we'd eaten, the children were encouraged to say a few words or sing. The evening was made even more special when little Jean – one of our younger children – stood up and sang a couple of songs that he'd made up – it was so sweet. Eugène and his family had to leave early because of the German curfew. After they'd left our children continued with the celebration, each taking turns to sing different songs. The following day we heard that the Germans had closed all the roads leading to Carentan for a few hours saying they were on exercise. We thought there might be some other reason for their action.

In 1944 Thérèse Dieudonnè (née Jacquet) was just 12 years old. Her parents lived in a detached house in the center of town just west of the church. Part of the building had been requisitioned by the German commander and became his headquarters, which was known as the Kommandantur. Because of the increasing frequency of Allied bombing raids, relations with the Germans had steadily deteriorated. On the Sunday before the invasion children from several families had taken part in their first communion. After leaving the church the Jacquet family sensed a strange atmosphere, as Thérèse recalls: "Whilst returning home to our modest communion party we noticed the Germans were talking inordinately loudly to one another."

Living nearby, in the Place de la République, was the Hébert family. They possessed the only radio in the town not confiscated by the Germans. Their home had been commandeered as a billet and they shared the building with about 20 soldiers. One of these was an Austrian who was the German commanding officer's driver. William Hébert, who was ten years old in 1944, recalls:

> The driver didn't particularly like his colleagues and was very sympathetic toward the French. He told the German commander that he'd bought the radio from our family for his own personal use and even produced a receipt that we'd given him. Satisfied that everything was above board, the colonel allowed the radio to remain in our house. But of course it was all a ploy so that we could covertly listen to the BBC.

In 1944 20-year-old farm laborer Charles Destrès lived with his parents on a farm at La Croix, just over half a mile west of St-Côme-du-Mont. A German infantry company had occupied the farm but just before the invasion they moved out and set up camp in the surrounding fields. A short distance away is Le Manoir de Rampan (Rampan Manor), an imposing 15th-century house that has been inhabited by the Savary family for several generations. The manor is in a superb location with commanding views across the Pommenauque marshes toward Carentan and Méautis. When the Germans occupied the building, they made the entire family live in one of its ground floor rooms and built raised wooden machine-gun platforms in trees overlooking the marshes.

The German army still used horses and mules for transportation purposes, and some were stabled at the manor. A large blacksmith's forge was constructed and a veterinary officer and his aide lived in the house. One of the bedrooms on the upper floor had been converted into a jail whilst the surrounding farm buildings were used as barracks. (On D-Day the ground floor and basement were turned into a German aid station and one of the stables became a morgue).

On the night of June 5, the Laurence family went to bed early. At about 1am they were woken by the droning sound of aircraft approaching and the noise gradually became more and more intense. Gustave and Louise stumbled out of bed just as the German antiaircraft batteries began opening fire across the peninsula.

Soon the planes began to arrive overhead. The noise was so loud that it woke Louise's baby daughter Nicole, who had managed to sleep through everything up to that point. Gustave couldn't resist taking a look, even though Louise begged him not to. He opened their bedroom window at exactly the same time as hundreds of men began to jump from the low-flying aircraft. The German antiaircraft defenses and infantry were firing at everything they could, lighting the sky with thousands of rounds of tracer fire. To the Laurences it looked like a massive firework display that had a bizarre beauty all its own. Suddenly, because parachutists were coming down behind their house, the Germans lowered their guns and began firing in the Laurences' direction. Bullets bounced off the front wall, narrowly missing the windows. Louise ducked back inside, threw herself on the bed, and frantically started getting dressed.

MAP KEY

1. Gloria milk factory
2. Brick factory
3. Farmhouse where Ed Shames stopped on D-Night
4. 3/506 area of operations June 15–22 (divisional security)
5. Lock-keepers' houses (either side of canal)
6. Bailey bridge built June 16–17
7. German command post (CP) in farmhouse
8. Phosphate factory
9. 3/506 aid station at Fortin Farm
10. La Barquette locks
11. "Hell's Corner," 501 road block on D-Night
12. German 6 Para HQ and underground bunker
13. Rampan Manor
14. German 40mm antiaircraft gun position
15. Site of H/501 plane crash on D-Night
16. Destrés Farm
17. Villand Farm
18. H Co CP at Le Ferage, June 8–12
19. 3/506 HQ Co CP at Folleville Farm, June 9–12
20. G Co CP at Le Boujamet Farm, June 10–12
21. I Co CP at Le Vivier Château, June 10–12
22. Col Sink's CP, June 7–11 and G and I Co bivouac area, June 8–11
23. Les Droueries Manor
24. Tamerville, where barn was set alight on D-Night
25. La Haute Maison
26. Le Bel Esnault Château
27. Frigot Farm
28. Pfc Sosnak's additional aid station at Le Bordel
29. Les Rats farmhouse, site of plane crash on June 6
30. 3/506 sector, June 13

 Train station

— Metaled road

— Dirt roads

.... Tracks

3/506 Normandy overview,
June 6–22, 1944

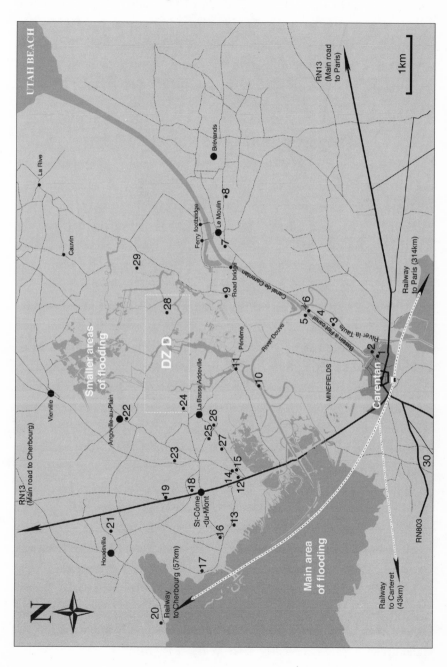

Gustave was transfixed and stayed by the window. Louise begged him to come away before dashing into one of the other rooms where her mother was staying with the children. In order not to panic them, she calmly told everyone to get dressed and lie on the beds until they knew what was going on. The family stayed inside the house until daylight. Then they ventured out into the street, where the question on everybody's mind was: "Is this really the start of the long-awaited invasion?"

The drop and chaos of D-Night

Despite the fact that the only "Eureka" beacon marking Drop Zone D was set up in the wrong place, the 3rd Bn had a much higher concentration of men dropped on target than the rest of the 101st Airborne Division. Out of a total of 45 sticks, eight landed on the actual drop zone and 26 were less than a mile away. However, the drop was not as accurate as the planners had hoped, and the battalion was spread over a much wider area than expected. The following accounts describe some of the difficulties faced by the paratroopers as they headed for the bridges; they are grouped under headings that best describe the areas where the men landed. During the authors' many interviews with French civilians, no evidence has been found to support claims in other historical works that more than one barn was set ablaze on D-Night. Also, contrary to what has been written in other publications, interviews with surviving veterans suggest that the soldiers who landed on the actual drop zone had an above average chance of survival.

St-Côme-du-Mont

As the formation headed toward St-Côme-du-Mont, the Rebecca receiver in Col Krebs's lead aircraft successfully detected the "Eureka" signal and Krebs prepared to switch on the red light. On board was Ray Calandrella, who was sitting opposite war correspondent Ward Smith. The two men had chatted briefly during the flight and Smith had asked, "Where are you from and how long have you been in the army?" Calandrella replied, "Nearly two years. I'm from Hamden; you've probably never heard of it, but it's near New Haven, Connecticut." Nodding politely, Smith handed his notebook over to Calandrella and asked him to write down his name and address. He then passed the book around the remainder of the stick. Cpl Jack Harrison of Phoenix, Arizona, leaned over and thrust a packet of cigarettes in his hand. "You might need them on the way back," he said. After returning to Exeter Smith wrote in his article "I Saw Them Jump To Destiny," "We've come back but our paratroopers haven't yet. At the moment they're too busy to tell their story. Just in case Cpl Harrison happens to read this, I'd like him to know that I'm keeping his cigarettes for him. Perhaps he might like a smoke on the way home. But if he can spare them I'd like to keep them always." Sadly, Harrison died from wounds received on D-Day morning and never read Smith's article.

Looking intently out of the window, Calandrella could see farm buildings burning below. Suddenly an antiaircraft shell burst adjacent to the plane, showering shrapnel against the aircraft's fuselage and snapping him back to reality. Then the green light came on and the plane's human cargo departed in under 10 seconds. Don Ross followed Sgt Nagy (an artillery spotter working for the navy) and Col Wolverton out of the aircraft into a stream of heavy tracer fire that seemed to be coming from all directions. The entire stick was about to land in an area containing a high concentration of enemy soldiers.

Within 30 seconds of leaving the aircraft, Wolverton and Nagy were dead. Tragically, both got tangled in trees before they landed and were shot still hanging in their harnesses – neither soldier touched French soil alive.

Ross landed next to a German command post and field kitchen at Le Ferage/Le Chasse Datin. About half a dozen enemy soldiers quickly surrounded him and dragged him off to a nearby hedge shouting what sounded like, "Schiessen Amerikanisch, Schiessen Amerikanisch" ("shoot the Americans"). Standing in front of the makeshift firing squad, Ross was just seconds from being executed when a German officer, who spoke English, arrived and stopped the proceedings. He had a brother who was a prisoner of war in the USA and wanted to ensure that the Geneva Convention rules were properly followed.

Ray Calandrella was one of the last men to leave the aircraft. During his descent he put his hand in front of his face in a vain attempt to protect himself from the thousands of bullets being fired into the night sky. The 'chute had only just opened when he landed in the corner of a large field on the edge of high ground, about 380 yards west of La Basse Addeville.

Following the lead ship was the no. 2 aircraft carrying Capt Barney Ryan, who was part of Maj Grant's stick. The men landed along a line between the southern edge of St-Côme-du-Mont and the flooded fields below L'Amont. The stick suffered many fatal casualties, including Maj Grant and the three naval observers. Barney Ryan recalls:

> The antiaircraft and small-arms fire was horrendous, and our plane began taking violent evasive action. As we stood up on the red light we were thrown about, and the plane didn't seem to slow down when we jumped. I felt a terrific shock as the 'chute banged open. The ground was ablaze with enemy fire. Tracer bullets seemed to be coming in all directions and I instinctively pulled my legs up to make a smaller target. I must have been in the air for about 30 seconds, which would have made our jump height around 400ft.

Johnny Gibson's plane was further back in the formation and he remembers some of the problems caused by the leg bags:

> When the green light came on we tried to jump as quickly as possible so that we all landed close together. However, somebody tripped and several seconds were lost while the man behind helped the fallen trooper to his feet. All the 81mm guys were wearing heavy leg bags that made it difficult for them to exit in a fast and efficient manner. Those of us toward the back of the stick were yelling at the guys to get moving. We were worried that the longer we stayed on board the less chance we had of getting out.

S/Sgt Tom Simms (HQ Co) was in charge of 16 men from the machine-gun platoon that made up chalk no. 27. The group was hooked up ready to jump when the aircraft's tail was hit by ground fire, forcing the plane to bank steeply to the right. Bobbie Rommel was no. 8 in the stick and recollects, "We all fell to our left and hung on to our strops and equipment with all our might – everybody stayed calm." The plane returned to level flight but was hit again on the port wing. The green light came on and seven men, including Tom Simms and Cpl Don "Dog" Gallaugher, went out. However, Rommel stumbled at the door and T/4 Ed Bluestone, the plane's crew chief, had to steady him. Bluestone then pushed Rommel out and he lost his leg bag on exit: "I was looking at the machine-gun fire. It appeared to be moving in slow motion and I tucked my legs beneath me. A bullet grazed my hand and a few more went through the canopy making popping sounds." Unfortunately Rommel's aircraft had been badly damaged and its pilot, 2nd Lt Alton Keller, was struggling to keep it in the air. It eventually crashed into the English Channel, killing the entire crew.

Capt McKnight's stick comprised 16 men from I Co and included Sgt Dueber, T/5 Joe Beyrle (McKnight's radio operator), Pfc John Houk, Pvt Manny Barrios, and T/5 Gene Kristie, who was last man out of the door. Unfortunately, most of the stick landed in fields to the east of McKnight's location. Gene Kristie would spend most of the night trying to round up a squad. Strangely, the majority of men he gathered together seemed to be members of the 502nd PIR! Unluckily Kristie was captured before he could make it to the battalion's objective, and was taken to the POW field at Le Ferage. John Houk landed on the roof of a grocery store on the edge of the square, whilst Manny Barrios came down in a freshly cultivated garden near the Rue des Croix.

Due to the amount of equipment he was carrying, Joe Beyrle jumped without a reserve parachute. However, his main 'chute deployed with its usual force and by some miracle he managed to keep his leg bag. Drifting toward St-Côme-du-Mont's church tower, he could see tracers whizzing through his canopy, leaving glowing entry holes. He pulled the cotter pin that held the leg bag in place and it dropped below. At the same time he tried to steer away from the building by pulling on the 'chute's front right-hand riser. His efforts failed and he slid feet first down the church's high-pitched roof but somehow managed to check his fall. He then carefully lowered himself from the roof's edge and dropped 20ft or so into the churchyard below.

Joe realized he was out of sight of the German machine-gun team located in the tower. A barn was burning some distance away at Tamerville, lighting up the area, and the Germans had turned their fire in its direction. Alone, Joe decided to head west back down the line of flight where he hoped to locate Capt McKnight and Sgt Dueber.

To lighten his load, Joe left some of the heavy items he was carrying near the base of the church. Then he crawled away, dragging his radio behind him. After clambering over the wall of the churchyard, he turned and fired a couple of bursts from his Thompson sub-machine gun at the Germans in the tower and then disappeared into the garden behind the Jacquets' residence. He struggled on through fields beside the Rue des Écoles/Rue Mary before stopping briefly to switch on his radio. All he could pick up on the company frequencies was static. He continued scanning every 30 minutes or so, but eventually gave up and buried the radio in a hedgerow.

Still alone, Joe moved back toward the main part of the town. There he spotted a mobile generator that was supplying the Germans with electricity – the civilian population had been without power for nearly a month. He then saw some parked vehicles and decided to slash their tires before attacking the generator with C2 explosive. Joe set the fuse for 45 seconds and was still looking for cover when the C2 blew up. The noise attracted the enemy's attention and Joe could hear soldiers moving toward him from the direction of La Croix. They stopped for a moment at the house opposite his position. Joe carefully pulled the pins from two grenades and rolled one down the road. He waited a few seconds and threw the other high in the air above the Germans. After hearing the explosions he ran off through fields toward the southwestern edge of the town where he spotted the Carentan–Cherbourg railway. He then realized he was heading in the wrong direction and began retracing his steps.

Crawling beside a hedgerow, Joe heard a rustling sound and clicked his recognition cricket. The reply he received was "*Hände hoch.*"

Unfortunately he had stumbled into a well-defended German MG42 position and was surrounded by enemy paratroopers. They went through his pockets and mistook him for an officer after finding his .45cal automatic pistol.

Two soldiers took Joe to an aid station in the town. The station had been established in the Jacquet family's home and was being run by Dr Stanley Morgan, who had been captured by the Germans. Joe joined other wounded soldiers lying on the floor and pretended he had a back injury. He looked around and saw Jack Harrison, who had been hit several times in the stomach and was in great pain. The 3rd Bn medics were struggling to save him. After a while Harrison's crying began to get Joe down and he decided to try and escape. With everyone occupied he crossed the room and made his way upstairs.

Just before daylight, the commandant of St-Côme-du-Mont decided to put a red cross on the roof of the aid station and take a closer look at a dormer window in the attic – he thought it might be a possible point of entry. A soldier was sent upstairs with Msr Jacquet to see if he could get onto the steep sloping roof through the window, but it proved difficult to get outside. As the soldier was about to leave the junk-filled attic something made him look behind an old bedstead that was leaning against a wall. The soldier jumped back in surprise when he saw Joe Beyrle peering at him. Joe had been trying to get out through the same window when he heard footsteps and hid behind the largest thing he could find. He was dragged back downstairs, marched out of the building and taken north along the RN13 to a prisoner-holding area at Le Ferage.

Les Droueries

Local French sources suggest that three artillery pieces, located in positions near Les Droueries Manor, had been aimed at Utah Beach – by June 6 these appear to have been moved. Nearby was a camp occupied by soldiers from a German foreign legion unit (Ost-Bataillon 795). Its men were scattered throughout the fields and orchards in the area, and it was here that many 3rd Bn paratroopers met their deaths.

2nd Lt Bill Wedeking was jumpmaster on plane no. 5. There were 16 men in his stick and they started landing somewhere near Le Chasse Datin. Their casualty rate was high; six were killed by small-arms fire, including Pvt Phil Germer, who was still in his harness when his body was found days later. Four others including Sgt George Dwyer and Cpl Clarence Kelley were captured, whilst Wedeking was wounded in the wrist. After jumping, George Dwyer lost contact with the rest of his stick and recalls, "I kept making my way toward the sound of battle. However, late on the third day I was trapped in the corner of a hedgerow and taken prisoner by an enemy machine-gun squad."

First man out of plane no. 8 was 1st Lt Howard Littell, who was closely followed by Sgt Gil Morton and Cpl Jim Bradley. Last, and 15th, man to jump, was medic S/Sgt Mike Weiden. Many of the stick were captured whilst still trying to get out of their harnesses. Gil Morton was luckier:

> My plane load landed close to a wooded area containing a group of tents, where the enemy was camped. Four of us had gotten together to try to find our way to the objective. We decided to follow the road we found hoping we were going in the right direction. At this time we didn't recognize any landmarks. I took the lead scout position with the others at intervals behind me. We came to a crossroads at which time I began crouching down to my knees, trying to decide whether to proceed. I heard a noise and a German said "*Halt!*" I hit the ground on my stomach and fired three times at him. He fell forward. I jumped up and ran back down the road telling the others to follow. Before I got to the first man another enemy soldier shouted "*Halt!*" and fired, hitting my helmet. It stung so bad I thought I'd sustained a head wound. I was light headed for a few minutes but managed to pull myself together and got out fast.

Ray Calandrella had also landed in the Les Droueries area and recalls:

> After cutting myself out of the risers I set about chopping a small piece of nylon from my reserve 'chute as a souvenir. I pulled the D-ring and the brilliant white canopy burst out announcing for all to see that I had

arrived! In a panic I gathered up the billowing 'chute and wrapped it inside my camouflaged main canopy. I then lay quietly on the ground trying to calm down. Thankfully the only person to have noticed me was Sgt Tom Newell, the medic from my plane, who came over and asked if I was OK. I suggested we should wait for a while and then move out together. After about 5 minutes he decided to scout around to see if he could find any injured men. That was the last I saw of him.

I lay motionless for another 15 minutes or so before I saw the hunched shape of a man creeping toward me through a gap in a hedge. He was big and thickset and I found it difficult to determine what type of helmet he was wearing... American or German. As he got closer I began to run a couple of scenarios through my head – should I use the bayonet or squeeze the trigger? I didn't want to do either but time was running out, so I nervously used my cricket. Click-clack – no response. I repeated the process: click-clack – there was still no response and I raised my rifle to shoot. Suddenly I noticed a jump rope hanging from the guy's belt – it was 1st Lt Howard Littell, our 81mm Ptn leader.

After introducing myself I whispered, "Why the hell didn't you use your cricket?" In a hushed voice Littell replied, "I'm sorry, but I just couldn't find it." "Couldn't find it!" I said in disbelief, "I came that close to pulling the trigger." Littell just shrugged his shoulders and told me he'd got separated from the rest of his stick and that I should join him. Before leaving we unclipped our gas masks and threw them away [naïvely the men felt the masks were unnecessary].

Later that night Littell and Calandrella met up with seven other strays from the battalion. Within the group were privates Earl McGrath and Fred Neill as well as S/Sgt Zolman Rosenfield, who was the last man to join Littell's party. Fred Neill and Ray Calandrella had been friends for a couple of years and both were relieved to find someone they knew in the patrol.

Rosenfield was jumpmaster on his aircraft and had the job of looking after two door bundles that contained rubber rafts for assaulting the bridges. Both bundles were pushed out by the plane's crew chief just before the men jumped. Cpl Warren Nelson was in Rosenfield's stick and found the rafts shortly after he landed. He decided to stay with them until Zol arrived, but lost his life whilst waiting. The rafts never reached the footbridge.

Littell and his group struck out for the assembly area. Carefully following hedgerows, the men came across a road that ran between La Basse Addeville and L'Amont. Watching the road, and unseen by the Americans, was an enemy machine-gun position. As Littell and his group started to cross, all hell broke loose. During the ambush Rosenfield was hit a number of times and fell. Littell pulled him into the relative safety of a ditch, shouting, "I'm sorry, but we're gonna have to leave ya, kid!" Following the skirmish a German medical team promptly treated Rosenfield before sending him to the aid station in St-Côme-du-Mont. He was later moved to an underground hospital in St-Lô. For the rest of the day Littell and the remainder of his group moved around trying to stay out of sight. Unfortunately they were going round in circles and never managed to leave the area where they had landed.

Carentan

Just as Ed Shames was about to jump from his plane, it rocked violently and the man in front stumbled. The delay only lasted a few seconds but was critical, as Ed recalls:

> By the time we got him to his feet the plane had traveled past St-Côme-du-Mont and was over Carentan. I had plenty of time to look around as I was in the air for about 50 seconds, which meant I must have jumped at around 1,000ft. I was heading toward a burning industrial area and fighting desperately to control my drift. I landed amongst some cows in a muddy yard near a milk factory. The building was on fire and I could see a tall chimney. Below it was a logo depicting a pink carnation and a cow. That image has remained with me to this day.
>
> I knew that I'd landed in Carentan and the words "avoid at all costs" kept running through my head. I cut the risers that connected the main 'chute to my harness and moved out toward the Bassin à Flot [a 1¼ mile-long canal that connects Carentan with the river Douve. The water

within the basin is maintained at a constant level by a lock at its seaward end]. I was actually inside the factory compound and as I clambered over the perimeter fence I could hear the cows mooing. I believe the noise they were making covered my sounds and ultimately saved my life! I didn't see anybody else from my aircraft and, as I was one of the last out, most of them would have landed across the city. Poor bastards wouldn't have stood a chance.

Another man who landed close to Carentan was Sgt Gordon Yates (H Co Communications) and he takes up the story:

We were flying north to south when the green light flashed on and 1st Lt Meason was first out. I was right behind him and landed on the south side of the Douve River about 1,800 yards south of the DZ. The last man out hit Carentan's church steeple on the way down. I started crawling along hedgerows. Eventually six of us joined up and we headed toward the objective. Just after dawn we met seven other men and a little later were pinned down by fire coming from some houses. Sadly, we failed to reach the bridges on D-Day.

2nd Lt Peter Madden (H Co) and his stick landed near Carentan, close to minefields protecting its northern edge. During his descent Madden was unable to release his leg bag and was knocked unconscious when he landed. "When I came round the first thing I heard was Germans talking. I managed to untie the bag from my leg and crawled toward a hedgerow, dragging the container behind me." Two German soldiers saw the bag moving and opened fire. Madden paused and looked around for better cover, but none was available. Thankfully the bullets missed and the soldiers were distracted and moved away. Breathing a sigh of relief, Madden began sorting out his equipment and then set off toward the objective. A little while later he noticed a solitary figure walking toward him. He clicked his cricket, but there was no reply. He then whispered "Flash," hoping he would receive the response "Thunder" – still no reply. Crawling behind a tree, he got his jump knife ready. The figure came closer and closer, but just as he was about to strike Madden noticed the man was wearing an American helmet – the soldier had lost his cricket and forgotten the password!

It wasn't long before the two men realized they were on the wrong side of the river Douve and had to find a place to cross. After walking a short distance they found themselves in the middle of a field near an old racetrack. It was then they noticed a sign that filled them with dread. On it were stenciled the words "*ACHTUNG MINEN*." Both men froze. Then Madden had an idea. He had noticed a cow grazing nearby and encouraged the animal to walk across the minefield. Both men followed in its path. Once clear they crossed a marshy area and started to pick up more men.

Fred Bahlau, H Co's supply sergeant, landed close to the Douve and like Madden was also on the wrong side of the river. Every now and again the moon would appear from behind clouds, casting its eerie light all around. As Bahlau was cutting himself out of his harness he noticed movement in bushes nearby. "After getting out of my 'chute I got my Tommy gun ready. I must have been a little nervous because I fired a burst into the ground. Luckily, with all the noise going on around, the enemy didn't seem to notice." Bahlau used his cricket and cautiously approached the bush. To his relief it was another H Co man and both chatted briefly before moving off.

Later, whilst attempting to cross the river, Bahlau spotted a German patrol – fortunately they did not see him. "I saw a German squad marching along the other bank. At first I thought they were our own men and decided to cross over. I dropped into the water but couldn't touch the bottom and had to be helped out. It was then I realized the other squad were Germans."

Bahlau and his colleague moved further along the bank looking for another place to cross. Then they spotted the diminutive figure of Pfc Trino Mendez walking toward them. Mendez was one of Madden's small group and Bahlau noticed that his M1 rifle was broken in two. "Mendez's rifle had been hit in the middle by a German bullet," recalls Bahlau. "I said, 'Mendez, what in the hell are you going to do with that broken rifle?' and I gave him my pistol on the understanding that he return it within two days. A couple of days later, as promised, he gave the weapon back."

Moving around in the same area was Ben Hiner, who recalls, "I saw some guys lying on the ground in the shadows. I kicked the nearest man's backside and told him to get moving. It turned out to be 2nd Lt Sutfin and men from the 81mm mortars. As Sutfin jumped up, he grinned and I could see the light of battle reflected on his gold fillings. He then disappeared into the night with his men."

Meanwhile, Ed Shames was moving in a northeasterly direction away from Carentan and had reached a small swing bridge spanning the Bassin à Flot. He crossed the bridge, passed the entrance to a brick factory and then found himself in an area dominated by large warehouses. A couple of minutes later he could see, silhouetted in the moonlight, two rows of trees lining either side of the waterway. Ed now knew exactly where he was and that a mile or so ahead were two lock-keepers' cottages. He decided to move away from the road he had been following and shadow it from open ground to his right. This was a lucky move – he did not realize it at the time but a number of German vehicles were parked under the trees! It was shortly after this that other paratroopers from the battalion began to join him and he ended up leading a group of about a dozen men.

A little later Ed and his group passed an isolated farm that was set back from the road. He was amazed that they had got this far and not been seen by the enemy. They moved on and soon came to another farm. It looked as though it was occupied and Ed decided to ask for help. This was not without its risks.

I reasoned that it was probably safer to approach an isolated building. If we were challenged we could easily withdraw and carry on down the road. I deployed the men around the building and a couple of us walked up and knocked on the door. An old man opened it and I said, "I am an American and the invasion has begun." He must have understood and almost collapsed with shock. From somewhere behind a woman started to scream hysterically. I forced my way past the man, clamped my hands over the woman's mouth and carefully lowered her to the ground.

After she calmed down a little, I got on the floor beside her and encouraged the old man to do the same. I wanted to show the Frenchman my map. The pair of us got under my raincoat and I switched on my flashlight. I pointed at Ste-Mère-Église and the old man pointed at Brévands – this was a settlement near our objective. He then showed me the location of a minefield and vehicle park. He didn't seem to think there were any enemy soldiers between his house and the Douve. We left the farm and doubled up the road toward the lock-keepers' cottages. We then noticed two figures staggering toward us. They were Germans returning from a night out. Both were drunk and had no idea what was going on! I ordered the guys to deal with them and left them lying in the middle of the road – we just didn't have time to mess around with prisoners.

Shortly afterwards, Shames's group reached a bridge that crosses the river La Taute at St-Hilaire-Petitville. The river drains into the Douve just east of the Bassin à Flot lock gates. Ed knew that crossing the bridge would mean almost certain death, and as the tide was in it was too treacherous to wade through the river at this point. The lock gates were fitted with a metal footbridge and Ed decided to use this route to get over the waterway and then try and find a better place to cross the river. The group soon found a more suitable spot and Ed decided he should be the one to go first. "I tied a jump rope around my body and two men held the other end as I slipped into the water. I couldn't reach the bottom and was forced downstream by the current. The two guys hauled me back to shore and we continued along the bank toward the lock at La Barquette." A little further upstream the group ran into S/Sgt Bob Webb and T/4 Stan Stockins. Webb recalls, "Ed Shames and I decided to set up a defensive perimeter with a couple of outposts. It was getting late and somehow I got left behind when the group moved out. I couldn't find a soul when daylight came."

Close by, but a little further downstream, Madden and his group were also attempting to cross the river. Slipping into the water, they held their weapons over their heads and began wading across. Madden looked behind him and saw Trino Mendez disappear below the surface, leaving just the very top of his helmet showing. Madden quickly pushed the butt of his carbine into Mendez's stomach giving him something to grab hold of. Once safely across the group made their way over fields toward the dirt road at Pénême and then on toward the junction at Pont de l'Esseau. This area later became known as "Hell's Corner."

L'Amont, Le Mont, and Frigot Farm

L'Amont lies on the edge of high ground to the southeast of St-Côme-du-Mont. Nearby, at Le Mont, is a large farm that during the war was owned by the Frigot family. About 200 yards to the west, the Germans had established a 40mm antiaircraft gun position in a field known locally as Clos des Brohiers. They were using the farmhouse as a billet. The dining room had been converted into a mess and the men slept upstairs in one of the bedrooms.

Suddenly, just before the invasion, the gun crew departed and were replaced by a platoon of Mongolians. Politically Mongolia was aligned closely with the Soviet Union. Many of its countrymen served in the Red Army and a number were captured during the Germans' invasion of Russia in 1941. Some were persuaded to switch their allegiance because, like their Georgian counterparts, they felt it might eventually help end Russian influence in their country. The Mongolians soon began digging foxholes along a hedgerow that overlooked the Douve plain, which had been deliberately flooded by the Germans.

The marshland south of the farm acts as a drain for the surrounding high ground. During the winter months, an area of about 20,000 acres is often under water. The locks at La Barquette are on the seaward side of the marshland, and as the tide goes out the gates swing open, allowing fresh water to drain into the sea. When the tide comes in they automatically shut, preventing salt water from contaminating the fertile plain. As an anti-invasion defense, the Germans had taken control of the locks and fixed them so that the marshland was always under water, no matter what the season. During summer months, the stagnant water attracted mosquitoes that created health problems for people living nearby.

Before the invasion, rumors had spread that Allied agents had been dropped into the region to help organize local resistance groups. Jacqueline Frigot (née Devautour), then aged 17, recalls, "The Mongolians forced my dad and 15-year-old brother Michel, with gun barrels pushed into the backs of their necks, to open up the haylofts and stables near the house. Because the Germans were overstretched they mobilized the "Civils" (civilian defense force) who were made to search the homes of people they knew."

On the day before the invasion, the Mongolians prevented the Frigot family from leaving their home and the atmosphere became very strained. Jacqueline picks up the story:

> That afternoon my father felt we needed to move to another building and he ushered us out of the house and across the courtyard. The soldiers pointed their rifles in our direction and forced us back inside. Later that night we began to hear the sound of aircraft. We gathered together in our parents' bedroom but the frightening noise forced us out onto the landing. There, through the hall windows, we watched antiaircraft fire light up the night sky.

Johnny Gibson's C-47 was heading in the direction of Frigot Farm. "I was not as heavily laden as others in my stick and managed a good push out of the aircraft. Despite this my body position was poor and the opening shock of the parachute was severe. Red tracer seemed to be all around but luckily it missed me. I oscillated only twice before striking the ground." George Rosie jumped before Gibson and was struggling with his overloaded leg bag. As he was falling, he briefly noticed the Frigot family looking up at him through a large window in their farmhouse. Jacqueline recalls, "As we stood at the window, not thinking of the danger we were in, we could see white parachutes descending and four paratroopers landed near our courtyard."

Rosie's leg bag hit the ground and he followed a few seconds later. On landing he was pitched forward against a roadside fence and a post split open his mouth, smashing his two front teeth. The damage exposed

This picture was taken looking north toward St-Côme-du-Mont. In 1937 work started on repairing and widening the RN13 highway (note the piles of stones). (Nicole Laurence and Michel Léonard)

A prewar picture of St-Côme-du-Mont looking west, with the Place de la République in the foreground and the church beyond. After the war the square was renamed Place de Judels in honor of 1st Lt Robert Judels and his family who helped finance the rebuilding of the village. (Remy Villand and Michel Léonard)

The mayor's office (mairie) is still housed in the same building as in 1944.

The wartime home of the Jacquet family on Rue des Écoles. During the occupation the left hand side became the German commander's headquarters, known as the Kommandantur. In the days immediately following the invasion, the rooms on the right became an aid station where Dr Stanley Morgan and his medical team worked.

FROM TOP TO BOTTOM:

Carentan as it looked just a few days before the invasion. The Gloria Milk Factory is in the top right hand corner of the picture. (Jim Martin)

During the war the house in the center of the picture (with garage door) was the home of the Laurence family.

Rampan Manor.

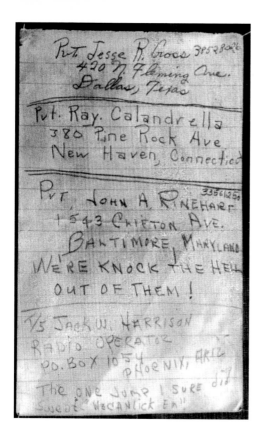

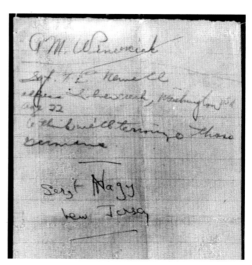

As they flew toward France on the night of June 5/6 every member of Col Wolverton's stick signed war correspondent Ward Smith's notebook. Sadly most were either killed or captured on D-Day.

CLOCKWISE FROM ABOVE:

Pvt Jesse Cross – Reconnaissance Ptn (wounded June 6)
Pvt Ray Calandrella – Reconnaissance Ptn (POW June 7)
Pvt John Rinehart – Communications Ptn (who wrote "We're knock the hell out of them!" (KIA June 6))
T/5 Jack Harrison – Communications Ptn (who wrote "The one jump I sure did sweat! We can lick em!" (died from wounds June 6))

S/Sgt John Taormina – Communications Ptn (who wrote "A plane, a jump and a God-damn good chance to get even" (POW taken to St-Lô at 1200hrs June 6))
T/5 Bill Atlee – S1 Personnel (KIA June 6)
Dr Stanley Morgan (POW June 6, remained in St-Côme)
1st Lt Alex Bobuck – adjutant (POW June 6, remained in St-Côme)
LtCol Robert Wolverton – commanding officer (KIA June 6, Le Ferage)
Pfc Don Ross – S3 Planning and Operations (POW taken to St-Lô at 1200hrs June 6)
Sgt Joe Gorenc – S3 Planning and Operations (POW June 8)
T/5 Charles Riley – HQ Co armorer (POW taken to St-Lô at 1200hrs June 6)

Pfc Harry Howard – Communications Ptn (POW taken to St-Lô at 1200hrs June 6)
Sgt Bill Pauli – Communications Ptn (broken pelvis POW June 6; remained in St-Côme)

Pvt Anthony Wincenciak – S4 Supply (KIA June 6)
Sgt Tom Newell – Medical Detachment (who wrote "I think we'll terrorise those Germans" (POW June 6 in St-Côme))
Sgt Nagy – Marine Artillery Observer (KIA June 6, Le Ferage)
(Ray Calandrella and Bob Webb Jr)

TOP:

The point where Ed Shames crossed the Bassin à Flot. The building in the background was a lock-keeper's cottage.

BOTTOM:

Northern side of the church – I Co radio operator Joe Beyrle landed on the church's high-pitched roof directly above the two windows. The odd-shaped mounds in the foreground form part of a monument to French soldiers who died from typhoid during an epidemic in 1870.

A modern-day aerial view of Frigot Farm. (Philipe Frigot)

This prewar picture (taken from the Douve's northern bank) shows the seaward side of the lock at La Barquette looking south toward Carentan. The gates are fully open, indicating that the tide is going out. The trees on the horizon line the Bassin à Flot canal and to their right are the brick factory and Gloria Milk plant chimneys, plus the town's church steeple. (Remy Villand and Michel Léonard)

Pvt Walter Hendrix from E Co 506th stands beside the burnt-out remains of 75th Troop Carrier Squadron C-47 "Butchski II," which crashed near Frigot Farm on D-Day. The plane was carrying men from H Co 501st, who all jumped to safety before it crashed. Unfortunately its crew were not so fortunate and Capt Seymour Malakoff (pilot), 2nd Lt Thomas Tucker (co-pilot), 1st Lt Eugene Gaul (navigator), Sgt Paul Jacoway (flight engineer) and S/Sgt Robert Walsh (radio operator) all perished in the inferno. (Forrest Guth picture, Carentan Historical Center)

Pfc Jimmy Martin (2 Ptn G Co). (Jim Martin)

This picture was taken in England during April 1944 and shows members of I Co's 3 Ptn 60mm mortar squad. Note how the Screaming Eagle shoulder patch has been removed from the picture by the Army censor. L to R: Pvt Harold Stedman, Pvt Claud Tucker, and Pvt Frank Lujan. (Harold Stedman)

This photograph was taken on the morning of June 6 and shows the 2nd Ranger Bn command post at Pointe du Hoc. Sitting to the right and slightly below the Red Cross flag is Pvt Lenny Goodgal from 1 Ptn I Co, who recalls, "We were drinking coffee and eating peanut butter and jelly sandwiches sent in by the battleship USS *Texas*." (US Navy)

S/Sgt Roy Burger (81mm Mortar Ptn). (Bob Webb Jr)

This track is about 400 yards north of Fortin Farm and during the war was the main access route to the road bridge. In the background is the river Douve and in the trees beyond are the villages of Le Moulin and Brévands.

raw nerve endings, but adrenalin took over and temporarily masked the pain. Rosie was no more than about 200 yards from a Mongolian machine-gun post. As he was struggling to get out of his harness he heard the sound of soldiers, wearing hobnailed boots, coming down the road toward him. He started to run but was still tangled in his rigging lines and they held him back. He kept his head and quickly cut himself free before scrambling through a hedge into the field beyond. The enemy ran past heading in the direction of the farmhouse, no doubt looking for the rest of the stick.

Because Gibson was a medic, he was unarmed apart from his M3 trench knife and switchblade. On landing he stuck the knife in the ground and waited for a few moments. He then began to work himself free and unbuckled his parachute harness. He was in a large field close to Frigot Farm and a startled horse was galloping around. Terrified that the animal would give away his position, Gibson made his way across the field to a high stone wall near the farmhouse. Fearing that the Germans were occupying the building, Gibson took refuge in a ditch beside the wall. Heart pounding and breathless, he desperately needed to locate other members of his stick, but where were they?

The German 40mm antiaircraft gun was in the next field. Flames from the burning barn at Tamerville were lighting up the night sky, giving the gun crew a clear view of planes caught in its glow. On board one of those aircraft was 1st Lt Joe Doughty: "I was standing in the door and just before the green light came on a burst of antiaircraft fire raked the aircraft from door to tail. We must have jumped from 400–500ft because it didn't take long to hit the ground. From that point onwards the party got pretty damn wild!"

Meanwhile, Gibson had removed the Red Cross armband issued at Exeter. Unlike his other armband it was made from a shiny material that reflected every muzzle flash and it stood out like a sore thumb. Looking along the ditch to his rear, Gibson saw some movement and his heart skipped a beat. Partly hidden by the shadow of the wall, a figure was creeping slowly toward him. With knife and cricket at the ready, Gibson waited until the figure got to within 15ft before making the recognition click-clack sound. A second later he received a positive response. Gibson picks up the narrative: "It was Pvt Charlie Lee, the last man out of our plane. 'You scared the hell out of me,' I exclaimed. He said the feeling was mutual and we then whispered a few words about finding the others. Both Lee and I were shocked at just how much firing was going on around. Neither of us expected such a hot reception from the enemy."

The two men moved cautiously off along the line of the wall toward a hedge. A few minutes later they discovered George Rosie hiding under a tree. He was overjoyed to see them. They remained hidden in the hedge for a while wondering what they should do. Suddenly Rosie pointed in the direction of the farmhouse and muttered something through his broken teeth that sounded like, "Jesus Christ. Look!"

A C-47 had been hit, its port engine was on fire and it was banking sharply to the right. The men watched as the aircraft leveled out and its paratroopers started to jump. As the last man left the aircraft it became totally engulfed in flames. It was then that Gibson, Lee, and Rosie realized that it was heading directly toward them. They flattened themselves against the ground and the stricken plane tore through power lines and swept 20ft above their heads before exploding in a ball of flame at Clos des Brohiers. Just moments later they were surprised to see four men, silhouetted by the inferno, sprinting toward them. A water-filled ditch briefly interrupted their run, but they waded in and quickly scrambled out. Watching in amazement, Gibson's small group could not believe their eyes. Before them, covered in mud and dripping wet, were Cyrus Swinson, Leo Krebs, Phil Abbey, and Francis Ronzani. All four had jumped from the same plane as Gibson. They had been hiding in a field and the burning plane forced them out.

Dr Barney Ryan had landed in the flooded area close to L'Amont and could see something burning furiously on higher ground nearby. He had met up with three other men and led them toward the fire. Ryan recollects, "I couldn't be sure what was burning at the time but thought it was an aircraft. We were shot at by figures running around the flames. As we weren't supposed to open fire until daybreak we guessed they must be Germans." The figures were probably Mongolian soldiers who could see Ryan's group illuminated in the flames. Their firing forced Ryan and his men to dive under the water and swim away.

The burning plane had been carrying 18 men from H Co, 501st Bn. They had been scheduled to jump on Drop Zone C, which was about 3 miles north of the crash site. All the paratroopers got out safely but unfortunately the plane's five-man crew perished in the inferno. The aircraft was piloted by Capt Malakoff from the 435th Troop Carrier Group's 75th Troop Carrier Squadron, based at Welford in Berkshire. It was probably hit shortly after crossing the French coast and fell back in the formation. Losing altitude and unable to reach the drop zone, the pilot switched on the green light allowing the paratroopers to jump to safety before the plane crashed.

After swimming away, Ryan became separated from his men and spent the best part of an hour trying to find a safe way out of the marsh. Whenever he approached dry land he could hear German voices. He knew that he needed to find cover before it got light and eventually crawled into a large bush. With water up to his neck, he waited in the cold, stinking, mosquito-infested marsh for dawn to break.

Meanwhile, back at Frigot Farm, the family had moved downstairs. It was about 3am. Jacqueline recalls:

It seems stupid, but the only things we could find to protect our heads were some old brass cooking pots. We cowered under a heavy wooden table and waited. During the course of the following day our house was hit six times by naval gunfire, filling the hallway with dust, smoke and rubble. Each time one of the shells exploded we huddled closer and closer together. Our dog, Utrecht, was also under the table. He was shaking with terror and urinated uncontrollably over each and every one of us. We didn't think we'd get out alive and prayed for someone to come and save us.

~6~

"For Christ's sake, let's go"
D–Night part 2

Drop Zone D

Jim McCann was one of those lucky enough to land in the middle of the drop zone. After seeing the aircraft's red jump light come on, McCann stood up. However, he soon began to sense a problem. Standing in the no. 1 position was 2nd Lt John Williams, and the young officer was showing signs of extreme anxiety. McCann was directly behind him and decided to place his left foot in front of Williams so that he could force the lieutenant out of the way if he failed to jump. All he wanted to do was get himself and his bazooka out of the plane as quickly as possible. Sure enough, when the green light came on, Williams froze and McCann had to push his way past. Ralph Bennett was standing at the back of the same stick and remembers:

> When the red light flicked to green nobody moved. I could hear people shouting, "For Christ's sake let's go, let's get out, what's happening up there and why aren't we moving?" I was the "push out man" and it was my role to clear the plane. I started pushing and shoving furiously from the back and suddenly the stick began to move (I think this delay may have actually saved our lives). When I got to the door Williams was still on board and was tucked to the left hand side of the opening. He must have jumped, because he turned up a few days later.
>
> On the way down I oscillated twice before slamming into the ground. Despite all our problems we had a good drop and landed close together. However, we lost contact with Pvt Lawrence Davidson. He

eventually turned up three or four days later, after fighting with the 501st at La Barquette.

The stick landed about a mile from its objective and was supposed to form up, together with the rest of the battalion, on a blue light and bugle call, but this never happened. McCann recalls the moments after landing: "While getting out of my 'chute I saw two silhouettes and immediately clicked my cricket. I recognized one of them as T/5 Joe Bickhart and asked if they were hurt. Bickhart said that a bullet had grazed his forehead and that shrapnel had damaged his watch. We made our way to the objective and picked up a few men along the way, but had no encounters with the enemy."

Pvt Don Artimez was in the same stick as McCann. As he floated to earth, an enemy soldier armed with a Schmeisser machine pistol fired and hit him 23 times in the legs and lower body. When he landed, he had no feeling from the waist down and was unable to move. The German soldier thought that Artimez was dead and cautiously approached. He then sat astride him and started going through his pockets. Luckily Artimez's arms were by his sides. He managed to pull his jump knife out of his boot and plunge it into the German's kidneys. The man let out a terrifying scream and collapsed on top of him. He was now trapped under the German's body and stayed in this awful position until he was discovered the following day by a group of passing troopers. Artimez survived his ordeal and astonishingly made a full recovery, but he never returned to duty.

Machine gunner Ken Johnson was no. 2 in the door behind his platoon leader 1st Lt Ken Christianson. The plane was flying fast and low. As Johnson's 'chute deployed, the machine gun (fastened to his body) was ripped away by the opening shock and the 31lb weapon broke his ankle as it fell. As he landed, Johnson instinctively tried to protect his injured leg. Lying on the ground he felt sick and disorientated. As he came to his senses, he could see the glow from the burning barn at Tamerville. Hearing familiar voices he realized Ken Christianson and Pfc Sam Porter were moving toward him. On hearing about Johnson's machine gun, Lt Christianson went off to look for it and to try to find something to use as a crutch. Sam Porter remained and helped Johnson out of his parachute harness.

Christianson returned without the gun, but he had found a large fence post and after a short while Johnson was ready to move. The lieutenant took point and the three-man group set out for the road bridge, which was about 1¼ miles due east. It soon became clear that Johnson was jeopardizing the safety of the small group, and he fell further and further behind. Ken Christianson came across a shell hole occupied by two other wounded men and ordered Johnson to get in and stay put. "I watched Ken Christianson and Sam Porter disappear off into the darkness and that was that," recalls Johnson. "I stayed in the shell hole with the other guys for two days and how we were never discovered is beyond me."

For some unknown reason, all four squads from HQ Co's machine-gun platoon had been mixed together on three different aircraft for the flight across. Among those on board 1st Lt Robert Machen's plane was squad leader Sgt Charles Easter and section commanders corporals Ralph Fischer and Tom Bucher. Bucher recalls:

Andy Bryan, my second gunner, was in front of me in the stick. As we went through our equipment checks I noticed that he had taken off his reserve parachute. When I asked him where it was he shouted back, "If I need it then I'm in trouble – besides I can't wear it anyway because of the tripod." At the last minute he had decided not to put our tripod into his leg pack but had strapped it directly to his harness. At about this time we became aware of chunks of metal hitting the underside of our plane and were worried that some might come through the floor. I was halfway down the aircraft carrying the machine gun. Everyone in front of me, including Andy, was jumping with leg bags and it took a long time for them to get out of the aircraft. The opening shock of my main parachute forced my hand into the D-ring of my reserve. The white parachute spilled out only to collapse and dangle below me. Not wanting to be a bigger target than I already was, I was started to pull the 'chute in and was still doing this when I hit the ground. It then dawned on me just how low we had jumped because I had been in the air for only a few seconds. Shortly after landing I saw some movement in the darkness. I tried to use my recognition cricket but it snapped in half! I then gave the password and a voice came back with the correct reply. I knew immediately that it was Andy Bryan because of his broad accent (he was from Richmond, Virginia). Although he had lost his leg bag and all our spare ammunition he still had the tripod. Despite all my problems I had landed safely with the gun, a small amount of ammunition and all my other equipment!

La Basse Addeville

Bill Galbraith came down close to the small settlement of La Basse Addeville on the southwestern edge of the drop zone area: "On landing the first person I saw was 1st Sgt Paul Garrison, who'd broken his ankle. I stayed with him and tried to help him along. He could barely walk and we couldn't keep up with the men around us. As the group moved ahead into an open field, a flare went up and the enemy opened fire killing many of them."

G Co's 2nd Lt Tom Kennedy landed in shallow water and recalls, "I had my legs curled up under me as tracers were flying by. I landed in about 12 inches of water and was startled by a tethered horse. About 5 minutes later I met up with another paratrooper." Kennedy had a pretty good idea where he was because he could see the church steeple in Carentan, nearly 2 miles away. As he moved toward his objective, other men joined him and he sent scouts out ahead.

At around 0300hrs one of the scouts reported back and told Kennedy that he had run into the 501st's commanding officer, Col "Jumpy" Johnson. Kennedy decided to shadow the colonel's group and followed them to Pénême. There Johnson ordered his men to establish a roadblock and pitch a tent, which became his command post. Kennedy and his men waited in a field nearby.

A little while later Johnson strolled over to Kennedy's area and asked, "Have you sent out a patrol to the lock?" Kennedy replied, "No, sir. I'm 506th and my objective is the footbridge at Brévands." The colonel said, "Lieutenant, the 506th didn't make it and you're now with me. Is that clear?" Kennedy had no choice but to agree, but had no intention of staying a minute longer than was necessary. When Johnson and his group eventually moved out, Kennedy's patrol quietly slipped away toward the footbridge.

Jimmy Martin landed in marshland south of La Basse Addeville:

> The loneliest feeling I ever had in the world was hitting the ground and realizing there was no one else in sight. I lay on my back unbuckling my harness – why I didn't cut myself free I'll never know! Just as I was making final adjustments to my equipment a mortar shell plopped down about 15ft away. I moved out and then noticed someone sneaking along. I challenged him and discovered it was my buddy Spiller, a machine gunner from 2 Ptn. After a while S/Sgt Charles Skeen and my squad leader Sgt Don Austin joined us. We eventually formed a small group, which comprised about a dozen men from several companies, and made for the bridges.

On the way they saw the C-47 crash near Frigot Farm. "Suddenly there was a brilliant ball of flame traveling in a half circle. It crashed into the ground and flames billowed hundreds of feet into the air. The roaring fire could be seen and heard long afterwards. A little while later we met Capt Shettle who suggested we join his group. We declined his offer and continued our journey to the bridges."

La Barquette

Some 3rd Bn troopers, including Bob Webb and Bobbie Rommel, came down near the 501st's objective at La Barquette lock. Struggling to stay afloat, Webb had landed in the river Douve about 875 yards southwest of the lock. He recalls:

> As I floated down, shell fire from an antiaircraft gun followed me. When I hit the water I was surprised how far under I went. When I surfaced I couldn't get my head up because my life preserver was under the back edge of my helmet. Water was filling the parachute canopy and dragging me downstream. However, my leg bag acted like an anchor and stopped me moving too far.

Grabbing hold of an overhanging branch, he pulled himself to the bank and was hauled ashore by T/4 Stan Stockins.

In fields north of the river German engineers had erected poles to act as glider obstacles. Rommel was amused when he noticed that cattle had been using one as a back scratcher. After checking his compass bearing he moved out toward the bridges. Within minutes the area came under fire from the antiaircraft gun at L'Amont and Rommel was forced back toward the lock.

On the way he met Cpl "Dog" Gallaugher and a soldier from another outfit. As the three men reached the lock they could just make out, in the pale moonlight, a parachute draped over the lock's parapet. Bent double, they made their way across the lock toward the keeper's cottage. The water was much deeper on the landward side of the lock gates and the parachute's rigging lines disappeared under the surface. Looking over the side, they could just make out a helmet bobbing up and down in the water. Grabbing the parachute, they hauled a body up onto the parapet. Rommel recalls:

> This guy had come down and hit the wall of the lock. He must have knocked himself out and drowned as he sank into the water. We unbuckled his helmet and it rolled onto the ground. Inside the liner was a picture of his wife and kids. I immediately recognized him as a newcomer to the platoon who'd bunked above me back at Ramsbury. I can't for the life of me remember his name, but he was way older than the rest of us and we called him "Pop."

Leaving the body by the lock, Rommel and his group eventually made their way successfully to the bridges.

Vierville

The plane carrying Pfc Teddy Dziepak was about 1¼ miles north of Drop Zone D when the green light came on:

> Many of the guys on my plane took off their reserve 'chutes thinking that at combat height there wasn't enough time to deploy them anyway

– but we kept our life preservers on! Some of the guys were praying, smoking cigarettes, or being sick. As we crossed the coast the red light went on. The enemy fire coming up at us was heavy. You could hear shrapnel ripping through the fuselage and we wanted out!

As Dziepak jumped, everything suddenly went quiet. He could no longer hear shells hitting the plane or flak zipping through the fuselage. Less than half a minute later he landed, together with the rest of the stick, on marshy ground a couple of hundred yards southeast of Vierville. Seconds later wind re-inflated his parachute, dragging him further into the marsh, but he quickly cut the risers and freed himself. His musette bag containing K-rations, a first aid kit, chocolate bars, and cigarettes came adrift on exit. Luckily he managed to keep the rest of his equipment: "As I lay on my back I could see German searchlights lighting up the planes and our men jumping out."

A little while later Dziepak found himself part of a group led by 1st Lt "Jeb" Holstun. They moved east and followed a raised road, avoiding the drainage ditches and flooded fields that were a feature of the area. Whilst on the road, a German machine gun opened fire and Holstun was killed instantly. Everyone scattered to the roadside and they were pinned down for about 5 minutes. Soon word came down the line that the gun had been neutralized and the men regrouped. Further along the road they came under fire from another machine gun and scattered into the surrounding flooded fields, where Dziepak remained until daybreak.

Northeastern end of the drop zone

As he floated to earth, Cpl Hank DiCarlo released his leg bag, put his feet and knees together and tucked his chin into his chest. The leg bag thumped into the ground and DiCarlo followed a second or two later. He struggled out of his harness and started to sort out his equipment. After assembling and loading his M1 he donned his bandoliers and started out in search of friendly company. He made his way to a nearby road. However, he could find no features that were familiar to him and recalls, "So much for those sand table orientation sessions. A Mickey Mouse cartoon would have given me just as much usable information and been far more entertaining."

DiCarlo dropped into a ditch beside the road and took a compass bearing. Just as he was about to leave, he heard men running toward him and a few moments later three German soldiers, silhouetted against the light of battle, came into view. "While the mental side of me was dealing with the shock of seeing real enemy soldiers, the physical side lifted my rifle and I fired eight rounds at them – they all hit the ground. I reloaded and approached them from behind. I checked the bodies and discovered that all three were dead."

DiCarlo cautiously continued his way along the road. Sporadic small-arms fire was going on all around. Suddenly, over to his left, he heard the identification "click" of a cricket and could see someone hiding in the bushes. Nervously, DiCarlo gave the appropriate response. The figure of Pfc Otto Dworsky stepped out of the bushes and was overjoyed to see DiCarlo. The pair moved off in a westerly direction and soon ran into a small group of US soldiers. The group was made up of men from different units, including a number from the 82nd Airborne Division.

DiCarlo and one of the 82nd men, whom he knew only as Roy, were detailed to work together, and the pair acted as scouts on the right-hand flank of the group. When they were about half a mile from the footbridge they heard someone calling in a loud voice "Guzman! Guzman!" DiCarlo recalls:

I later learned that this was a common German name. However, it was new to us and for some reason Roy found it hysterically funny and started laughing uncontrollably! I quickly put my hands over his mouth and tried to keep him quiet. We were hiding in a bush and could see a German soldier, with a Schmeisser machine pistol slung over his shoulder, striding toward us. On reaching the bush he unbuttoned his fly and urinated over the pair of us! I was amazed that he couldn't hear it splashing off our helmets and clothing.

As soon as the German returned to his position, DiCarlo and Roy retraced their steps and then headed toward their objective.

Ste-Mère-Église

Two of I Co's sticks were dropped near Drop Zone A in the 82nd Airborne Division's area of operations. Pvt Harold Stedman, from 3 Ptn's 60mm mortar squad, jumped from a very low altitude. His parachute had only just opened when he landed in 3ft of muddy water. The heavy load he was carrying quickly dragged him under the surface, and whilst struggling to cut himself free from his parachute he lost both his knives.

Between gulps of air Stedman frantically began click-clacking away with his recognition cricket. Within seconds Joe Madona came to the rescue and grabbed Stedman's head, keeping it out of the water. Meanwhile Pfc Lloyd Rosdahl and Pfc Wilbur Fishel arrived and helped untangle a very relieved Stedman from his parachute and equipment. Both were machine gunners who had lost their gun and equipment.

Stedman's small group was soon joined by Pfc Bill Kidder (I Co's medic) and Pvt Frank Lujan (pronounced "Luhan"). The men had no idea where they were or what they should do. Eventually they decided to move toward the sound of fighting, and took with them as much equipment as they could carry. Stedman had his rifle and the 60mm mortar tube whilst Lujan carried the ammunition. Unfortunately neither was able to find the mortar's base plate or its C2 sighting device. They soon came across the body of a paratrooper who was lying face down in a drainage ditch. It was obvious that he had got tangled up in his rigging lines and drowned. Had it not been for Joe Madona's quick thinking, Stedman would have suffered the same fate.

East of the Vire Estuary

The C-47 carrying stick no. 24, piloted by 2nd Lt Zeuner from the 96th Troop Carrier Squadron, had been badly damaged as it passed over the drop zone. Its starboard engine was on fire and the wing had dropped, making it impossible for the paratroopers to jump. USAAF field order no. 16 stated that: "In the event the DZ is missed on the initial run-in, troops will be delivered within the combat area. In the event the coastline is reached and troops have not been delivered, aircraft will execute a right hand turn and deliver troops in the DZ area." The pilot was desperately trying to follow orders, but his plane was too badly damaged. Len Goodgal was on the aircraft and recalls:

> Once over the French coast we hooked up and I could see water below – all was calm. Suddenly all hell broke loose. The plane was tossed around and I thought we'd been hit in the tail – Pfc Niels Christensen then told me that the right engine was on fire. Initially the plane went into a dive and then started to climb just as the green light came on. As we exited I was hanging on to Christensen. My 'chute opened and I watched the burning plane crash into the sea. Looking down I realized that I was heading for open water. I jettisoned my leg bag, and as much other equipment as I could, and landed in shallow water just off the beach – I was completely lost. Then someone called out; it was Pvt Ray Crouch. We got together and tried to work out where we were. We later discovered that Christensen and 2nd Lt Johnston were the only others to get out of the aircraft alive.

The names of the paratroopers who died are as follows: S/Sgt Jim Japhet, Sgt Bev Manlove, Sgt Victor Turkovich, Pfc Bryant Hinson, Pfc Harry Berg Jr, Pfc Newton Weatherby, Pfc Alvin Poynter, Pfc Chris Smith, Pvt Keith Bryan, Pvt George Fernandez, Pvt Robert Kinsey, Pvt Roy Mezo, Pvt Jesse Hawkins, Pvt George Karalunas, and Pvt Edwin Finder.

After wading ashore, Goodgal and Crouch wandered along the beach trying to figure out where they were. Goodgal recalls:

> We later discovered that, had we walked in the opposite direction, we'd have been on Omaha Beach! Moving west, we soon reached some cliffs but couldn't find a way up. As dawn broke a boat came into view – it was carrying US Rangers. I waved some white clothing at them hoping they'd pick us up, but the boat sailed on past. We walked on along the beach to a headland (Pointe du Hoc) that was being attacked by the Rangers, and came under fire.

165

We started to take care of the wounded and Crouch attempted to retrieve first aid kits from the boats, but was beaten back by rifle fire. As I recall the USS *Satterlee* [a destroyer] shelled the gun position – then we went up the cliff. Once on top we continued to be attacked from all sides, and it took two days to secure the point. The Rangers' commanding officer, Col Rudder, ordered me to stake out a flag on the ground so that we wouldn't become targets for friendly fire. A little while later I was sent back to retrieve it and put it on a pole as a recognition sign for ground troops approaching from our front.

S/Sgt Roy Burger was in command of 14 men from HQ Co's 81mm mortar platoon. As their aircraft crossed the drop zone its green light failed to come on. The plane then dropped to ground level and headed out to sea. The interphone link between the pilot and his crew chief was broken and Roy Burger decided to visit the cockpit. "I asked the pilot where we were. He told me we were over the Channel and heading back to England. I ordered him to turn the plane around and jump us in France, which he did." After banking to the right the plane headed inland, crossing the coast again between Pointe du Hoc and Vierville-sur-Mer. Later, a rumor was spread that Burger had pulled a .45cal automatic pistol on the pilot and threatened to shoot him if he didn't turn the aircraft round. It was a great story that Burger dined out on for many years, but totally untrue.

Bob Dunning was at the back of the stick:

I remember the plane getting peppered with shrapnel. We were told to wait in the door until we were back over land. Pvt Herb Spence, who couldn't swim, lost his nerve while we were over the water. He unhooked his static line and sat down. As we turned back toward the French coast the crew chief told us he had no idea where we were. When the green light eventually came on everybody, except Spence, jumped out.

After his return from Normandy, Herb Spence had a lot of explaining to do. However, much to everybody's surprise, he never faced a court martial.

Burger's stick came down in a large area of marshland just east of the River Vire near Isigny-sur-Mer. They were about 7½ miles due east of their objective. Some men jettisoned their leg bags before landing and everything they contained, including personal weapons and ammunition, was lost. Roy Burger recalls:

We were badly scattered. I joined up with Cpl Allison and we eventually made our way out of the marshes. It was dark and we were lost. However, shells fired from the battleships were constantly going overhead and this helped us work out where the coast was. At daylight, dodging German troops, we headed toward the sea. The naval bombardment was terrific and we assumed our troops must have landed on the beaches. We entered a deserted town and started walking along one of its streets. Rifle fire from an upstairs window soon greeted us. We hot-tailed it out and took refuge in a bomb crater in a nearby field.

Meanwhile, after landing in the marshes, Bob Dunning had spent the best part of 16 hours trying to find his way out. He then met up with Jack Manley and the pair headed in a southwesterly direction toward what they thought was Omaha Beach – they were actually heading for Pointe du Hoc. By this time they had met up with a number of fellow paratroopers from another regiment, who had also been dropped off-target, and soon came under heavy naval bombardment. On the assumption that shells don't usually fall in the same place twice, Dunning and Manley spent their time dodging from crater to crater and trying to avoid the minefields that seemed to be all around the area.

At dusk on June 6, Burger and Allison, still in the crater, were surrounded by enemy soldiers and had to surrender. Burger remembers:

We were taken back to a German field command post. There we were stripped of everything we had including watches, knives, belts, and bootlaces. The next morning we were loaded into a German command car and driven away. An officer and his driver sat in the front while Allison and I were in the middle. Beside us was a wounded German and a guard sat directly behind. Several times we had to take cover from Allied aircraft. Eventually a P-47 appeared from the rear and strafed us, killing all the Germans. One shell passed through the body of the guard and into Allison's leg. At that moment I pushed Allison out of the door and we ran through a ditch into a field. The P-47 made another pass and completely destroyed the car. I treated Allison's wound with sulfa powder and we hid for a couple of days.

Moving toward the bridges

As Hank DiCarlo and Roy (the 82nd Airborne trooper) neared the bridges they joined a group of men led by Sgt Ralph Bennett. DiCarlo recalls:

One nervous trooper fired at an imaginary German column during the march to the bridge, sending us all into the shelter of roadside ditches. As our group increased in number the NCOs split us into six-man units, as we were frequently coming under hostile fire. I was amazed that we hadn't received more attention from the enemy. We were moving alongside a hedgerow and Roy decided to take a look over the top. As he peered over a German soldier did exactly the same thing. The two of them stared at each other for a few moments before slowly sinking back to the ground. As we scuttled away I threw a grenade over the hedge. If the German had left as quick as we did then I am sure it did him no harm.

Ralph Bennett adds to the story:

The men I'd sent out to act as scouts were my eyes and ears that night. They would report to me every hundred yards or so. I put the word out that crickets were not to be used and that if anyone came under fire they were to return it without hesitation. I was constantly telling people to put out cigarettes or stop talking! Guys were acting like it was some sort of stroll in the park – I couldn't believe what I was seeing.

In the darkness Bennett missed the bridge and led his men half a mile or so past it before arriving at the Pont de l'Esseau road junction (a 501st check point). He then heard three men talking in hushed voices. Stopping his column, he approached the group in order to find out what was happening. One of the men was Capt Charles Shettle who was discussing his whereabouts with two other officers. Shettle was clearly lost, as Bennett heard him say, "I have just walked in completely the wrong direction." The captain acknowledged Bennett's arrival and they began to study a map. At that moment recognition crickets were heard and 2nd Lt Peter Madden and his group arrived on the scene.

A few moments later Bennett heard his men shouting; "We've got a Kraut, let's shoot the bastard, let's shoot him!" and went to investigate. He told them to shut up and demanded to know what was happening. A German paratrooper had given himself up and Pfc Bob "Whitey" Hoffman (H Co), who could speak German, told Bennett, "The Kraut says that he left his unit a couple of days ago and has been waiting for us to arrive. He's been walking with us for several hours without us knowing and wanted to give himself up." Bennett frogmarched the soldier up to Capt Shettle and asked what they should do with him. Shettle said, "Oh bring him along, it's time to move out." Bennett decided to call the German "Schultz" and he stayed with the group helping to dig foxholes. He remained with them until June 7 when he was sent to a POW pen.

Shettle's group was now 30–40 strong. He decided to head east along the Pénême road in the general direction of the bridges, avoiding one or two isolated farms along the way – Shettle didn't want to be drawn into any unnecessary skirmishes that would have delayed his arrival at the road bridge. At around 0445hrs, the group reached a farm owned by Théophile Fortin. About 200 yards further on, branching off to the right, was a road that led to the objective.

It was now daylight and the group was spotted by enemy soldiers on the southeastern side of the river, who started firing at them. They left the road and followed low ground to its right before reaching the base of a dyke that gave them excellent cover. The dyke formed part of the river Douve's flood barrier, was about 10ft high and topped by a single track road. A second lower dyke some 200 yards away marked the edge of the river.

At this point the group split up, leaving Sgt Bennett and his squad to fall back and prepare their 60mm mortar for the bridge assault. Shettle and the rest of his men continued for about 380 yards along the base of the dyke toward the road bridge where they found 1st Lt Ken Christianson waiting for them.

Meanwhile 2nd Lt Tom Kennedy's group was still struggling toward the bridges. They came upon a farmhouse and decided to stop and ask directions. The family was overjoyed to see the Americans and helped them locate the objective. On arriving in the area, some men headed off to check in with Shettle whilst Kennedy and the remaining soldiers made their way to the footbridge.

After making their way from Carentan and successfully crossing the Douve, Ed Shames and his group met five soldiers from the 501st led by a captain. They were from the same stick and were clearly lost. The officer asked Shames, "Who are you, where are you going, and do you know where you are?" Shames replied, "I'm Col Wolverton's operations sergeant from 3rd Bn 506th and yes, I know where we are, sir." The officer said, "Sgt Shames, we go where you go."

They followed an easterly bearing that took them across open ground. As it started to get light, Shames began to pick up the pace and he told the group, "I'm not waiting around, you either keep up or get left behind, it's entirely up to you." Some of the men started to moan but fell in behind the operations sergeant like ducklings following their mother.

We hadn't gone far when we met Col Johnson, the 501st's commanding officer. Johnson demanded, "Which way's the God-damned lock?" I showed him on the map and pointed. He set off and took the 501st people in my group with him. It was nearly broad daylight and I stepped up a gear as we approached the bridge.

On arrival Capt Shettle shouted, "Boy, am I ever glad to see you and why on earth are you still wearing your parachute pack tray?" Due to the shock and excitement of landing in the milk factory I'd forgotten to take it off and was wearing it like an extra layer of clothing. This may sound crazy but it made me feel safer in some strange way. Shettle continued,

"For the time being I want you to act as my temporary executive officer whilst we try to sort out this mess." I wondered if Shettle was trying to butter me up because normally he was not as friendly as this.

Approaching the road bridge from the southern side of the Pénême road were "Dog" Gallaugher and Bobbie Rommel. Rommel recalls:

We came across an officer who'd taken control of a few men from my company, plus one or two from Regimental HQ Demolitions. There must've been about 15 of us in total. The officer then decided to blow one of the concrete electricity pylons beside the road. We watched in anticipation as he instructed the demolition men to place C2 charges onto the pylon's latticework structure. When the C2 detonated, nothing happened and they gave up. We then all continued our march along the road.

It was just starting to get light when we spotted a group of soldiers moving in the same direction as us. Our officer got a little spooked and decided to crawl into a small chicken shack and ordered us to protect him! One of my buddies thought this was really funny and started to cuss the officer. After being called a chicken shit for the umpteenth time he reluctantly got out of the shack and threatened the enlisted man with insubordination – what a stupid man! We carried on toward the bridge and soon came under attack from the 40mm antiaircraft gun at L'Amont that was air-bursting shells above us again. At that point we left the road, making directly for the bridge, arriving just after first light. That damned officer immediately reported my buddy to Shettle. When things calmed down a bit I was summoned and questioned about the "chicken shit" incident. I told Shettle that the officer deserved it and that's as far as it went. The kid in question was put down for transfer but before it came through he took a bullet in the backside and was evacuated.

First light, June 6

Pvt Phil Abbey was leading John Gibson's small group eastward away from the farm at Le Mont toward their bridge objective. He had been skirting around the worst of the flooding and using ditches and hedgerows for concealment. By dawn the patrol was near La Basse Addeville and was following a ditch that ran across an open field. The ditch slowly began to get shallower and eventually disappeared. Abbey ordered the group to make for better cover beside a grassy berm.

Abbey and Ronzani reached a fence and passed through a gate. Suddenly, Gibson saw a German helmet. Before he could shout a warning about a dozen Germans rose from waist-high grass and opened fire with machine pistols. Abbey and Ronzani were hit several times and fell to the ground.

The others turned back and ran for cover. Gibson and Swinson managed to crawl on all fours along a drainage ditch. Rosie and Krebs were trying to follow but were captured. Somehow Lee managed to slip away. Gibson recalls:

> The Germans hit us so fast that I don't think we fired a single shot in return. The entire terrible experience lasted about 5 minutes and we stood no chance. There must've been a full company of those bastards just waiting for daybreak and someone to ambush. They started to hunt for Swinson and myself with fixed bayonets and I made one last desperate attempt to hide myself. They got closer and closer and soon I was looking at the point of a bayonet. The soldier ordered me out and I got to my feet and half raised my arms. He made no attempt to use his weapon but his face and voice showed signs of extreme agitation. Seconds later a P-47 Thunderbolt, with its throttle wide open, crashed near us and made a terrific noise as its bomb load exploded. The Germans paid little attention and seemed more focused on processing us!

One very young-looking German soldier walked over to the prisoners and placed a pistol between Gibson's eyes. Fortunately he was just fooling around and laughed as he put the gun away – Gibson breathed a huge sigh of relief. "Shortly afterwards my medical kit, wallet, watch, and knives were taken from me, so I no longer had medical supplies to tend the wounded." Gibson was furious with the way he had been treated.

His Red Cross armband was clearly visible but the enemy soldiers were showing no respect. For a moment he seriously thought about using his M2 knife, which was concealed in his jumpsuit. However, before he could do anything about the situation he was marched off to where Ronzani and Abbey lay wounded.

It was a horrible sight that greeted Gibson. The two paratroopers were on their backs gasping for breath. "I was shocked. Blood was pulsing in spurts 6in high out of their chests. I tried to assist but was forced away and both men died before my eyes." The four surviving Americans were rounded up and guarded by a couple of very young-looking Germans. Meanwhile Charlie Lee, who was hiding in bushes about 50 yards away, opened fire, narrowly missing the two guards. Gibson recalls, "We watched as several German soldiers discussed how they were going to get Lee. They ran off down a track, outflanked him and within seconds we knew that he was dead – Lee had a one-year-old son whom he'd never seen."

From the ambush point, the men were marched a couple of hundred yards to Les Droueries Manor, which was surrounded by defensive positions. Georgian soldiers from Georgisches Infanterie-Bataillon 795, easily identified by sleeve patches inscribed GEORGIEN, defended the site.

The Americans were surprised to see well-constructed trenches nearby that were designed specifically for horses. Each trench was about 3ft wide, 15ft long, and deep enough to protect the entire animal. The German horses were much smaller than those kept by local farmers.

The group was then separated and Gibson marched off with his hands behind his head toward Carentan whilst the others were taken to an outbuilding. Rosie was in terrible pain as the nerves in his broken teeth were exposed. Leo Krebs could speak a little German and approached one of the guards about Rosie's predicament. The German consulted with an older soldier who was cooking nearby. The two men approached Rosie and sat him on a bale of straw whilst Krebs and Swinson held his arms.

The older German clamped a rusty pair of pliers onto the damaged teeth and began ripping them out, together with bits of gum. The pain

TONIGHT WE DIE AS MEN

from this amateur extraction was unbelievable, but as soon as it was over Rosie felt immediate relief. Shortly afterwards the three paratroopers were taken to the prisoner-holding field at Le Ferage, before being marched to Carentan.

A French woman, who may have had German sympathies, hurled abuse and spat in Gibson's face as he arrived in Carentan. Other civilians he encountered seemed more reserved. For the remainder of D-Day Gibson was passed from the care of one weary guard to another. Whilst moving around he saw Charles K. Lewis (B Co 506th), an Indian from Tensid, Idaho, sitting awkwardly on the back of a horse-drawn cart. He had lost a leg, was clearly in need of urgent medical care and died a couple of days later.

Gibson spent the night of June 6 in a pigsty together with a wounded 101st trooper. The soldier had lost part of a leg from just below the knee. His skin was progressively losing color and he was shivering uncontrollably. As the night wore on Gibson desperately tried to keep him alive, whilst at the same time protecting the unbandaged stump of his leg from pig excrement! A couple of German guards took it in turns to watch over the prisoners, but neither showed any concern or sympathy toward the wounded soldier. The following morning Gibson was taken from the pigsty at bayonet point and forced to join a shabby-looking collection of wounded soldiers. There were 29 Germans plus three Americans in the group and, with the exception of the guards, Gibson appeared to be the only able-bodied person.

In charge of the wounded was a German officer who was clutching a small suitcase. He was a hard-faced man and despite his wounds gave Gibson and the other two Americans as hard a time as he possibly could. They moved off in the direction of St-Lô and 7½ miles later stopped in the small town of St-Jean-de-Daye. Allied bombing had damaged many of its buildings. It was very hot, and using sign language Gibson asked the officer if he could fetch a bottle of water from a bombed-out store.

He said no! He wouldn't even allow us to drink from a nearby puddle! Before I could say anything more we were all taken to an empty building and crowded into a small room. I sat there reflecting on the past 36 hours and feeling very empty and alone. I turned toward a wall and began to sob making sure nobody, especially that son of a bitch officer, heard a thing. It only happened the once and I knew that if I was going to make it I would have to shape up and focus on survival.

After a short while the men were ushered outside into a waiting bus, which had been commandeered to take them to St-Lô. It was in a poor state of repair and had a large red cross painted on the roof that would have hopefully protected its occupants from air attack. Just before nightfall, as the bus was approaching the northern outskirts of St-Lô, it ran out of fuel. The men continued the remainder of their journey into the burning city by foot and were taken to a building near the convent at Bon Sauveur. Straw had been thrown on the floor but the officer made it clear that it was for German use only and the Americans had to sit on the bare stone.

Not far from La Barquette, Paul Garrison and Bill Galbraith were hiding in a hedgerow waiting for first light. As dawn broke the two men discovered they were in an area busy with German activity. Garrison was fearful that they might become a target for Allied naval artillery and sent Galbraith to scout around. "As I moved along the hedgerow I came across a naval observer and some enlisted men," recalls Galbraith. "I told the observer about Garrison's concerns. He replied, 'Don't worry – I'm in radio contact with the navy and I'm not about to call anything in on us!' When I told Garrison what the observer had said he almost choked on his D-bar [D-bars were solid dark chocolate, not very sweet but useful to trade. They were generally disliked by GIs but European kids loved them]. He then told me to take his maps (he didn't want to get caught with them) and attempt to make contact with soldiers we'd seen about a thousand yards away."

Galbraith could see a line of woods in front of him that ran to his left. The woodland joined the Pénême road that passed within 100 yards of the lock at La Barquette. As he moved across a field he spotted an equipment bundle. It contained machine-gun ammunition and he bent down to pick up a couple of boxes. Suddenly a bullet whizzed past his ear: "I could feel and hear the round pass by and dived into a slight indentation in the ground. Bullets started peppering all around the edge of the dip and I knew it was only a matter of time before one found me. I dumped one of the ammo boxes and ran off toward a stream and jumped in. Working my way toward the woodland I eventually found the men we'd spotted earlier. They were from the 501st PIR."

At Ste-Mère-Église, enemy resistance was fierce. Stedman, Madona, Fishel, Rosdahl, Lujan, and Kidder were hiding in a water-filled ditch. With them were three wounded soldiers. With the exception of medic Bill Kidder, who stayed behind to look after the wounded, the men took it in turns to go out and find other paratroopers and eventually rounded up five soldiers from the 506th.

By first light Kidder had managed to stabilize the three wounded men, but everybody was cold, wet, and miserable. Suddenly about 50 paratroopers from the 82nd Airborne Division turned up. The 3rd Bn men were pleased to see them but shocked to learn how close they were to Ste-Mère-Église.

Stedman and his colleagues accepted an invitation from the 82nd to assist in their efforts to take the town. The group had no defined leader but everybody seemed to get along together. Stedman recalls, "At about 1000hrs that morning we came across a couple of equipment bundles full of 60mm ammo. That kept us busy again and we raised a little hell." Their first target was the village of Vaulaville. Stedman and Lujan softened up the place by firing more than 100 rounds into the settlement before the 82nd made their assault. During their mortar bombardment Stedman told Lujan, "That's the first day of Kraut season well and truly open." Stedman and his five colleagues remained with the 82nd until after the liberation of Ste-Mère-Église. Stedman recalls, "When the main fighting for the town was over Col Sink had all the 101st troopers (there were about 50 of us) sent back to our respective outfits. The 82nd issued us with notes that we handed to our platoon leaders stating where we had been and what we had been doing – just in case there was any doubt over our absence."

As the first light of dawn began to appear at La Barquette, S/Sgt Webb was carefully picking his way behind some German positions. He recalls, "I moved toward a barn near the lock-keeper's house, not 50 yards from the lock. I could hear Germans talking and spotted someone up in the loft. As I got closer I could make out one or two of our guys." Hiding in the barn were Ben Hiner and five other men from 3rd Bn; the group also included an unknown soldier armed with a machine gun. All the men had weapons, which made Webb feel a lot safer. He climbed up into the loft and could see that crossing the Douve via the lock was out of the question. Looking up the river toward the Bassin à Flot (just under 1,600 yards away) Webb spotted a line of trees and thought it would make good cover: "I suggested that we make our way to the canal and try to steal a boat. I put the idea to the vote and they all insisted that I lead. We moved out cautiously, staying close to the river and waiting every once in a while to listen for enemy activity."

When the patrol reached the trees the machine gunner set up his weapon on the northern side of the canal near the bridge at St-Hilaire. Suddenly a shot was fired and the soldier slumped over his gun. He had been hit between the eyes and died instantly. On either side of the canal were two identical-looking houses belonging to the lock authority. The sniper was on the second floor of the house nearest to Webb and his team. The group quickly removed the bolt from the machine gun before abandoning it, along with any idea of stealing a boat. Then, fearing more soldiers were nearby, they moved out. Hiner thought that, for some strange reason, the sniper was female: "I don't know what she was doing there, but she saw me and waved. The next thing I knew shots were being fired. I realized it was this blonde and fired back with my M1. We didn't stick around to see what happened but I think I may have killed her."

Moving northwest along the southern bank of the river, they noticed a German paratrooper walking toward them. Webb recalls:

He seemed to be in a world of his own. He just kept coming toward us – by the time he'd walked up the embankment I had my pistol out and leveled at his head. He was no more than 3ft away before he realized we were there! We dragged him off and discovered he was an artillery observer with a map case full of vital information. Using sign language I ordered him to lead us back along the riverbank. We eventually found a narrow place to cross and forced him at gunpoint to swim the river. He carried across some jump ropes, which he then used to pull us over.

Safely on the northern bank, Webb's patrol headed off in the direction of Pénême. Along the way a captain from the 501st approached them. The officer said he needed Webb and his men for an attack that was about to take place at La Barquette lock. Webb protested that he had his own agenda, but the captain responded by telling him that the 3rd Bn had been wiped out. "All the more reason to accomplish our mission, sir," Webb replied, as he turned and marched his men away.

Meanwhile Bill Galbraith was moving along the tree line just north of La Barquette when he came across Pfc Marion Hove (I Co), who was with some men from the 501st. Bill talked Hove into going back with him to get Paul Garrison. As they left the safety of the woods they were surprised to see Garrison heading in their direction. "I could not believe my eyes, he was hobbling over the field that I'd recently had so much trouble crossing," recalls Galbraith. "Not one of those German bastards took a shot at him. I looked on dumbfounded and couldn't figure out where the enemy had gone. Garrison seemed to be doing pretty well so Hove and I went back to the trees and shouted words of encouragement." Once Garrison reached the safety of the trees the medics treated him. Galbraith and Hove then joined the 501st for the attack on the lock. Afterwards both wished that they had headed for the bridges, but at the time it seemed safer to stay with the crowd.

After crossing the Pénême road, the pair took cover behind a berm that ran parallel to the river Douve. They were being heavily shelled by what they thought was mortar fire and had been abandoned by the rest of their group. It soon became apparent that the firing was coming from the antiaircraft gun at L'Amont. At the end of the berm, close to the lock, they found a wounded man. "Most of his face was missing and I felt sick, so Hove had to fix him up," recalls Galbraith. "We left him sulfa powder and water and for some stupid reason went back to our original position, which was still under fire. We were both terrified and nobody from the 501st gave us any direction at all – we just made things up as we went along!"

Eventually the firing stopped and the two men crawled into an empty German foxhole that was about 275 yards from the lock. Galbraith recalls, "Later that morning somebody from the 501st came over and said 'Do you guys wanna die? If you stay here you will.' He then asked what outfit we were from. I said that I was a machine gunner and Hove was my assistant; he wasn't, but I didn't want to be left with people I didn't know. We were given a spare .30cal LMG [light machine gun] and repositioned in a ditch beside a track leading to the lock, which was lined with tall trees." The naval observer Galbraith had spoken to earlier was now working with the 501st and had begun calling in naval artillery support from one of the battleships (USS *Nevada*) out in the Channel.

It was late in the morning before the *Nevada* began firing. The first 14in round whooshed over like an express train and landed in open ground about 65 yards behind Galbraith and Hove's position. Luckily the area was waterlogged and absorbed most of the impact. After a reprimand from Col Johnson, the observer made adjustments and called for more fire. The following bombardment was awesome and the men cheered as they watched shells come down around L'Amont. This shelling, however, had devastating consequences for Allied prisoners being moved from St-Côme-du-Mont to Carentan.

As the day wore on, mortar and small-arms fire grew louder. Galbraith and Hove were unaware of what was happening just half a mile or so northeast of their current location. The German I.Bataillon/Fallschirmjäger-Regiment 6 had been trapped when glider-borne troops landed on the afternoon of the 6th. The Germans faced two options – they could either stay and fight or withdraw to their Regimental HQ at St-Côme-du-Mont. They chose the latter; at first light the following morning they were spotted by elements of 3rd Bn 506th and a battle began that lasted most of the day.

∾7∾

"A real feeling of victory"
D–Day – June 6, 1944

St-Côme-du-Mont

At some time around dawn, unaware that he was being watched, George Kenfield was cautiously moving through an open field about 550 yards south of St-Côme-du-Mont. Fellow pathfinder Dave Morgan was about 20 yards to his left hidden in a hedgerow. "He ignored me even after I'd called out the password," recalls Morgan. "So I went out into the field and told Kenfield where I'd been hiding, but he just knelt motionless. I returned to the hedgerow expecting him to follow." A couple of hours later, on Morgan's far left, a German soldier stepped out from cover and began walking in his direction, casually throwing grenades over the hedgerow as he went.

Morgan aimed his rifle at the soldier's head and took a deep breath, "I let him get closer before firing the shot that killed him. I then waited a while to see what might happen and a line of German soldiers soon appeared. I started firing as quickly as I could and used about a clip and a half before they pulled back. Rushing into the field I found Kenfield and suggested we leave. I could see the church steeple and decided to circle the village keeping it in sight."

The RN13 was about 160 yards away and, keeping under cover, the two men made their way toward it. As they crossed an open field they were fired upon and fell to the ground. Morgan recalls:

> I crawled over to Kenfield but he was dead. Every time I moved a spray
> of bullets went over my head and I couldn't work out where the firing

was coming from. All of a sudden a trickle of blood ran down the bridge of my nose and into my eye. It scared the hell out of me and I surrendered. The firing came from an outpost on the edge of town and, thankfully, the wound turned out to be a superficial cut! The Germans took my water bottle and wallet but left a little prayer book my aunt had given me when I joined the army – plus a picture of my girlfriend.

Morgan took one last look at Kenfield's body before he was marched out of the field into captivity.

A little earlier Louise Laurence had caught her first glimpse of captured parachutists:

The soldiers had their arms in the air and were escorted by German guards. Some of the prisoners had lost their boots and were walking in bare feet. As these brave soldiers passed by they glanced in our direction, winking and smiling. These simple gestures instilled a real feeling of victory in us and we knew a huge operation, in which they had supreme faith, was underway. I don't think many of them thought they'd be captives of the Germans for long.

Louise dared not smile or speak to the prisoners for fear of German reprisals.

By February 1944 Mayor Gustave Laurence's sentence had expired and he was a free man again. He met his first American during the morning of D-Day:

A lot of parachutists had come down on the eastern side of the RN13. Two landed in my back garden. One of the men disappeared before I had a chance to greet him but the other remained, as I think he'd been wounded. From this moment onwards we felt free! We wanted to mark our gratitude toward our liberators in some small way but unfortunately the Germans had looted everything including our wine. It was wine that most of the soldiers asked for but they ended up drinking cider, as it was all we had left to offer.

At about 0800hrs Gustave, his brother-in-law, and one of their neighbors went to help the parachutist who lay wounded in his garden. In spite of the soldier's obvious suffering he gave each of them a cigarette. All three Frenchmen shook hands with the American but the language barrier made it difficult to communicate.

Shortly afterwards Gustave met his second American and recalls:

> Another soldier, who we thought was dead, was lying on the roof of Melle Mauduit's grocery store. He lay motionless, his feet were caught in an electric cable and his back was against the roof. The Germans had been firing at him periodically for some time and thought they'd killed him.
>
> Around mid-morning the Germans came looking for me. I was a roofer by trade and they wanted me to get him down. After putting ladders in place my brother-in-law and I climbed up and crawled across the roof to where he lay. To our surprise he turned his head and looked at us. I asked him how he was (in French of course). He smiled and seemed pleased to see civilians rather than German soldiers. The American was very tall and had hurt his back.
>
> We cut through his parachute cord and started lowering him to the German soldiers below. He tried his best to assist us but found difficulty in moving his body, which had been in the same position for nearly 9 hours. I was amazed at just how much a fully laden parachutist weighed. On reaching the ground, the Germans searched him and took his weapons. We then took him to the newly established aid post in Mme Jacquet's house. Quite a few paratroopers were already at the aid post and an American doctor was treating them.

The soldier Gustave had rescued was Johnny Houk from I Co. The American doctor was Capt Stanley Morgan who had sprained his ankle on landing. Following capture, he persuaded the Germans to let him set up an aid station in St-Côme-du-Mont. Pfc Henry Ritter could speak German fluently and was acting as his interpreter. Morgan was working in unison with a German medical team and by 0600hrs on D-Day the aid post was fully established. "A Red Cross flag was hurriedly placed on the roof of our house," recalls Thérèse Jacquet. "Many wounded men lay next to each other on the floor. After spending two days in a slit trench close by, we joined another displaced family at Maitre George's place."

During the course of the morning more and more wounded were brought in, including medics S/Sgt Mike Weiden, Sgt Tom Newell, and Sgt Mainard "Cliff" Clifton. Newell had been wounded in the leg and Clifton had a piece of his steel helmet lodged in his scalp. Weiden had fractured a bone in his foot on landing and was finding it difficult to move around, but he tried his best to help the medical team who were struggling to cope. As things got progressively worse, Dr Morgan decided to ask the Germans to evacuate the more seriously wounded. They agreed and plans were made to move them to an underground military hospital in St-Lô. Later that afternoon Morgan, Weiden, and Ritter traveled to the hospital in an ambulance with the wounded. Weiden had his foot treated and volunteered to remain with the patients in St-Lô whilst Morgan and Ritter returned to St-Côme-du-Mont.

One of the evacuees was 23-year-old Pvt Robert Cone, a 506th demolitions expert. Cone was Jewish and had the letter H (for Hebrew) stamped on his dog tags. After being brought into the aid post, he was processed by 1st Lt Alex Bobuck (for some reason the Germans thought Bobuck was part of the medical detachment) who had the good sense to remove his identification – Cone was to remain a POW until the end of hostilities.

Joe Beyrle, together with a number of other prisoners (including his company commander John McKnight), had been held in the POW field near Le Ferage since dawn. Just across a dirt track, not too far from his position, was an orchard. Hanging from two apple trees were a couple of paratroopers. Their bodies were swollen and bulged as if about to explode. German reinforcements coming from the direction of Houesville were using them for target practice. With each burst of fire the blood-caked bodies twisted in the trees and one man's head was nearly severed. One of Joe's guards came over and gleefully told him that the nearest body was a colonel. Then the penny dropped and Joe realized it was Col Wolverton. He began to cry – the feeling of loss was overwhelming. After regaining his composure he asked if the colonel and the other man could be cut down and buried. The guard shrugged his shoulders and the bodies remained hanging from the trees.

The guards started selecting NCOs for interrogation and several prisoners, including Joe, were marched to a field near ObstLt von der Heydte's Regimental HQ at L'Amont (now known as Dead Man's Corner). The position was located in the basement of a house and was occupied by Hptm Preikschat (I.Bataillon/Fallschirmjäger-Regiment 6) who was using it as a command post.

One by one the prisoners were led away for questioning and soon it was Joe's turn. He was taken through an orchard and down some steps into a small room in the basement of the house. Seated in front of him was a German lieutenant who spoke the most perfect English. Following his interrogation Joe was sent to another room that was supposedly occupied by representatives from the German Red Cross. Sitting on a table in the room, with her legs crossed, was a girl who bore a striking resemblance to a young woman Joe had met in Ramsbury, and sitting behind was a German officer. The officer appeared to be anti-Russian and started talking about the Communist threat. Every now and again the girl chipped in with 3rd Bn casualty figures.

The interrogation continued for some time, but Joe would not cooperate and was eventually taken back to the POW pen at Le Ferage. As he left the bunker he saw Fred Berke (C Co 326th Airborne Engineers) waiting to enter the interrogation room. "Watch out for the English bitch," he murmured as they filed past.

A little earlier in the day, on the western side of the town, Charles Destrès and his father were walking along a track called Chemin des Campagnes (now renamed Route des Fardelles) that links La Croix with the Houlland farm. Some American soldiers approached them. Charles recalls, "Five or six big men with blackened faces came through a gate. They were dressed like nothing we'd seen before. They showed us a small map and kept pointing to 'Les Droueries.' My father and I tried to make them understand that they were nowhere near the place and that German troops were in the town. They went back into the field and camouflaged themselves in a sunken cattle wallow."

An officer from the 501st was leading the group Charles and his father had met. With him were a couple of men from his own regiment plus Sgt McCallum, Joe Gorenc, Bill Atlee, and Jack Brown from the 506th. The officer wanted to break cover and move out, as McCallum recalls:

Rather than risk the lives of his own men, the officer made Atlee and myself scouts. I told him that we had no real experience in this line of work and he raised his Tommy gun and pointed it at us. Joe Gorenc responded by calmly telling him to watch where he was pointing that thing, as he was also armed. Joe was feeling very confident because, just after the drop, he and Atlee had attacked and killed several enemy soldiers riding on a horse and cart. However, the situation soon calmed down as I agreed to carry out the officer's instructions and Atlee and I went on ahead.

We left the field and started to cross a sunken track [Chemin des Campagnes] when we were suddenly hit by fire from a group of German paratroopers. Atlee, who was no more than 3ft from me, was killed instantly. I left him on the ground and went back the way I came, spraying the Krauts with automatic fire as I went.

Charles Destrès recalls the incident: "During the day there was a lot of firing from the Germans and a parachutist was killed by a bullet that went through his throat. That night we returned to the field, covered his body with a blanket, and took away his helmet and fighting knife. We later discovered the soldier's name was Atlee, as both items were named."

As late evening of D-Day approached, so more gliders carrying soldiers and equipment started landing in fields north of St-Côme-du-Mont. Louise Laurence was watching the aircraft circle over the town:

We had a lot of trouble stopping ourselves from shouting for joy as we pointed in disbelief at the giant gliders. That evening we all went to bed fully dressed and all through the night listened to the shooting. At one point we heard incoming mortar fire and realized that the battle for St-Côme was stepping up. The following day [June 7] the battle grew in ferocity and German reinforcements came in by foot from Lessay.

Sometimes we felt that the battle was coming nearer to our home, only for it to move away again. Then the Allied attack seemed to ease off. We later learned that supplies dropped by American planes had landed in the wrong place and were captured by the Germans. Like the previous night we went to bed fully dressed, making sure that our shoes were at the bottom of the stairs and our coats placed at the foot of each bed.

Moving the prisoners

At noon on D-Day, around 80 prisoners, including about 30 men from 3rd Bn, were marched from Le Ferage along the RN13 toward Carentan. As the group passed through St-Côme-du-Mont they were alarmed by the number of German reinforcements (mostly paratroopers) entering the town. Joe Beyrle was marching in company with Capt Harwick and Pfc Lambert Tucker. They had been on the road for about 15 minutes when shells, probably fired by an Allied ship in the Channel, hit the ground nearby. The explosions threw everybody into a panic and they all desperately ran for cover. Beyrle, Harwick, and Tucker slipped into the marshes on the eastern side of the road. Joe had been hit on the backside by a small piece of shrapnel, although he did not realize it at the time. The men stumbled into a flooded field where they came across two soldiers from G Co, who had been hiding in the area since the drop. One had lost both legs during the barrage and the other (Pvt Richard Johnn) was also seriously wounded. They were unable to give much help but carried both men to the edge of the RN13 where they were treated later by medics. Then, from a safe distance, they watched whilst the Germans rounded up the other POWs and marched them off toward Carentan. The three men split up and Harwick managed to make good his escape.

After dark Joe Beyrle, who was hampered by his wound, hobbled across to the western side of the RN13 and hid among the reeds. Before he knew what was happening, German soldiers had him pinned down in the mud. Joe had no weapon or helmet and the Germans guessed that he had escaped from captivity and took him to another prisoner-holding field (probably near L'Amont, where his dog tags and jacket were taken.

On arrival in Carentan, the POWs joined more prisoners to form a group of around 200, which included a number of British and Canadian soldiers. There the men were packed onto trucks and driven 19 miles south to St-Lô. One vehicle in the convoy was marked with a red cross. On board were Dr Morgan and his two colleagues, who were taking wounded from St-Côme-du-Mont to the underground hospital in St-Lô.

Shortly after the convoy left Carentan, it was attacked by a couple of Spitfires. Many of the prisoners were killed or wounded and the dead were buried by the roadside. Dave Morgan remembers, "We saw aircraft coming toward us and the trucks pulled over. We began waving white sheets and one man leapt out of a truck – a guard was about to shoot but I managed to bump into him, giving the man time to escape. The first plane flew over without shooting but the second fired one burst and everybody jumped out of the trucks."

The convoy arrived in St-Lô during the early afternoon of June 6. The men were then marched past Gen Marck's HQ at Immeuble de Commines to a compound on the northeastern side of the city. The complex consisted of a number of stable blocks and was known as Dépôt de Remonte. It was once part of a large stud farm called Vieux Haras and was near the church of Ste-Croix, whose steeple could be seen from the stable compound. On arrival some of the prisoners, including George Rosie, were taken away for further questioning.

Later that day the Allies started bombing St-Lô. The first raid began at about 2000hrs and destroyed the Feldkommandantur's headquarters, the Caisse d'Epargne bank, Banque de France, the town hall, and many civilian dwellings. A further 50 B-17 bombers came at 0030hrs on June 7. The attack lasted 10 minutes and there were two more raids before daylight. Fortunately the bombing missed the stables and church area, but the western part of the town was badly damaged and enormous columns of smoke rose from the inferno. During the afternoon the large civilian hospital at St-Joseph was hit and its 700 patients evacuated to the nearby German underground hospital. The hospital, built below the medieval part of the city, was overwhelmed and the following day most of its wounded prisoners were moved to Mortain. Civilian patients went to a nearby convent at Le Bon Sauveur – 326 civilians lost their lives during the bombing of St–Lô.

The road bridge and Fortin Farm

1st Lt Ken Christianson, Pfc Sam Porter, and Pfc Don Arminio were the first 3rd Bn men to arrive at the road bridge. At this point there should have been around 250 men at the position, but by the time Capt Shettle and his group arrived the total was around 40. The bridge area was surprisingly quiet and the officers wondered if the invasion had been postponed, leaving them stranded behind enemy lines. 2nd Lt Pete Madden was looking at the men around him when suddenly a damaged P-47 came screeching overhead and crashed in flames 1¼ miles due north at Les Rats Farm (the same aircraft seen by John Gibson while at Les Droueries Manor).

Sgt Bennett and his squad had set up their mortar 380 yards north of the bridge on the western side of its access road. At that point the road, which ran along the top of a berm, turned west through 90 degrees and ran for about 550 yards toward the farmhouse owned by Théophile Fortin. The berm provided excellent protection from German fire coming from the opposite bank of the Douve. Peering through the early morning mist, Bennett could just make out the church tower at St-Côme-du-Mont some 3 miles away. About 220 yards of open ground lay between his position and the riverbank, and he recalls, "A little later on somebody sent out a couple of machine-gun teams who dug in nearby."

From around 0500hrs Christianson had been asking for volunteers to scout across the bridge – he had devised a rough plan to test the enemy's strength by drawing their fire. No one showed any interest until Don Zahn stuck his hand in the air and got the ball rolling by taking the position of lead scout. Christianson noticed Hank DiCarlo nearby and ordered him to join the group. At that very moment (about 0530hrs) the northeastern horizon lit up, followed by a deep rumbling noise. The Allied naval bombardment of Utah Beach had begun, signaling that the invasion was under way – everyone breathed a deep sigh of relief.

Road bridge and surrounding positions, June 6, 1944

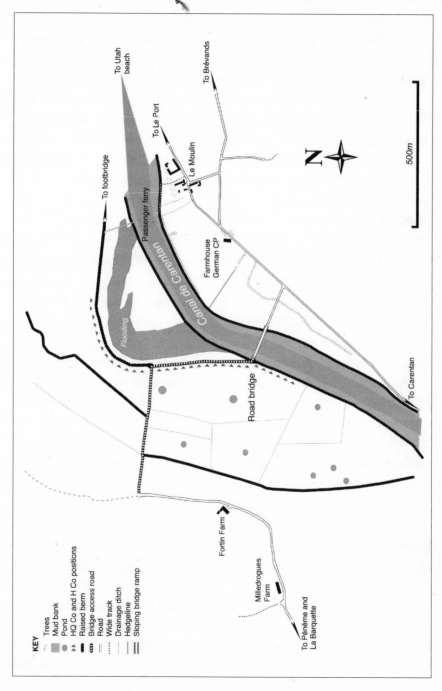

At about the same time a solitary Me109, throttle wide open, passed low overhead and made off in the direction of Carentan.

Impatient for action, Bennett approached the bridge to see Christianson. The lieutenant was somewhat preoccupied, so Bennett decided to take a look over the berm with his field glasses. Before he had a chance to steal a glance Christianson shouted, "Mind your own God-damned business, Sergeant. Get back to your squad and wait for further orders."

Christianson eventually sent five H Co men across the bridge. They were DiCarlo, Zahn, Arminio, Montilio, and S/Sgt Bahlau, who was in charge of the patrol. DiCarlo followed Zahn along the left bridge rail whilst the others worked their way along the right. DiCarlo recalls:

> As I got on to the bridge, I realized it was built of heavy timbers and absolutely flat. I followed a little way behind Zahn and we made no conversation. When I got about halfway across he jumped over the rail onto the bank below. I then noticed movement in the bushes and fired a couple of rounds. There was no response and I followed him off the bridge. Looking back I could see the others who one by one dropped into the mud and made their way upstream. Zahn, who was moving in the opposite direction, had disappeared around a bend in the river and I set off after him.

While DiCarlo and the others were crossing the bridge, Lt Christianson ordered Cpl Tom Bucher and Pfc Andy Bryan, who had arrived earlier with Capt Shettle, to set up their machine gun and provide covering fire. "We clambered up the berm just to the right of the bridge and began to fire short bursts at the opposite bank," recalls Bucher. "Just then a burst of machine-pistol fire from across the river tore into the bank spraying dirt into our faces, which forced us to relocate."

Meanwhile, on the other side of the river, the men were struggling to make progress through the soft, exposed mud banks. As DiCarlo followed Zahn downstream he suddenly noticed movement above him. Looking down from the berm was a German soldier who was kneeling and pointing a Walther P38 pistol. The German fired and the bullet struck DiCarlo in the upper right chest, knocking him to the ground. Flat on his back, he watched helplessly as the enemy soldier peered over the embankment and fully expected him to fire again. Meanwhile Zahn, who had heard the shot, was making his way back upstream. As soon as DiCarlo spotted him he pointed at the German. Only a couple of seconds had elapsed since the pistol shot, but it seemed like forever. As soon as the German soldier saw Zahn he panicked and started running toward a line of trees. Zahn leapt up onto the berm and killed him with a burst of fire from his Thompson submachine gun.

The rest of the group had heard the commotion, and leaving Montilio in position, Bahlau and Arminio made their way downstream to see what was going on. Finding DiCarlo, they started dressing his wound while Zahn, who was about 40 yards away, gave covering fire. It was clear that DiCarlo's wound was serious.

There was a lot of German small-arms fire coming in their direction but they were protected by the berm and it was going high above their heads. The problem now facing them was how to get DiCarlo back across the bridge. After about 10 minutes they came up with a solution. Nearby was an 8ft wooden plank left over from the bridge's construction. Although Hank was finding it very difficult to walk, he could crawl on his hands and knees. Ten prefabricated trusses supported the bridge. The plank fitted perfectly between these and there was just about enough room for a man to get through. The berms on either side were higher than the bridge trusses and unless someone was actually standing on a berm the bridge was out of view. They thought Hank could use the plank as a kind of shuffleboard and crawl along underneath. It soon became apparent that this was going to be the only way the rest of the group would get back, as the Germans had started firing mortars and the shells were dropping all around.

Whilst this was going on, Bennett had been instructed by Christianson to target his mortar onto an area just to the right of a farmhouse, which was set back about 100 yards from the bank, on the enemy side of the river. This action was to support Bahlau's small team. He began to fire and Bahlau shouted corrections from the far side of the river, which were relayed to Bennett. In the meantime Christianson was organizing another group, led by 2nd Lt Pete Madden, to cross the bridge and help the stranded men. The enemy soldiers were getting nearer and nearer. Knowing that Bahlau's team could not hold off a larger-scale attack, Shettle and Christianson ordered that the bridge be rigged for demolition.

Bennett was now moving his mortar in small increments so that the rounds fell at about 25-yard intervals between the farmhouse and the bridge. All this was done blind, as the berm obstructed his view, but he hoped it would disperse the approaching enemy forces.

Lieutenants Christianson and Madden were concentrating on the problems facing Bahlau whilst Capt Shettle was keeping the rest of the force occupied. Ed Shames was looking after defense and recalls:

> Shettle ordered me to go and scout around and find out what the ammo state was. He said, "If you find anybody with 60mm mortar ammo who's not part of a mortar squad, then get them to drop it off next to that C2," and pointed to a large pile of explosive that had been brought in earlier. He then continued, "Hold the line and make sure everyone knows it. Oh yeah, don't forget to tell everyone to keep their heads down, we don't want anyone getting them blown off, do we?"

Whilst Ed was scouting around he found a 60mm mortar tube, minus its base plate, and also came across Trino Mendez. He was with another soldier and neither man had a weapon! Ed returned to Shettle, reported his findings and left the tube beside the C2 explosive and some mortar ammunition.

Bennett was struggling to support Bahlau's group, and Ed decided to give him some assistance. He ordered Stan Stockins to throw blocks of C2 across the bridge toward the Germans, telling him to keep well below the cover of the berm. It was an unenviable job. Stockins had to insert slow burning waterproof fuses into the ends of each heavy (1lb) C2 block then pause momentarily before throwing them as far as he could. Unfortunately all the explosives fell short and most ended up in the river.

Suddenly Stockins stopped throwing the explosive. He had been hit in the face by a German bullet and died instantly. Pvt McCann was nearby and saw what happened, "Stockins had stayed in the same position for too long and the Germans had a bead on his location. I think the bullet hit his submachine gun in the breech area and ricocheted up through his face." Ed Shames was the first person to reach him. "I think the shot came from a two-storey house across the river. I turned him onto his back and dealt with his dog tags. Then Father McGee came across and said a few words. Later in the day Stockins's body was moved to Fortin Farm for temporary burial. The explosives idea was essentially sound and I used it again after dark, this time much more successfully."

Within seconds of Stockins's death, Tom Bucher had been hit. He remembers:

As I traversed the machine gun to the right, a burst of enemy fire bounced off the barrel jacket of the gun, severely wounding me. One bullet went into my shoulder and the other hit me in the neck just missing my jugular. It was as if I'd been electrocuted – that's the best way I can describe the pain. My fingers clamped so hard on the trigger that Andy Bryan had to prise them off one by one. By this time blood was spurting from my neck and I was paralyzed. Andy placed a field dressing onto the wound and kept it under pressure, which saved me from bleeding to death. Then one of the medics gave me a blood transfusion before going for help. As I lay semi-conscious on the berm waiting to be evacuated, I clearly remember Father McGee trying to give me the last rites... I had no intention of dying and yelled at him to get lost! Shortly afterwards three or four guys turned up with a stretcher and Andy helped them carry me to the aid station.

After Stockins was killed, Shames got permission to use the 60mm tube he had found. Shettle thought it was worth a try even though the mortar's base plate was missing. Placing the tube on the ground, Ed used his left hand to adjust the angle and his right to drop the shells into the tube. He had no idea where they were landing but hoped it would keep the Germans away from the bridge.

In the meantime, DiCarlo was beneath the bridge sliding along on the plank. He stepped off as he reached each wooden support and pushed the heavy board toward the next truss. It was a painful process as he inched his way slowly across the bridge's 130-yard span – all the while his colleagues were doing their best to give him covering fire. As he crawled forward, Hank could see his blood dripping into the murky water below. As he neared the friendly bank Pfc Bill Briggs (H Co) and another soldier hauled him up and dragged him off behind the berm, leaving him beside Stockins's body. "A medic turned up to check me over," recalls Hank. "I didn't recognize him but he said I was going to be OK and told me to remain still until he could get someone to take me down to the aid station." DiCarlo's attention was then drawn in the direction of Ed Shames who was still working the mortar. With each shot the tube sank a little further into the soft earth until the muzzle was 3in or so below ground level. At that point Shames sensibly decided to stop firing.

A few minutes later, Shettle and Christianson decided to send Madden and his group across the bridge. Their job was to protect regimental demolition engineers who were rigging the crossing with explosives. As the group reached the far side, they broke right and joined up with Bahlau and his men. The group, which was now about a dozen strong, formed a defensive line along the berm upstream of the bridge. Madden spotted a German some distance away and fired; the soldier fell and became the one and only man he shot during the entire war!

Because of overwhelming enemy fire, the demolition team had to abort their mission. Madden could see that there was no point in his group staying any longer and during a brief lull withdrew. Had it not been for Bennett continuously firing his mortar, the withdrawal would have been almost impossible. Most of the enemy had fallen back but one German remained and, despite the mortar barrage, positioned himself on top of the berm. He was trying to get a bead on Madden's group as it moved back under the bridge. Madden was leading and had three M1 rifles slung over his back (they belonged to some of the men who had been wounded). Using the same route as DiCarlo, he set off across the bridge but the rifles slipped, throwing him off balance, and for one terrifying minute he was left dangling below the bridge trusses.

Bulrushes obscured the German's view, but he heard Madden struggling and opened fire. As Madden pulled himself back up, five rounds slammed into the woodwork just in front of him. The German stood up for a better view and Madden tried to shoot, but his weapon was clogged with mud and it misfired. In a moment of desperation he threw the gun at the enemy soldier, who promptly picked it up and ran off. Getting across the bridge was difficult enough, but climbing over the exposed northern bank would be suicidal. However, Christianson's men had an idea and threw their jump ropes over the berm. One by one Madden's group grabbed hold of the ropes and were pulled over the bank to safety. The only man who failed to join them was S/Sgt Harry Clawson, who disappeared whilst scouting upstream. Montilio won the Distinguished Service Cross for his part in the action, the first man from the battalion to do so, whilst Bahlau and Clawson were awarded the Silver Star for their efforts.

Shettle's group was getting low on ammunition and he ordered 2nd Lt Jack Esco to retrieve some bundles that had landed in the river. A lot of machine-gun fire was zipping across the top of the berm and any man going over faced certain death – Esco refused the order. There was no reasoning with Shettle at this point, as he was desperately trying to retain control of the bridge and was under immense pressure. Furious, he relieved Esco of his duties and sent him back to Fortin Farm. Once at the farm Esco placed himself under close arrest and helped out with basic medical duties. After Madden's return, the immediate need for ammunition passed, and Shettle wisely decided to leave the bundles in the river.

Meanwhile, a couple of soldiers had arrived to help get DiCarlo to the aid station at Fortin Farm. In a direct line the farm was only 550 yards away, but the ground was exposed and too dangerous to cross. Therefore, keeping under cover of earth banks and supported by the two men,

DiCarlo took a longer, 1-mile route – as the day wore on this became the only safe way in and out of the bridge area. When Hank arrived, Mme Odette Fortin, together with eight-year old Georgette Revet who was helping out on the farm, directed him past a number of wounded American paratroopers to a room at the back of the house, where they laid him on a small bed.

The room was about 8ft wide, 15ft long and had a low ceiling supported by wooden beams. The only light came from a small window that was too high up for Hank to see out of. There were two opposing doors; one opened out onto a yard whilst the other gave access to a cowshed. In normal times it was occupied by a herdsman.

About a dozen 3rd Bn medics had made it to the farm, as well as Capt Nick Sorenson (a surgeon) and Pfc Hank Rossetti from the 501st's 2nd Bn medical detachment. They had brought with them a bundle of medical supplies, but these were soon used up and the best that could then be done for the wounded was to make them as comfortable as possible. Many wounds were treated using the first aid kits that every soldier carried. Sorenson asked Odette Fortin and her husband to find as many red and white bed sheets as they could. S/Sgt Talford Wynne (3rd Bn 506th Medical Detachment) then made them into a red cross that was placed on the roof of the farm.

DiCarlo's injury was assessed by T/5 Harold Haycraft, who injected him with morphine. Medics popped in from time to time checking on his condition, and that afternoon Father Maloney paid him a visit. He jokingly asked, "Aren't you glad you took communion yesterday?" Hank was hugely relieved that Maloney didn't give him the last rites, but the attention he was receiving concerned him. To this day he believes they didn't expect him to make it, but that thought made him even more determined not to give up. Hank recalls:

> The external bleeding had stopped and that worried me. I was getting a heavy bloated feeling in my right chest and I guessed, correctly as it turned out, that this signified internal bleeding. My right side was so swollen I couldn't feel my collarbone. Sixty-five years on and I can still

smell the riverside and the foliage that grew there. I found myself in many other dangerous situations later in the war, but nothing came close to the emotional ride I experienced during my time at the bridge and its immediate aftermath.

German prisoners soon started arriving at the aid station, and to make room the American wounded were moved into the western half of the building.

Back at the road bridge the situation had calmed down enough for everyone to start digging in. As the day progressed, more people arrived and they were allocated positions along the berm. From his mortar position Bennett watched as the front line crept closer and closer. Eventually foxholes crossed in front of him and straddled the access road to his left. Soon the line of holes joined others being dug by men defending the footbridge further downstream. On several occasions he saw Ken Christianson dash across the road. "Every time that lanky SOB made the crossing we all thought he was going to get hit, but it was the only way the lieutenant could keep in touch with his men on the other side," recalls Bennett. Before too long, Shettle ordered Pfc John Agnew from regimental demolitions to blow a trench through the road, making it much safer to cross.

Bobbie Rommel and Don Gallaugher arrived and settled down behind the berm waiting for someone to tell them what to do. Nearby was an unattended machine gun and tripod. After checking its serial number, Rommel realized that it was his section's gun and was puzzled as to the whereabouts of Tom Bucher. Somebody eventually came over and told them that Tom had been shot a couple of hours earlier. Rommel took over as gun corporal, moved the weapon nearer to the bridge, and waited for Andy Bryan to return from the aid station.

As Ed Shames started to dig in, he began wondering what had happened to Col Wolverton and the rest of the battalion.

I was behind a levee on the northeastern side of the bridge and Capt Shettle and Chaplain McGee were beside me. Rooting around inside my wet musette bag I pulled out a handy talky portable radio, which was full of water and the only communication equipment we had. After a while I got the thing working but we couldn't believe what we were hearing – it was the BBC World Service presumably broadcasting to ships off Utah Beach. Shettle's face was redder than ever but we both agreed that it was better than no news at all, though only just!

Throughout the day stragglers drifted into our position. Once we had established who they were, Shettle and myself questioned them to try and find out what was happening around the area. We were anxious for news about Wolverton, our company commanders, and of course our friends, but nobody seemed to know what had happened to them. Many of the new men brought in additional supplies and the occasional bottle of Calvados or cider. One guy who came in was badly shaken up. He was 2nd Lt Rudy Bolte. As Shettle and I started talking to him we realized he was having trouble functioning. Shettle told him to go and find a place to dig in and return as soon as he'd calmed down. Well, that was the last we saw of Bolte and that evening Shettle sent me down the line to try and find him. I discovered him in the bottom of a foxhole still shaking and behaving very strangely. I crouched down and said, "Excuse me, sir, but Capt Shettle wants to know why you haven't rep... " I stopped in mid-sentence as Bolte lifted his head. He was crying and clearly very screwed up. I went back to Shettle and reported what I had seen. After a few moments' thought he said, "What the hell, let's leave him where he is – there's no harm in that." Had it been an enlisted man I'm sure his response would have been totally different!

Cpl Hiner and a couple of other men had been sent out by S/Sgt Webb to look around the drop zone for lost equipment. Hiner recalls:

As I moved around I noticed the ground was scattered with all sorts of stuff, including a lot of hand grenades. Some of the guys couldn't have secured the pockets of their jump trousers properly and they must have fallen out. I came across the body of S/Sgt Othis Shepherd from Service Co. He was in the fetal position and his parachute hadn't deployed from the pack tray. A closer look revealed that the static line had been severed by ground fire. We left Shepherd's body in situ and reported his location to Eddy Shames.

Capt Shettle also had men scouting around. During the afternoon he sent a small group, led by 1st Lt Meason, to recover bundles and look for radio equipment in the drop zone area. Whilst patrolling swampy ground near Fortin Farm they came across a dozen enemy soldiers. Meason raised his pistol to take a shot. Everybody laughed, as they knew he would be lucky to hit a target more than 20 yards away with a .45cal automatic. Meason fired, the soldiers scattered, but amazingly one bullet found its mark. Everyone in the group looked on open-mouthed including Pfc Zahn, who said, "That man was meant to die, sir." The enemy soldiers, who were Ukrainian volunteers from Ost-Bataillon 439, promptly surrendered. When their weapons were taken from them they were found to be rusty and badly maintained.

On Meason's return, Shettle looked at the sorry bunch of prisoners and ordered him to "Shoot every last one of them." Don Zahn refused to take part and told Shettle, "I can't do that sir, I just can't do it, not in cold blood." The captain then began to realize that he had overstepped the mark and backed down. Then Zahn came up with a solution. "Sir, why don't we get Hoffman to tell them [some Ukrainians understood basic German commands] that we're going to put them in a barn and if they try to come out we'll kill them all, how about that?" The two officers both agreed and the prisoners were taken to the barn at the aid station, blissfully unaware that Zahn had just saved their skins.

A patrol was sent out to Les Rats where the P-47 had crashed. "I was sent along with a few others to try and recover the machine guns from the plane," recalls Pvt Miles Allen (G Co). "Unfortunately the weapons were twisted and bent beyond use."

As darkness fell, Shettle ordered five men from C Co 326th Airborne Engineers to rig two of the bridge trusses with explosives. The job of placing the fuses fell to John Kutz and Quinten Prussman. Kutz remembers:

I was carrying two charges, one under each arm. One end of a roll of primer cord was tied to my cartridge belt while the other was held on our side of the river. I crawled along beneath the bridge until I reached the truss nearest the enemy bank. I anchored the primer cord and dropped one of the charges on the left side and the other on the right. Cpl Russel, Sgt Shalpak, and Sgt O'Laughlin were behind me and it was their job to position the charges and wire them in place. When we returned to our foxholes Sgt O'Laughlin, who was in charge of our squad, gave me the fuse lighter to look after.

It was after dark before the engineers eventually completed the task of mining the bridge, and it was at about this time that Harry Clawson reappeared. His pockets were full of items taken from dead enemy soldiers, which established his reputation as a first-class looter. Fred Bahlau recalls:

It was after dark when Clawson returned. I was mad as hell that he'd stayed out there for so long, but he was happy. He'd walked along the riverbank looking for dead Germans and then climbed the berm and searched the fields beyond. He stripped all the bodies he found of medals and badges. When he showed me what he'd done I told him that if he ever got captured the Germans would kill him, and that's exactly what happened in Holland.

During the night, enemy activity increased and there was an exchange of rifle and machine-gun fire. Once again Ed Shames started throwing fused C2 over the berm (darkness making the job a lot safer) and together with Bennett's 60mm mortar the activity simulated an artillery barrage. The Germans then pulled back and things quietened down again. Ed recalls, "Shettle said, 'You really ought to be an officer, you know, I think you'd do well.' At first I thought he was joking but soon realized he was deadly serious. I nodded and moved off down the berm, encouraging the men to stay alert and remain focused."

Footbridge and surrounding positions, June 6, 1944

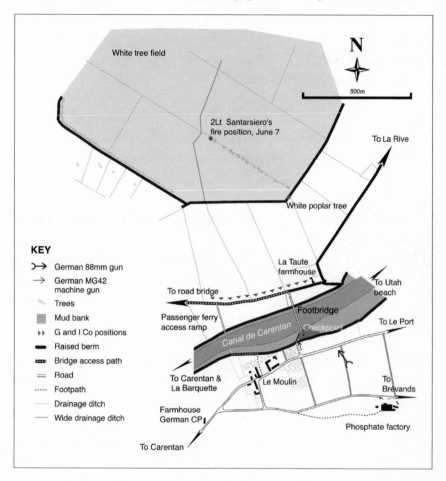

The footbridge

The footbridge was just wide enough to get a horse and small cart across and was 27 yards longer than the road bridge. Its southern end was laid onto a disused stone wharf that had originally been built for a phosphate (bone-ash) factory that was on the hill above the small hamlet of Le Moulin.

The Germans had positioned an 88mm gun on the lower slopes of the hillside below the factory. It had been in the area for some time but during the week leading up to the invasion was moved into a hedgerow near the river and hidden beneath camouflage netting.

Near the northern end of the bridge was La Taute farmhouse, owned by Bienaimé and Victorine Laurent. They used the bridge on a daily basis to get to the dairy at Bellamy Farm (near Brévands) where they both worked, and nearly always took their four children with them. The gun was close by and they got to know its crew fairly well. A small guardhouse on the southern bank controlled the passage of all civilians. The Laurents started work early each morning and the guards normally waved them through, rarely checking their *Ausweiss* (movement pass). Eight-year-old Amand Laurent often scrounged sweets from the dozen or so Germans who manned the "88" and the machine gun that was dug in near the old quay.

One of the first men from 3rd Bn to arrive at the footbridge was 1st Lt Joe Doughty who, together with his assistant 2nd Lt Linton Barling, reached the crossing at approximately 0500hrs. (Soon afterwards ten men including 1st Lt Turner Chambliss, 1st Lt John Kiley, 2nd Lt Clark Heggeness, Cpl Vic Szidon, Pfc Oakie Hilderbrand, and Pfc Stan Clever arrived). At about the same time Msr and Mme Laurent decided to cross the bridge and return to their home, leaving their children with the Bellamys. They wanted to collect some bread, as the Bellamys had run out, and only intended to be away for a short while. Amazingly, despite all the action going on around, the Germans let them cross. On reaching the other side, they were met by one of the American officers who decided it was too dangerous for them to go back. They were asked to move away from the bridge and were kept under guard in their own garden until somebody could figure out what to do with them. The Laurent children had no idea why their parents had failed to return and feared the worst – it would be a long and anxious week before they saw them again.

Joe Doughty's orders were to take control of both sides of the bridge as soon as possible, and in the half-light of early morning he took a closer look at the crossing. "As I made my way along the wooden beams below the bridge a German machine gun, hidden in the trees on the far bank, opened up. The bullets went high, hitting the wooden beams above my head and forcing me to retrace my steps." Following his return Chambliss and Heggeness made a similar attempt to cross, but were beaten back by the same gun.

Joe then ordered everyone to dig in and wait for Capt Van Antwerp (G Co commander). He did not know it at the time, but the captain had been killed on D-Night along with many other officers from 3rd Bn's command group. Joe recalls, "1st Lt Jim Morton broke his ankle on the jump but was able to rejoin the company later. Two machine gunners from my 3 Ptn broke their legs on landing because their leg bags failed to release."

1st Lt Nye and Cpl Elmer Gilbertson knew they were close to the objective when they spotted the large white poplar tree identified in the briefings. Although the poplar tree has now gone, the French still call this place White Tree Field. They had been lucky so far and seen little of the enemy, but things were about to change. As they made their approach an unknown soldier joined them, and when they were about 300 yards from the objective they saw Cpl Jim Millican waving. He was positioned in front of the first of three berms that separated them from the bridge. At 17, Millican was one of the youngest members of I Co. He told Nye's group about the 88mm gun and directed them to the bridge. It was being targeted by enemy mortar and artillery fire, most of which appeared to be coming from the factory.

To reach the bridge the new arrivals had to scramble over the berm, then crawl along a ditch on the other side that led up to a second berm near the Laurents' farmhouse. As they crept over the first dyke, the German gun crew spotted them and opened fire. A shell hit the poplar tree and exploded, killing Millican instantly and wounding the unknown trooper. Gilbertson did his best to patch the man up before continuing his journey to the bridge.

A dozen men, led by S/Sgt Charlie Skeen, were crossing the same field when they were spotted by a machine gun hidden somewhere on high ground near the "88". Bullets kicked up dirt around the patrol and then the 88mm gun opened fire. Sgt Don Austin and Pfc Jimmy Martin gave covering fire with their rifles. Martin recalls, "The first shell made a terrific bang that made my ears ring. They fired five rounds at us before we got under cover. Nine of us back-tracked and ran smack into an enemy light machine gun. Everyone opened up, forcing the enemy to retreat with their wounded."

The intense shelling caused several casualties including Pfc Spiller, who was badly hit. As Austin was crawling away, he pointed at muzzle flashes he could see near Le Moulin. There was a continual threat of enemy machine-gun teams setting up fire positions north of the footbridge. Skeen decided to patrol the White Tree Field area, where his team remained for nearly 24 hours. During that time they successfully prevented five German machine-gun crews from targeting the footbridge.

At around this time, a damaged and burning P-47 aircraft came in from the south, passed low overhead, and crashed about 1¼ miles from the bridge. Amand Laurent remembers his father telling him that the plane jettisoned two bombs. Both bounced off the ground near the poplar tree and failed to explode. Joe Doughty sent out a small patrol (led by Clark Heggeness) to the crash site to see if anything could be done for the pilot. The men returned with the dead airman's dog tags.

1st Lt Chambliss was hoping that Rosenfield would turn up soon with the rubber rafts, and with that thought in mind decided to look along the river for a suitable place to launch them. The original plan was to place the 60mm mortars and other heavy equipment on the rafts. Then, under cover of darkness, a number of strong swimmers would tow them across. From his position 30 yards west of the bridge, Joe Doughty could see Chambliss repeatedly popping his head above the berm, when suddenly a sniper's bullet struck him in the mouth, leaving a gaping exit hole in the back of his neck. Clark Heggeness and Sgt Addison Marquardt (H Co) were close by and immediately went to his aid. Other soldiers gathered round as Marquardt cradled the dying officer in his arms. Just before he passed away he asked if any 2 Ptn (G Co) people were around. Marquardt told him that nobody else from the platoon had arrived so far. Struggling to breathe and coughing blood, Chambliss kept asking a bewildered Marquardt, "Why did my platoon stencil West Point on their jackets, were they mocking me... why? I just don't understand."

Fifteen minutes later 2nd Lt Tom Kennedy arrived. "Joe Doughty told me the news about Chambliss. I was deeply shocked, as Turner had been a good friend. Joe then went on to say that because Capt Van Antwerp was absent he was the ranking officer and taking responsibility for the small bridge force."

All the men could do was dig in and hold on. Kennedy recalls, "I was between the house and 1st Lt Doughty. Gunfire from the 88mm was sporadic and all it damaged was the house and our morale. Other than the bridge there wasn't much else to hit!"

Barling seemed oblivious to the danger, and kept returning to the house in an attempt to spot the troublesome enemy gun. The gable end of the two-storey building was at right angles to the river and Barling had made a hole in its wall. Despite this he was still unable to get a clear view of the "88" that was hidden behind trees on the far bank. It wasn't long before the Germans spotted the hole and opened fire, forcing Barling to evacuate. The Laurents, still sheltering in the garden, looked on helplessly as several rounds went straight through the building. Incredibly the heavy stone structure remained relatively intact.

Doughty could see Allied planes flying around and knew he had to do something: "I got Cpl Szidon (Doughty's radio operator), who had some signal panels, to lay out a message saying, 'Bomb 1,000 yards' with an arrow pointing in the direction of the '88.' The distance was an educated guess but we really needed that gun out of action. Unknown to us Division had ordered the air force to bomb the bridge and it was only a matter of time before the inevitable happened."

~ 8 ~

"No word from 3rd Battalion, 506th PIR"

D-Day +1

June 7 – the skirmish in White Tree Field and the bombing of the bridge

As dawn broke on the 7th, S/Sgt Charlie Skeen and his group were crossing the White Tree Field on the final leg of their journey to the bridge. Unknown to Skeen, 300 yards behind were two companies of German coastal artillerymen who were following the same course. They had been manning gun positions behind Utah Beach and were inexperienced in close combat fighting.

From his position on the northern side of the bridge, 2nd Lt Charles Santarsiero (I Co) was looking in Skeen's direction through his binoculars. Suddenly he noticed the rear of the German column. Santarsiero was lying on the edge of a 300-yard-long tree-lined ditch that ran northwest toward Skeen's approaching patrol.

At almost exactly the same time as Santarsiero and his men opened fire on the enemy, the Germans attacked Skeen's group. All hell broke loose and after a brief firefight the leading enemy company withdrew into trees that bordered the western perimeter of the field. A couple of Skeen's men made it into the tree-lined ditch but others, including Jimmy Martin, were stranded in the field with just grass for cover. "We were being raked with machine-gun and rifle fire," recalls Martin. "Don Francis lay to my left and was hit in the right forehead by a bullet. Suddenly a group led by 2nd Lt Santarsiero came in on our left flank." Francis never regained consciousness and died the following day at Fortin Farm.

Santarsiero told Barling to stay at the observation post and moved the rest of his men forward along the ditch. They established fire positions just 80 yards from the nearest German, which prevented the enemy from regrouping and launching a counterattack. Meanwhile, men at the bridge heard the gunfire and headed out to assist. Santarsiero remembers this in his 1985 article "My Most Memorable Meeting with General McAuliffe":

I was greeted by a very frightened paratrooper. He said, "Boy, am I glad to see you!" Time was critical and the Germans disorganized. I said to the soldier, "I am going to engage them and you have a choice. You can come with me or you can join our forces at the bridge," pointing in the direction of the Douve.

I found a slit trench in the hedgerow that was in a perfect position. Fifty yards in front of me were two German officers shouting at a group of men. Within the group were six captured paratroopers who were bearing stretchers. As soon as they moved out of my line of sight I opened fire. Still hanging on to their stretchers, the troopers ran in three different directions toward the relative safety of the hedgerows. Then an enemy machine gunner found my position. Luckily his fire cut into the bank to my right, showering me with dirt and rocks.

The Germans began to panic and a squad ran in front of my position from left to right. I fired at the last man in the line and worked my way up to the first. Then another squad ran in the opposite direction and I continued firing until I ran out of targets. I then remembered the trooper that had joined me earlier, but he was no longer there. I assume he must have joined our forces at the bridge.

Tom Kennedy was involved in the same action and recalls:

I came across a wounded Kraut. The guy was begging me not to shoot him and showed me his wedding ring and some family pictures – he was obviously dying. I stayed with him for a short time and held his hand until he fell unconscious. I then returned to our position. There was very little command and control at this time, just individual pockets of action. While I admired Santarsiero's bravery, I couldn't help thinking that he should have been leading whatever was left of his platoon. However, I'm sure he had good reasons for what he did.

By 1030hrs the fighting was over, and the field was alive with Germans wanting to surrender. Jim Martin recalls, "We disarmed them and several of our men, including a medic, began dealing with the wounded. After about 10 minutes an enemy soldier walked from the bushes with an MG42 on his shoulder. I'm convinced that if we had not been treating the wounded from both sides equally he would have killed us all with his machine gun."

The 3rd Bn men returned to the bridge with their prisoners, and the wounded were given first aid before being taken to Fortin Farm. Santarsiero handed the captured MG42 machine gun to a trooper, increasing the position's firepower. Moving upstream behind the protective cover of the berm, Santarsiero and Barling marched the prisoners along to the road bridge. On arrival they learned from Capt Shettle that the battalion had been unable to establish any contact with either Regiment or Division.

Skeen, Austin, and Martin had dug in near the wooden pier used by the chain ferry. It wasn't long before they saw the body of their platoon leader, Turner Chambliss, being carried past their position toward Fortin Farm. Someone then told them what he had said to Marquardt just before he died. "I cried tears of shock, frustration and shame, as his body passed by," recalls Martin. "I kept wondering why he failed to understand the great pride and affection we all felt for him."

The shock of seeing their platoon leader's body affected the men in different ways. Charlie Skeen became more and more convinced that La Taute farmhouse was being used as a German observation post. He eventually persuaded Jimmy Martin to go with him and check it out. Of course the house was empty, but as the two men were about to leave Skeen thought he could hear voices coming from the basement and threw two grenades into the darkness. Skeen's actions troubled Martin, who wrongly thought that he had killed some French civilians. Skeen was not an easy man to get on with and was never very popular with the men. Many said they would shoot him if they ever got a chance. Nevertheless Skeen did his job well, but his antagonistic nature eventually got him transferred to Service Co.

Returning to the footbridge, Santarsiero and Barling told Doughty that they had been ordered by Capt Shettle to try and establish contact with Regiment. At around 1330hrs the two officers departed on their mission, and about an hour later a couple of P-51 Mustangs flew in low and fast. Joe Doughty thought that at long last somebody had seen his marker panel and the planes were going to attack the 88. But instead of targeting the gun the returning aircraft attacked the bridge, dropping at least three bombs. One landed near the riverbank 75 yards from the American positions, narrowly missing the bridge's wooden walkway. A second took out the entire section that straddled the berm, and the third landed in the middle of the Douve and blew out five or six of the bridge trusses. Luckily, Doughty and his men were well dug in behind the berm and nobody was injured.

After this incident, and for their own safety, Msr and Mme Laurent were moved to the Milledrogues' house, which was along the Pénême road.

Operation Memphis

The arrival of 62 C-47s dropping food, ammunition, and medical supplies marked the beginning of Operation *Memphis*. This early morning resupply mission gave the 101st Airborne Division enough fresh equipment to support them for several days. The 40mm gun at L'Amont had been relatively quiet until several C-47s strayed over Drop Zone D. These should have been over Landing Zone E between Hiesville and Ste-Marie-du-Mont some 2½ miles further north. Flak burst all around the planes, but they flew on undamaged. Bill Galbraith, who was watching from his position near La Barquette, was left in no doubt over the enemy gun crew's tenacity and devotion to duty. Ralph Bennett recalls, "Three C-47s came from the direction of Utah Beach dropping supply bundles onto an open area north of Fortin Farm, and patrols were sent out to recover them."

Bobbie Rommel was on one of these patrols and recovered a bundle that contained a bazooka and its rockets. Enemy small-arms fire eventually forced them back to the bridge. "Capt Shettle gave us permission to use the bazooka," recalls Rommel. "We could see a factory on a hill in front of us and thought it was being used as an observation post. It was around 1,500 yards away, but the range didn't put us off." Damage to the factory was negligible but Rommel and his colleagues hit several houses in Le Moulin.

A little while earlier Galbraith and his team, who thought the 40mm gun had been knocked out by the previous day's naval barrage, fired their machine gun in its general direction. "After one round we had a stoppage. Then, to our utter amazement, a couple of 40mm shells came whizzing back. After all the naval shelling that damned gun was still operational! We then hastily field stripped, cleaned and oiled our machine gun."

Following another night without sleep, and after leaving Hiner in charge, Bob Webb went to Fortin Farm to snatch a few hours of well-earned rest. He made himself comfortable in the loft of one of the outbuildings and was just getting settled when Pfc Elwood Kendall (Shettle's runner) turned up. Kendall was in a bit of a flap, as Webb recalls:

> He told me he'd seen Germans, about 600 yards away, moving past a gap in the trees north of the farm. I looked in the direction he was pointing and sure enough there they were. I didn't like what I saw and told him to let Shettle know what was going on. Looking through my field glasses I began counting the figures crossing the gap. I got to 100 and they were still coming! The runner returned and I immediately sent him back to Shettle with my estimation of enemy numbers.

The Germans were heading west in the direction of St-Côme-du-Mont. It wasn't long before Ken Christianson and three other men arrived on the scene. The lieutenant had a plan, and taking four of Webb's men crossed the Pénême road. Webb looked on in disbelief as they ran toward the enemy yelling and firing wildly into the air. It was a crazy move, typical of Christianson, which took the Germans completely by surprise and they turned back. Clearly pleased with the outcome, Christianson returned Webb's men and headed off to the road bridge.

When dawn broke on June 7, 1st Lt Littell and his small group were near La Haute Maison farmhouse just east of St-Côme-du-Mont. They were making slow progress and looking for cover when they came across a hedge about 8ft thick. They found a hole that was just large enough for Littell, Pfc Neill (H Co), and Pfc McGrath (HQ Co) to squeeze into. In front of them was an apple orchard and on the far side, partially hidden by a row of trees, was La Haute Maison. There was no room for Calandrella at that point, but he managed to find a hole about 5 yards away just beyond a small path that split the hedge in two. He crawled backward into the dense foliage so that the orchard was behind him. It was a very confined space and the thick vegetation made rapid movement difficult. The only way he could see his colleagues was by cranking his head round to the left.

An hour or so later confidence in their hideout was confirmed when a German soldier wandered past without seeing them. "I watched the soldier come walking toward me from my right," recalls Calandrella. "He wasn't a paratrooper because he was wearing the regular steel helmet. He was so close that I was able to look straight at his face, but he had no idea I was there!"

A short while later Littell directed Calandrella's attention toward another German soldier, who was running a communications cable across the orchard. The men were unconcerned by the activity and felt safe and secure. The warmth from the early morning sun, and the fact that they had been awake for nearly 48 hours, brought on an overriding urge to sleep. One man should have remained on watch and this lapse had devastating consequences, as Calandrella recalls: "The next thing I remember was being woken by the sound of machine pistols firing. Bullets raked the base of the hedge where Littell, McGrath, and Neill were hiding. If the enemy issued a challenge then I didn't hear it." Fortunately for Calandrella his presence went unnoticed. Closing his eyes he put his head down and tensed himself, but the shooting stopped and the Germans vanished.

At that point I saw Neill and McGrath burst out from the hedgerow. Neill shouted "Calandrella, help me, help me!" I crawled out to see what I could do for my wounded comrades. There was a gaping hole in McGrath's right buttock and he was shouting hysterically. I fumbled for his morphine before pouring on sulfa powder and dressing the wound. Neill was nearby continually calling for my assistance. Littell was lying motionless and I put my arm into the hedge and shook his boot, but it was obvious he was dead.

I then crawled over to Neill. He was on his stomach and there was a large exit wound in his back that was big enough for me to put my entire hand into. He was having trouble breathing and kept trying to raise himself up onto his arms. I didn't stop to think and jabbed some morphine into his thigh. It didn't seem to help and he started to deteriorate rapidly. Struggling to catch his breath, he began talking about his wife and told me he couldn't understand why his marriage had collapsed. Not knowing what else to do, I asked if I could baptize him. He seemed unconcerned, but halfway through the act of perfect contrition began repeating my words and died moments later.

Most of H Co secretly knew that Neill's best friend Pvt Bruce Paxton, who had known him since childhood, had been responsible for his marriage breakdown. They chose to conceal this fact from Neill, knowing full well that he would have killed Paxton had he found out.

Throughout the time Calandrella had been treating Neill, his back had been turned toward McGrath. He had no idea what was going on behind and as he turned around was shocked to see two German paratroopers frantically trying to resuscitate him. In the meantime half a dozen of their comrades were moving across the field toward him and he briefly considered resisting, but thought better of it and surrendered. Initially the Germans ignored him and he watched as they vainly attempted to save 17-year-old McGrath's life.

After about 3 minutes a very young paratrooper was sent to remove Calandrella's weapons. Calandrella asked the soldier, "Do you speak English?" He replied "A little!" and spat in his face, prompting

Calandrella to keep his mouth shut. He was then hastily searched and interrogated before being marched off toward the prisoner collection point near St-Côme-du-Mont.

An eerie silence had fallen over the town of St-Lô following a night of terrifying air raids. A dense blanket of smoke darkened the sky turning day into night. The Germans decided to move the Allied prisoners they were holding at Dépôt de Remonte to Hôtellerie Notre-Dame, another temporary prison located 7½ miles south of St-Lô in the village of Troisgots. A shortage of trucks meant that some of the 200 or so POWs had to walk.

The Hôtellerie Notre-Dame was a three-storey Catholic Institute (mistakenly called a monastery by the prisoners) beautifully situated on a hillside overlooking the village of Troisgots. Before the Germans took control the building had been used to train novice monks and it later became a boarding school for children evacuated from St-Lô. It had a large courtyard that was bounded on two sides by a 10ft-high wall and on the third side by part of the institute. A wire fence linked the institute to one of the walls, creating a rectangular enclosure that made an ideal prison compound.

Pvt Morgan was among the first group to arrive: "The Germans removed our belts and bootlaces and there was a lot of confusion. I was disappointed in the general behavior of many of my colleagues whose main focus was food – understandable in the circumstances. They were constantly squabbling in front of the Germans over who was getting the biggest piece of bread. I thought, 'For Christ's sake look at yourselves, we're American paratroopers – let's have some dignity!'"

Because of the shortage of food, the soldiers nicknamed the place "Starvation Hill." Most of their meals consisted of a very thin soup that they called "whispering grass," which was made from turnip greens and boiled animal bones. As the days passed the food gradually began to improve but the men were always hungry, a situation that was compounded as more prisoners arrived. The German paratroops running the camp interrogated all new arrivals. Don Ross recalls, "All I gave them was my name, rank, and serial number. I was hit a few times but on the whole we were treated reasonably well – a lot better than what was to come!"

Back at the road bridge, around dawn of the second day, Ed Shames had been assessing the situation:

It seemed to me that the Germans were withdrawing into Carentan. Most of us stayed near the bridge as per orders. However, one or two patrols were sent out to try and make contact with other units. The first couple of days were chaotic and we were just trying to stay alive. We couldn't see the footbridge from our position – it was about 1,000 yards away beyond a bend in the river – but could hear the 88mm gun, and Shettle knew the men there were having problems. In an ideal world we should have passed all the G and I Co guys that arrived at the road bridge onto their original objective, but we had troubles of our own and kept them all.

Earlier that morning I'd heard gunfire in the distance and a little while later Santarsiero arrived. He had been responsible for some of the noise, was clearly very excited by the action and was jumping around like some kind of macho flea. He'd brought along some prisoners and wanted to know what to do with them. We sent him to Fortin Farm and he returned later with another bunch of Germans. He told me that because he had no platoon to command he was spending his time out on patrol causing as much chaos as he could – I thought he was a bit of a nut!

The bombing of the road bridge, 1200hrs

Around midday at the road bridge Santarsiero was preparing to move another group of prisoners to Fortin Farm. At about the same time Bobbie Rommel was making his way toward Ralph Bennett's position and recalls, "Sgt Easter had given me permission to look at the Kraut that had been captured by H Co. I was returning to my position when four Thunderbolts swept overhead from the direction of Brévands and I watched as they disappeared from view. There were a lot of guys milling about and nobody seemed to give the planes much thought, as Allied aircraft were constantly buzzing around."

In fact, Divisonal HQ had been increasingly concerned by the lack of radio communication from 3rd Bn and as a result assumed their mission had failed. Therefore a backup plan was called into play that involved the US Army Air Force making two separate attacks on the bridges.

A few minutes later the P-47s returned and made two low passes from the direction of Fortin Farm, dropping ten 500lb bombs. Rommel had nearly reached his foxhole when the attack started:

> I was about 20ft from my position when I saw the first bomb. My immediate reaction was to dive into the nearest empty foxhole. Its owner, who was nearby, shouted at me to get out and we argued for a few seconds! Then the bombs hit the bridge and my world turned upside down. The ground shook and the explosions sent water and bridge parts high into the air. The second plane's bombs missed and one landed in a field on the German side of the river.

The bridge was partly destroyed. One bomb dropped about 160 yards short, leaving a large crater. The third aircraft passed much lower than the rest and for some reason its pilot lost control, as Rommel recalls: "I decided to make a dash for my own trench and caught a glimpse of the third plane. It banked to the left and started to cartwheel through the air, before erupting in a ball of flame."

From their position beside the Pénême road Bob Webb's men watched in horror, as Ben Hiner recounts: "The pilot of the third plane let his bombs go and as he barrel-rolled the aircraft I think he struck one of them. The plane erupted in a mass of flame and began to tumble end over end before hitting a hill. The fourth plane continued its attack and dumped its bombs close to Shettle's position. Then the other P-47s returned and began strafing the bridge with cannon fire."

Ed Shames has vivid memories of this attack:

> One aircraft began firing its eight .50cal guns. I was out of my foxhole and started running toward the nearest trench as the cannon shells thumped into the ground behind me. I jumped in feet first and landed on Chaplain McGee's back! The second plane was circling and preparing for its attack. I shouted to McGee, "Smoke, we gotta let 'em

know." I had some orange smoke grenades and air recognition panels in my musette bag.

I scrambled out of McGee's foxhole and expected him to follow. I then started to "pop" the grenades and jumped frantically up and down waving the smoke all around. I looked behind and McGee was still in the hole. I shouted, "Get your ass out here now and grab the air panels before we all get killed!" That got him moving and he crawled over and pulled the panels from my pack.

The second aircraft was now well into its dive and firing. We were both out in the open, I had the smoke and McGee was on his feet waving the air panels. The cannon shells went wide and we realized there was no point carrying on and both tumbled back into the foxhole. Fortunately for us the pilots must have realized they'd made a terrible mistake because they aborted their attack and flew away.

Bennett initially thought the planes were German and moved his squad 100 yards further away from the bridge:

We hunkered down in some brushes near a pond and flattened ourselves against the ground. Then one of my men shouted, "Bennett they're ours, they're ours!" All we could do was watch as the planes began their attack. One of the aircraft screamed in at very high speed and disappeared from view. The sky lit up somewhere over the other side of the river and we assumed it was naval gunfire, but I guess it must have been the plane crashing. Then two planes returned heading toward the bridge from the direction of Fortin Farm. One aircraft was slightly behind the other and they began firing their machine guns. I saw someone throw an orange smoke grenade on top of the berm.

Incredibly, only one person was killed during the attack. The sandy soil around the bridge area allowed the men to dig deep foxholes and these undoubtedly saved many lives. However, the pressure wave from the solitary bomb that left the large crater caused some painful injuries. Jim McCann was dug in on the western side of the bridge and his eardrums

FROM TOP TO BOTTOM:

Eastern side of the Place de la République – Pfc John Houk from I Co landed on the roof of the building in the center of the picture.

1300hrs June 6, 1944, near the northern edge of St-Lô. The first prisoners to arrive were marched down the rue St-Georges past Gen Marck's HQ at Immeuble de Commines. The POW cage at Dépôt de Remonte was a few hundred yards left of this point. (ECPAD)

A view from the church tower at St-Come-du-Mont looking northeast. Col Wolverton landed in apple trees in the far left hand corner of the large field in the center of the picture.

1400hrs June 6, 1944, Dépôt de Remonte – stable block B. Sitting amongst this group of prisoners are six men from HQ Co 3rd Bn 506th. (1) Cpl Clarence Kelley (Machine Gun Ptn), (2) possibly Pvt Joe Mielcarek (Machine Gun Ptn), (3) S/Sgt John Taormina, (4) Cpl Marty Clark (partially hidden) (Machine Gun Ptn), (5) Pfc Don Ross and (6) T/5 Charles Riley. (ECPAD)

1600hrs June 6, 1944, Dépôt de Remonte – stable block B. As the afternoon wore on the men were told to stand in line and were fed their first meal of the day – a watery soup! On the left a German officer and his team are interrogating a number of prisoners. In the background is the church of Ste-Croix. (ECPAD)

More of the group shown on the oppposite page: (4) Cpl Marty Clark, (1) Cpl Clarence Kelley and (2) possibly Pvt Joe Mielcarek. (ECPAD)

June 6, 1944, Dépôt de Remonte – stable block D. The time is about 1945hrs and I Co commander Capt John T. McKnight (third from left) watches Allied bombers approach the town of St-Lô. McKnight was held captive for 13 months and during that time his weight dropped to 67lb. (ECPAD)

3rd Bn medics. L to R: Cpl Walter Scmiege, S/Sgt Talford Wynne, and T/5 Harold Haycraft. All worked at Fortin Farm between June 6 and 9. (John Gibson)

LEFT:

Johnny Hahn from 1 Ptn H Co posing with a fully assembled 60mm mortar. This was the same type of weapon used to great effect by both Sgt Ralph Bennett and S/Sgt Ed Shames at the road bridge on D-Day. Rifle companies were supported by 60mm mortars, which were the responsibility of the 3rd squad from each platoon. Hahn was killed on September 22, 1944, at Koevering in Holland. (Don Zahn via Mark Bando)

OPPOSITE PAGE, FROM TOP TO BOTTOM:

June 6, 1944, Dépôt de Remonte – stable block D. S/Sgt John Taormina (center) is seen leaning against a concrete drinking trough spooning soup from his plate. In the background is part of the 10ft-high perimeter wall. Behind Taormina is D-Block, which was used to accommodate German soldiers. The prisoner in the foreground is still wearing his belt kit – often the first thing taken at point of capture. (ECPAD)

3rd Bn personnel began to gather in this area at first light on June 6 and used the berm on the right to shelter from enemy fire. The track leading to the road bridge ran along the top of the bank.

The remnants of the road bridge looking across the Douve toward the southern (German-held) bank where the initial five-man H Co assault took place. This photograph was taken shortly after dawn on June 6, 2004, the 60th anniversary of D-Day, when the tide would have been at exactly the same level.

This pre-World War I photograph is the only known picture of La Taute farmhouse. The building is partially obscured by the river's main flood defense berm. Nearly 90 yards in from the bank is a secondary berm that became the US front line between June 6 and 8, 1944. In 1942 the long-abandoned wharf was reused by the Germans to support the southern end of their newly constructed footbridge. (William Hébert)

At the time of the invasion Bienaimé and Victorine Laurent and their family (pictured here in 1947) lived on the river's northern bank, near the footbridge, in a farmhouse at La Taute. (Amand Laurent)

At dawn on June 7, 2nd Lt Charles Santarsiero led a small group of men from 3rd Bn in a successful counterattack against a German coastal artillery unit. (Charles Santarsiero via Mark Bando)

Fred Bahlau, H Co supply sergeant. This photograph shows Fred in a foxhole near the road bridge. The soft, sandy soil had the effect of lessening the destructive impact of high explosives, which undoubtedly saved many lives during the Allied bombing of the bridge on June 7. (Fred Bahlau via Mark Bando)

In this prewar photograph the Mildrogues family pose on the raised wooden walkway that linked the passenger ferry to the berm. The Germans used a similar design for the approach to their 1942 footbridge, which was further downstream. The white-roofed building in the background was the ferry's tollbooth and beyond is the village of Le Moulin. (William Hébert)

FROM TOP TO BOTTOM:

On the afternoon of June 7, 1944, the Hôtellerie Notre-Dame at Troisgots became a temporary prison for US POWs evacuated from St-Lô. It was named "Starvation Hill" by the prisoners because of a desperate shortage of food. The building was ideally suited for holding prisoners as it was partly surrounded by a high wall.

St-Côme-du-Mont. This picture clearly shows damage caused to the southern side of the church on June 8 by German artillery fire from Méautis. The bell (nicknamed "Marie Louise") was later removed and placed on a cradle in the churchyard where it remained for 21 years until the church's reconstruction finished in 1965. (Michel Léonard) had been perforated. He was in so much pain that he couldn't bear the sound of people talking to him and as the day wore on he found it necessary to write a note requesting evacuation to the aid station.

The northern bank then came under attack from German mortars and Pete Madden was blown out of his foxhole, receiving extensive shrapnel wounds to his back and right leg.

Shortly after the bombing, Santarsiero asked Shettle for permission to try to locate Col Sink's command post. Shettle ordered Barling to accompany Santarsiero and both men set off. However, after a brief encounter with the enemy they became separated. Undeterred Santarsiero pressed on and found an American antiaircraft unit. One of its officers knew where Sink's command post was located, and offered to take him there. It was about 3pm and following a short jeep ride Santarsiero was dropped off near a tent. He recalls:

> Inside was Gen McAuliffe [101st divisional artillery commander]. He wore a worried expression as I gave him the picture. He then walked over and said, "Charlie, thank God, you've brought great news." He then smiled, took me by the arm, pointed at his battle map, and said, "Look at the last entry I made before you entered." He'd placed a red circle around the bridges with a note saying, "No word from 3rd Bn 506. Unable to contact by radio, sent numerous patrols out but unable to get through due to enemy forces. We can assume that the 3rd Bn has been annihilated."

A very relieved McAuliffe then set about organizing a plan whereby Col Bud Harper's 327th Glider Infantry Regiment would relieve 3rd Bn as soon as possible. Santarsiero was given the task of guiding the regiment to the bridges.

Meanwhile, Ralph Bennett and his squad were still in position near the pond. He recalls:

> Earlier that afternoon 1st Lt Christianson ordered me to turn our mortar toward the rear. After discussing the situation with my men, I decided

not to fire the weapon as we ran the risk of hitting our own troops. We didn't fire a single round the whole time we were in that location!

A short while later two navy guys came over and wanted to speak to me. One was an officer [Lt Farrell] and the other a rating who was carrying a large radio. I guess they must have come over from the 501st at La Barquette. The officer said he was a forward fire controller for one of the battleships out in the Channel. He then asked if I could supply targets to keep the battleships busy, as they were hungry for action. I told him my targets were far too close for that kind of ordnance. However, as I was talking I noticed a man on a three-wheeled bicycle pedaling nonchalantly along the road some 500 yards from our position.

As a joke I pointed at the Frenchman and said "What about him?" They laughed, saying they would put a shell into an open area just behind him. It wouldn't do him any harm but would shake him up a bit! I didn't believe them but before I knew what was happening the officer was on his radio to the battleship! Within seconds a 1-ton shell came whistling over. It sounded like a freight train in a tunnel and sure enough slammed into a field just behind the guy on the bike. We watched through binoculars as the Frenchman threw himself into a roadside ditch. He then stood up, dusted himself down, and cycled away. We killed ourselves laughing and congratulated the officer. It was funny at the time but looking back I guess it wasn't the most sensible thing to have suggested – gave the Krauts something to think about though!

Since mid-morning the 501st at La Barquette had been in combat with German parachutists who had suffered heavy casualties. At around 1600hrs the Germans began to withdraw and were heading east toward the road bridge. Bob Webb recalls:

The enemy had formed a line of troops across our front and were heading in our direction. Capt Shettle had sent us 1st Lt Christianson and six riflemen, bringing our total strength up to 12. All the men were armed with M1s and we also had a box of .30cal machine gun ammunition and some extra M1 clips. Christianson was standing on the edge of the road, like Washington crossing the Delaware, and he made a fine-looking figure. He told us to hold fire and looked at the enemy through his binoculars. He then instructed one of his best riflemen to fire a tracer round in order to find their range. After several rounds the soldier said they were about 550 yards away. Everyone set their sights and got ready. Christianson told us to fire at will and said, "I want to see people falling down out there." The Germans kept coming and we kept killing them. It was like shooting fish in a barrel. A couple of times they played tricks on us by waving a white flag. When they reached our position they'd pull out a machine pistol and open fire. We didn't take any more of that nonsense and just kept on shooting.

After about 2 hours the Germans began to surrender and the Americans suddenly had about 190 prisoners to look after. Nobody knew quite what to do with them, as Bob Webb recalls: "We marched them down the road and put them all in a barn. These supermen didn't look that dangerous any more, but then I guess we didn't either. About 30 minutes later the barn came under the damnedest barrage of 88mm cannon fire I had ever seen. It was coming from the German position on the hill behind the bridges."

Meanwhile, back at the aid station, Théophile and Odette Fortin, who had been sheltering in the garden, decided to enter their house to look for something to read. After a short while Odette went back into the garden to fetch water from the pump, as some of the wounded soldiers were getting very thirsty. At that exact moment a shell from the 88mm gun exploded in the garden. Pete Madden, who had been wounded earlier, was recovering in the house and heard the explosion. It killed Odette and little Georgette Revet instantly. Powerless to help, he lay on the floor and watched the tragic scene unfold. Théophile was distraught and sobbing uncontrollably. Half an hour later Father Maloney arrived and gave last rites. Madden was torn apart by what he had seen and tearfully beckoned the Frenchman over to him. Grabbing Théophile's hand, he proceeded to give him everything he had in his pockets. It was a futile gesture but he felt he had to do something.

That evening a runner from the 501st brought Capt Shettle word that 260 Germans, all Fallschirmjäger, including 74 captured at La Barquette, were being sent to Fortin Farm – many were seriously wounded. Ten men, including Pfc John Kutz from C Co 326th Airborne Engineers, were ordered to bring them in. At about the same time Cpl Rommel and his gun team were dispatched to the aid station to act as security. When the prisoners were safely in the farm, the machine gun was set up beside the driveway. Rommel recalls:

> We had a good view of the front of the house. There were two doors about 12ft apart. The wounded from both sides were behind the door on the left with the remaining prisoners behind the door on the right.
>
> We had all suffered a degree of concussion damage and I could feel air being sucked through a hole in my right eardrum. We hadn't slept properly for 48 hours and drinking water was in short supply. I sent one of the boys to the back of the farm to take a look around. When he came back he told us he'd found two large barrels full of some kind of apple juice. It seemed mildly alcoholic but as we were so thirsty I told him to fill up our canteens. In the fields behind the farm we could see stragglers from the 6th Parachute Regiment still trying to surrender. Every time they tried to approach our guys on rear guard would open fire on them. Quite a few were killed but they continued to give themselves up! One of the prisoners, who arrived later, was a tall very dashing-looking officer. He was wearing a blue cape decorated with lots of gold braid. We watched in fascination as he was marched over to a small chicken shack near us and laughed as the guards crammed him into its tiny space.

As the day wore on, patrols were sent out to look for casualties and equipment. "That night I went on a scouting trip looking for medical bundles," recalls Bob Webb. "Working alone I went into the field where we had killed so many Germans. I returned soaked to the skin and empty-handed after falling into a ditch." Like many of his colleagues, Webb was on the lookout for souvenirs. "Back at our position I found two of my outpost guards sound asleep and threatened to shoot them for dereliction of duty."

Meanwhile, near La Barquette, Bill Galbraith had fired his machine gun at a shadowy group of 12 enemy paratroopers, but the instant he pulled the trigger the group melted away. Several minutes later a German holding a helmet approached the position. Galbraith was unable to see what he was carrying and ordered him to drop whatever it was or he would fire again. At that moment an American officer ran over from the 501st aid station and shouted something in German. "He then told us to let the guy through," recollects Galbraith. "It turned out that one of my bullets had grazed the top of the Kraut's head and knocked him senseless. Not long afterwards we had another flap when a German Junkers Ju88 aircraft flew across the area. It was so low that I could actually see the crew silhouetted against the night sky."

A few miles away, Harold Stedman and his group were heading south in an attempt to join up with 3rd Bn, and had entered the town of Blosville where the 101st had set up an aid station in the church. "I heard a noise like a cat meowing," recalls Stedman. "We entered the house where the noise was coming from and began digging in the rubble. Quite suddenly I found this tiny hand sticking out of the masonry. It belonged to a very young baby girl. She had severe head wounds and our medic, Pfc Alvin "Bill" Kidder, took her to the aid station. I've often wondered what became of her and hope that she survived." The Germans overran the town on June 8. Frank Fabian, a 101st medic, evacuated the walking wounded while Bill Kidder stayed behind and looked after the more seriously injured. Stedman and the others hid in the loft of a house. Shortly afterwards a dozen enemy soldiers occupied its ground floor, where they remained until the following morning. After they left, Stedman and the others snatched some much-needed sleep before sneaking out of the village.

∽ 9 ∽

"A pitiful sight"
D–Day + 2

The Allied net was closing around St-Côme-du-Mont. Three miles southwest of the town, German artillery positions at Méautis were attempting to destroy the church. They had been using its tower as an observation post and did not want it falling into American hands.

At around 3.15am, the Laurence family were woken by shells landing nearby. Louise recalls:

> The whole house shook and our bedroom was filled with light from the flames. Initially we thought one of the shells had landed on our house. We all ran downstairs and more explosions filled every room with dust and smoke. My husband Gustave took little Nicole in his arms and told me to follow him, but when he tried to open the backyard door it was jammed by debris. He forced it open and told us to go to Msr de Folleville's farm, which was some 800 yards north. With my mother's help we wrapped the two youngest children in blankets for protection against shrapnel. Gustave followed a little way behind with Jeannine and one of our elderly aunts who was on the verge of panic. As we left the rear of the house we could hear somebody calling for help nearby. Against my wishes Gustave ran off into the darkness to offer assistance. A few minutes later he returned and told me that because of the danger he was advising everyone to make for the farm.

Before long growing numbers of people were picking their way through the streets, which were now covered with all manner of debris. Louise continues:

As we passed my brother's house he asked where we were going. His wife Marthe pleaded with us to wait while she went back inside to get the pram [baby carriage]. At that point Gustave decided to go back for ours and we carried on without him. I was now at the rear of the group (which had grown to around 40 people) when we came under heavy machine-gun and rifle fire. It was not intentionally directed at us, but it threw everybody into a panic, and then another barrage of shells hit the town. As we approached the farm we came across a German roadblock where the soldiers had set up a machine gun that was facing toward St-Côme-du-Mont.

The soldiers told us to go back. We pleaded with them and said that our houses were being destroyed and that we had nowhere else to go.

Reluctantly the townsfolk turned around. On the way back they were stopped again by a small German patrol that questioned them about American troop movements. They were then forced into a ditch on the western side of the RN13 road. Louise remembers:

> The machine gun at the roadblock opened fire. Some of the bullets tore into the earth bank above me. My mother and I covered the toddlers with our bodies and made sure that the other children lay flat at the bottom of the ditch. Then the artillery at Méautis opened up again and as each shell detonated we held the children closer and closer but they never uttered a sound. Then things calmed down a little and I could hear Gustave shouting my name.

Louise was relieved to know that her husband was safe – he had been helping to fight fires in the town. About an hour later Gustave began evacuating people to the stables at Lemarchand Farm. Its walls were over 3ft thick and offered better protection from the shelling. Louise and her children were the last people from the group to reach the safety of the farm. Shortly afterwards the Maugers and several other families arrived seeking refuge.

"We learned that Albert Mauger and his 11-year-old son had been killed during the initial shelling. We tried to calm his mother down but she was terrified, grief-stricken and in shock. Ironically she had been diagnosed with terminal cancer and did not expect to outlive her son and grandson." Had it not been for Dr Stanley Morgan and his medical team, Albert's wife and many other civilians would have died that day.

Earlier that morning, more than 300 Germans had arrived at Rampan Manor. The road to the manor was littered with equipment, and dead men and horses. Watching from a window in the house was Jean Savary: "The Germans thought the manor was safe from air attack because of the large Red Cross on the roof and discipline had broken down. Then a German infantry officer arrived in the courtyard and fired several pistol shots into the air. He ordered the soldiers to evacuate the manor and sent them down the hill to the railway line, where they all marched off along the track toward Carentan."

At about the same time, a convoy of vehicles manned by Mongolians from Ost-Bataillon 795 was abandoned on the Rue Mary directly opposite Villand Farm. Henry Villand, who was then 16 years old, remembers the scene: "As the Mongols began to panic, a vehicle in the convoy was set alight and the fire quickly spread. A large tree and one of our barns were burnt and the damage can still be seen to this day. Many of the fleeing Mongols drowned in marshland as they attempted to reach the railway line about 300 yards due west. A few who couldn't swim spotted a raised causeway and used it to reach the safety of the railway."

After the Mongols had gone, Henry Villand and some of his young friends clambered onto the burning vehicles to look for food. "Ammunition was exploding all around us. We formed a chain and began frantically recovering as much material as we could from the convoy. My parents knew that what we were doing was foolhardy and tried to stop us, but we took no notice."

Earlier that morning, the Mongolians had captured Joe Gorenc and Sid McCallum. McCallum recalls:

June 8 was my 22nd birthday. The Mongols promised to hand us back to our own side as soon as they could, but they were lying and forced us out to the railway tracks through chest-high water. A couple of Allied aircraft flew low overhead and tipped their wings. Why they didn't attack I'll never know, because the enemy were right there for the taking. The two of us were force-marched down the railway line to Carentan and handed over to the German 6th Para.

On arrival at Carentan they joined about 50 other prisoners. One was Ray Calandrella, who remembers, "That morning the Germans hauled away some French prisoners and shortly afterwards rifle shots rang out. We were all terrified and thought they were going to do the same to us." The following morning the prisoners were moved to St-Lô and then on to the Hôtellerie Notre-Dame at Troisgots. As they were leaving Carentan, Calandrella looked around to see what the Germans had done with the bodies of the Frenchmen, but no evidence remained.

After 5 hours of shelling, the church tower was finally destroyed and by noon American forces began to establish control in St-Côme-du-Mont. During the afternoon Col Sink entered the town and visited the aid station before returning to his command post at Angoville. The battalion adjutant, Alex Bobuck, had spent three days working at the aid station and following Sink's visit went to Angoville for a debriefing session. There he handed in Robert Cone's dog tags, who was a POW, and a list of casualties, as well as the location of Bill Atlee's body.

While all this was going on, the Laurence family were still sheltering at Lemarchand Farm. Gustave decided to go out and get some food, as Louise recalls:

He went with my brother and another man to our house. When they returned we ate the meager rations they'd brought and learned that our house had been damaged but was repairable. After we'd eaten we ventured outside and watched the Germans disappearing in all directions as they tried to escape. We then decided to return to our homes. On the way back Gustave and my brother stopped to say hello to the American soldier they'd brought down from the roof of the grocery store on D-Day.

Their meeting came to an abrupt halt when a shell exploded across the street. It was fired from an enemy tank that was somewhere to the northwest of the town. During the days that followed, this tank and its crew caused many problems for the American forces in the area.

As soon as they arrived at their home the Laurences began to assess the damage.

> All the windows were broken and the entire place riddled with bullet holes. We had abandoned our dog in the earlier panic and found her unharmed hiding under a table in the yard. Our bedroom upstairs had received the most damage. It was covered in dust and there were a number of live bullets on what was left of our bed, plus 16 bullet holes in the wall. More had passed through the bedroom door and lodged in the corridor wall. Unbelievably a dozen eggs we had left in the cellar were intact, and although the house was in a mess, the valuables we'd hidden from the Germans in the loft survived!

The Germans were still in the vicinity as the terrifying day drew to a close. With her husband remaining at home, Louise decided to take her family back to Lemarchand Farm where they slept in the stables.

> As we walked to the farm I saw paratroopers patrolling the area astride horses that had been abandoned by the Germans – they looked like cowboys. We chatted with some but they made us feel they had more important things to do. In any case they didn't know who we were and probably felt they couldn't trust us. After all, we had spent the best part of four years living with the Germans and the region was full of collaborators, so who could blame them. As the days passed, the Americans allowed us to re-establish the mayor's office from where we were able to distribute daily news. Information about civilian casualties began to filter back and we learned that 13 people had been killed in La Basse Addeville on the 7th.

The total included almost all of the Langeard family, whose only survivor was 13-year-old Paul. He received treatment at the church in Angoville from two 501st medics (Pvt Robert Wright and Pvt Kenneth Moore). The bodies of the Langeard family remained in the rubble of their home until June 26.

Pénême and Fortin Farm

As dawn broke on the 8th, Bob Webb and his men were in foxholes beside the Pénême road eating a makeshift breakfast that consisted mainly of D-Bars. Suddenly a distraught well-built middle-aged woman appeared and shuffled passed heading east. The lady was Julia Letourneur, Odette Fortin's mother, and she had just received news of her daughter's death. Bob and several of his men followed her to Fortin Farm and tried to comfort her, but she was very bitter and blamed the Americans for what had happened. Soon after her arrival, and with the help of her son-in-law, she started to bury the bodies of Odette and little Georgette. (A couple of weeks later tragedy was to strike again when ten-year-old Lucienne Fortin, Théophile's niece, was killed whilst playing with a hand grenade near her home in Angoville).

Capt Sorenson had left Fortin Farm on the 7th and returned to his own unit, leaving S/Sgt Talford Wynne in charge of the wounded. In a barn nearby more men were being cared for by Pfc Andy Sosnak (nicknamed "dit-dot-dash" because of his pronounced stutter). Three members of the 326th Medical Co were ordered to evacuate the wounded and did so by using a horse and cart they found at the farm. As they left and headed for safety, they came across more casualties, like Ken Johnson, who was still on the drop zone:

After picking us up and putting us in the cart they took us to the church in Blosville. It was there that a young doctor told me he was going to try something new, and plastered my broken leg from knee to toe without gauze between the cast and skin. As a precaution against air raids I was placed beneath one of the pews and after a few hours the hairs on my leg began itching like crazy. I was then evacuated to Utah Beach and then on to a hospital in Southampton. It was there that I eventually found a knife long enough to fit behind the plaster so that I could scratch my leg – what a relief that was!

Back at Fortin Farm Bobbie Rommel was on guard duty. Ever inquisitive, Rommel decided to take a look inside the farmhouse: "I was about to go in when a young officer appeared. He was slim built and wearing a helmet and as I turned to leave he said, 'What a thing to have to do on my birthday.' It suddenly struck me that June 8 was my birthday as well! I was 20, the officer was 22 and we had a real good laugh about it."

By midday, communications had been firmly established with Sink's command post. During the course of the afternoon S/Sgt Talford Wynne was able to evacuate most of the remaining wounded in jeeps supplied by the 326th Medical Co. However, the collecting medical teams missed Hank DiCarlo, who was still in a room on his own. "When I first heard vehicles outside I thought they were tanks," recalls DiCarlo, "but they were trucks that took the German prisoners away." By the time the medics found him, all the transport had gone. Pete Madden was placed on one of the first vehicles to leave.

> We were loaded onto jeeps two at a time and taken to Utah Beach. On the way we passed wagons piled high with dead Americans and eventually stopped to pick up a German officer. Our jeep's driver and his buddy were both enlisted men and ordered the German to get into the back. He refused, quoting the Geneva Convention. The two enlisted men were having none of this and without warning put a gun to the man's temple and blew half his head away. I never reported the incident but it troubled me for years to come. The men left the crumpled body by the roadside and we continued our journey.

Tom Bucher was evacuated at about the same time but, unlike Madden, was not taken directly to Utah Beach. After being collected by jeep he was transferred to an ambulance and taken to Blosville church where he received further emergency treatment – it would be two months before he could walk again. The church was full of casualties and following his treatment Bucher was moved outside. He remained there for a couple of days before being shipped back to England. At the beginning of September, after four months in an English hospital, Bucher was repatriated to the United States on the troopship *Queen Mary*. Making the same crossing was none other than the British Prime Minister Winston Churchill, who was on his way to Canada for a meeting in Quebec with President Roosevelt. It would be another five months before Bucher was eventually released from hospital.

Barney Ryan had spent the previous 36 hours or so hidden beneath a parachute. After venturing out, he made contact with friendly forces at Frigot Farm and by late afternoon was making his way on foot to rejoin the battalion. He passed through the 501st area near La Barquette where he met John King (S4 supply officer), who was driving a captured German *Kettenkrad* (tracked motorcycle). King told him that Regiment had been completely out of touch with 3rd Bn but that things were now fine, before pointing him in the direction of Fortin Farm. A little later Ryan spotted Macrae Barnson (G Co), who was guarding a handful of prisoners held in a shack. Barnson gave him a German knife and asked him to tell 1st Lt Chambliss or 2nd Lt Kennedy of his whereabouts. "I arrived at the aid station during the evening when all the action was over," remembers Dr Ryan. "Wynne, Pelcher, Eckman, Haycraft, and Sosnak were outside cooking a cow they'd butchered. I think we stayed at the farm overnight before moving on to St-Côme-du-Mont." Wynne and Sosnak were decorated for their part in the care and evacuation of the wounded. Wynne got a bronze star and Sosnak a Distinguished Service Cross (DSC).

Bill Galbraith and Marion Hove were nearby and desperately wanted to rejoin their comrades after seeing the P-47s attack the bridges. "That afternoon we stopped a lieutenant who looked like he was in charge," recalls Galbraith, "I told him that 3rd Bn must be in a whole heap of trouble – otherwise why would the Air Force bomb the bridge – and asked permission to return to our outfit."

The officer told them to stay at their post or he would shoot them for desertion. Galbraith was overcome with anger and grabbing his equipment turned and moved away. Hove was worried that the officer was going to shoot, but he made no attempt to stop them and at long last both men were on their way to rejoining the battalion.

Following open ground and heading in an easterly direction, they passed a group of prisoners who were digging graves. They stopped briefly and spoke to the soldiers who were guarding them. "Some of the prisoners were crying," remembers Galbraith. "I wondered if they thought they were digging their own graves or were just saddened by the loss of their comrades."

On reaching the aid station Galbraith was shocked by what he saw:

> With the Germans in their gray uniforms it looked like a scene from *Gone with the Wind*. There were about 200 prisoners waiting to be collected; most were from the 6th Parachute Regiment. Some had been shot up pretty badly. We were told that the day before, as they were being marched up the road, the 88 across the river opened up and blew them into doll rags. There was no medication available and you had to feel a little sympathy for them – it was a pitiful sight.

Leaving the farm, the two men made their way to the bridges just as the 327th Glider Infantry Regiment was taking over the position. Galbraith was overjoyed to see Jim Brown and a dozen others from I Co, but nothing had been seen of 2nd Lt Windish and his squad. They all shook hands with one another and Jim Brown told Galbraith that Bob Young had been badly injured on the drop. There was a lot of talk from Santarsiero about the action he had been involved with near the footbridge. As he told his version of events (for which he was later awarded the DSC), Elmer Gilbertson, who had also been involved in the action, told Galbraith and Hove that "it was no great shakes and the Krauts were trying to surrender anyway." Galbraith then heard rumors about a gas attack near Ste-Mère-Église. Many soldiers, including Galbraith, had disposed of their respirators after the drop, and the story struck a fearful note. "Later that evening," recalls Galbraith, "I took a mask from a dead German, which stank of his decomposing body!"

By the evening of the 8th almost 150 men had reached the bridges (there were roughly 40 at the footbridge and 110 at the road bridge). The battalion was then placed in reserve and divided into three groups. After dusk H Co, with Christianson in command, was sent to an orchard at Le Ferage, whilst Santarsiero took G and I companies to a temporary bivouac field at Beaumont Farm that was near Col Sink's command post at Angoville. Around the edges of the field the Germans had left a system of well-dug fox holes that was concealed beneath overhanging trees. "When we left the bridges we were deployed here for a couple of days," Tom Kennedy recalls. "We were told not to walk or make any trails in the field that could be viewed from the air. A dead Kraut was propped up at the entrance and he must have been searched by nearly everyone that passed by. We managed to get some sleep here as this was our first proper rest since jumping in."

Meanwhile Shettle and Shames had taken HQ Co (minus its machine-gun platoon) and marched it to Folleville Farm, where they established 3rd Bn's command post. The command post acted as a hub, whilst its three rifle companies became spokes that allowed the decimated battalion to take control of a large area.

The next morning, just before dawn, the machine-gun platoon set off from Fortin Farm and made for Folleville. Along the way they passed through La Basse Addeville. "We came upon the twisted body of an American paratrooper lying next to a road junction," recalls Bobbie Rommel. "I didn't give the dead man a second thought; it just seemed like nothing to me. Later on in life images like these would replay themselves in my mind and it really screwed my head up. But at the time we had to trivialize these things and put them to the back of our thoughts."

Further along the road they passed half a dozen dead Germans who had no visible signs of injury. Presumably they had been killed on June 6 and 7 by concussion from Allied naval shelling. On arrival at Folleville Farm, a challenge rang out and Rommel responded by shouting his name. "They didn't like that," he recalls, "and got very jumpy. I then shouted, 'No, it really is me, Cpl Rommel, HQ Co,' and eventually they let us in."

Regimental surgeon Maj Louis Kent had been told that John Gibson's body was in the marshes below L'Amont. A search of the area was inconclusive and Gibson was posted as missing in action. At about that time Gibson was actually traveling south, together with two of his colleagues and a number of German wounded, from St-Lô to the evacuation hospital at Mortain. Transport was at a premium and they were being forced to walk. They had no idea where they were heading and had not eaten since their capture three days earlier. Whenever Allied aircraft appeared overhead, the men would dive into roadside ditches for cover.

After several hours of walking the German officer in charge spotted an old bicycle leaning against a tree. He took it, strapped on his suitcase and started to pedal away, but both tires were flat, making it difficult to ride. The officer screamed at Gibson and ordered him to take the bike and push it, which he reluctantly did. Shortly afterwards Gibson saw his chance to escape. The road began to drop downhill and in a second he was on the bicycle and pedaling like mad. "The old crate shuddered," recalls Gibson, "its flat tires rubbed against the frame but I soon reached the front of the column. Then came the inevitable shout 'HALT!' and I looked over my shoulder at the officer, who was threatening to shoot if I went any further."

Not long afterwards the group went cross-country in an effort to avoid the attention of Allied aircraft. Gibson remembers:

> Just before it got dark we stopped at a farmhouse. Our guards bought two large buckets of fresh milk from the farmer. The Frenchman seemed quite friendly and agreed to let us bed down for the night. Before turning in the Germans started to eat their meager rations of black bread, crackers, and cheese all washed down with a cup of that warm fresh milk – I looked on longingly. Eventually one of the Germans held his canteen cup up and gestured to me to have a drink. Twelve cups later I stopped and asked that my two wounded colleagues should have as much as they could drink as well.

After a good night's rest, the group continued their journey, but were following roads again. Along the way the German officer spoke to a

French priest. The clergyman then walked over to Gibson and handed him a small piece of cake. Thanking him, Gibson and his friends quickly divided it up and gobbled it down. Perhaps, thought Gibson, the German officer was not so bad after all.

A couple of miles further on they heard the sound of a lorry approaching (vehicle movement in daylight was extremely hazardous). The driver took pity and agreed to take the exhausted men the remaining 22 miles to Mortain.

Pointe du Hoc

After spending a couple of days on the run, privates Bob Dunning and Jack Manley were eventually captured. They had traveled just over a mile from Pointe du Hoc and were near the village of Cardenville. Dunning recalls:

> We walked right into a German patrol. The Germans were very nervous but appeared to be amused by our appearance. Jack and I had darkened our faces with potassium permanganate but it had washed off and left our mouths and tongues a weird purple color. The Krauts thought it was some kind of chemical warfare and at first kept us at arm's length, which was fine by me. Eventually we were searched, but they didn't find my invasion money, which was sewn into the hem of my shorts. Then things started to change for the worst. We were made to lean against a tree at a 45-degree angle. They wouldn't let us piss or give us water to drink. I told them I was a barber – that was my first mistake – and they responded by booting me several times on my ass. Then I told them I was a cook – second mistake, more heavy kicks – and so it went on.

A little while later, together with a number of other POWs, they were loaded onto a convoy of trucks that was heading inland away from the beaches. During the evening a flight of Mosquito fighter-bombers attacked the convoy. In the confusion, Dunning and Manley made their escape and hid in a flooded field nearby. When it got dark the Germans pulled out and the two men headed back toward Pointe du Hoc. "The invasion money came in handy," Bob recalls, "because we gave it as a thank you to some French people who'd helped us. The tough part of being captured was admitting it. So Jack and I never said a word until we saw Herb Spence back in England."

As they neared the coast, they ran into D Co from the 2nd Ranger Bn led by Lt Kerchner. They joined the company and went out on their first patrol with them later that same night. Bob Dunning has vivid memories of the events that followed. "The soldier in front of me was hit in the head by a sniper's bullet. As it struck the poor bastard, he fell forward and landed face down. What has always stayed in my mind was the way his legs continued to move in a walking motion even though he must have been dead by the time he hit the ground. It was a hell of a thing to witness."

The pair stayed with D Co for a couple of days. On June 11 they entered Isigny-sur-Mer, where they were astonished to find Lenny Goodgal and Ray Crouch from I Co. The Rangers then drove the four men 8 miles west to Folleville Farm, where they rejoined 3rd Bn. "When we arrived Sgt Morton wanted to know where the hell we'd been," recalls Dunning. "Lenny Goodgal still had the note from Col Rudder which put us in the clear. We half-jokingly told Morton that we'd been hunting for souvenirs, which really pissed him off."

Fellow 81mm mortar men Roy Burger and John Allison had also been hiding in the area south of Pointe du Hoc. They had managed to make contact with some local people, as Burger explains.

A Frenchman somehow got to know we were hiding in a hedge. After dark he came over and whispered while pointing toward a house saying "Boche." He then handed us two bottles of cider plus a loaf of black bread. This was the first food we'd eaten in three days and he returned the following evening with a similar treat. The next day the Americans attacked and we found ourselves in No Man's Land. A terrific battle ensued and after it was over Allison and I broke cover and turned ourselves in. Medics treated John, and I was moved out on the hood of a scout car belonging to the infantry unit that liberated us. The following day I told their commander that I needed to get back to my unit as fast as possible, but he refused my request because he needed everyone he could get his hands on. I eventually rejoined 3rd Bn and took over what was left of my platoon on June 22. Allison's wound healed up enough for him to return to the outfit pretty soon afterwards.

Because of the losses it had suffered (about 60 percent), the 81mm mortar platoon was not reconstituted as a fighting unit until after its return to Britain from Normandy.

~10~

"Don't shoot, we're Americans"
Regrouping and consolidation

Capt Harwick had been on the run for two days, but by 2030hrs on June 8 he had reached 506th Regimental HQ and reported to Col Sink. The following morning, Sink gave Harwick command of 3rd Bn and he immediately began the job of replacing the missing company commanders. 1st Lt Dick Meason took over H Co, 1st Lt John Kiley was given I Co (albeit temporarily), and 1st Lt Joe Doughty took command of G Co.

Meanwhile, elements of the 4th Division that had landed on Utah Beach on D-Day had reached Fortin Farm. During their short stay Dr Ryan arranged for a jeep from the division's medical detachment to evacuate Hank DiCarlo, and he was loaded onto a trailer next to an infantry sergeant who had a severe stomach wound. On the way to Utah Beach they stopped at a checkpoint where they were misdirected north toward Montebourg. Shortly afterwards they came under heavy mortar fire and the vehicle swerved off the road. "After a few moments I called to the driver to find out what was going on," recalls DiCarlo. "I received no answer, so I undid the webbing that held me in position and climbed out. The driver was nowhere to be seen and the sergeant on the other stretcher was dead."

After the mortar barrage stopped, DiCarlo stood by the roadside and waited for the driver to return. He soon began to feel light-headed and sat down on an abandoned ammunition box.

> I thought I was hallucinating when I started to see troops coming toward me. I couldn't motivate myself into moving and just sat there awaiting

my fate. Thankfully the troops were from the 4th Division's 22nd Infantry Regiment. A Maj Paulic ordered me to find a weapon and fall in with his men. I tried to explain that I was injured but it made no difference and I was paired up with a Pvt Carrigan. We then began to attack some Germans and the company I was in came under mortar fire. A shell landed nearby and blew Carrigan high into the air. His arms were waving about in all directions as he tumbled end over end – I felt like I was in some sort of dream. I then heard an order to move toward some woods up ahead. Struggling for breath and using every last ounce of strength I pushed forward. However, I couldn't keep up and collided with a tree before passing out.

Later that afternoon, when I regained consciousness, I found myself on a stretcher beside a hospital tent on Utah Beach. After a brief examination a medic informed me that I would be going out on the next available LST. He then gave me several syrettes of morphine and explained how to manage any pain – just in case I had problems during the next 24 hours.

There was a wounded German on the stretcher next to me who could speak English. I overheard him talking with one of the orderlies about the progress of the invasion. The German was predicting a massive counterattack that would drive us into the Channel and the medic was actually agreeing with him! I looked for my pistol (which had been my father's sidearm in World War I) but it was missing... no doubt taken from me earlier. I got so pissed off that I drew my jump knife, which was still strapped to my boot, and told them that if they carried on talking in that way I'd stab the pair of them. The orderly vanished and the German didn't utter another word after I told him that if there was a counterattack he could count on being the first casualty!

Two weeks after his evacuation from the beachhead, DiCarlo found himself at the 92nd General Hospital in Bristol. Here his chest was drained of fluids and gradually his condition began to improve. (Internal bleeding had put pressure on his right lung causing it to collapse, which saved him from drowning in his own blood). "Because the bullet was so close to my spine," he recalls, "the doctors wouldn't operate and told me it would eventually make its own way to the surface, which it did three weeks later. After this I was soon back on my feet and attended a number of functions in the hospital's recreation hall. At one of these dances I was surprised to see Pvt Carrigan, the guy from the 22nd Infantry who I'd seen blown up on June 9."

Hank was desperate to get back to Ramsbury and rejoin his platoon. "As the time drew nearer for me to leave hospital I began to experience feelings of guilt. Having been so ignominiously removed from battle on June 6, I desperately hoped my next mission would put everything right."

As H Co emerged from their "pup" tents at Le Ferage at dawn on the 9th, a grim sight greeted them. Hanging from apple trees nearby were the bloated remains of Col Wolverton and Sgt Nagy. "One of our officers detailed four men to cut the as-yet unidentified bodies down," recalls Ralph Bennett. "Their names were revealed the following day and it didn't take long for word to get around."

"Sgt Frank Padisak and I turned up just as the colonel's death was made official," remembers Cpl Lou Vecchi. "Up until then we had been hiding during the day and moving at night. By the time we rejoined the battalion it was all over. There was a huge sense of bitterness over the bodies because they had been left in the trees for so long." Padisak had more bad news for 1 Ptn. He and Vecchi had found Secundino Alvarez's body in a barn with his entire face shot away. They were only able to recognize him by his dark wavy hair (a feature of which Secundino was inordinately proud). Graves Registration asked the 506th to send out work details to retrieve dog tags from American bodies, as Ralph Bennett recalls: "When some of my guys returned to the orchard after 'pulling tags' I was disgusted and sickened to learn that they'd been robbing the bodies of people they knew – taking watches and rings etc."

Local civilians were also asked to help with the clear-up operation. "We were split into three groups," recalls Adrian Saint, who was aged 14 at the time. "The first group buried the dead. The second picked up material, and the third section (of which I was a member) collected dead farm animals. Decaying horses and cows were lying everywhere. We dug huge pits and using American fuel set fire to everything before covering the remains with topsoil. All this was done under periodic fire from the Germans, who were still located in Carentan, Auvers, and Méautis."

Despite a lack of running water in St-Côme-du-Mont, C Co 326th Airborne Engineers still managed to build a shower in the back garden of the aid station where the 506th's 3rd Bn medical detachment was based. On June 11 the detachment was moved to Carentan to work for Dr Kent. Doctors Ryan and Morgan took charge of a large abandoned house on the western side of town in the Rue Sebline. The owner, Dr Caillard, had been killed on June 8 while attending to civilian wounded during the naval bombardment of the railway station. "It wasn't long before somebody discovered the building's cleverly hidden wine cellar," recalls Barney Ryan, "It was stacked full with choice bottles of all vintages. Nobody bothered us for nearly 36 hours. The time was happily passed, drinking and partying, until Dr Kent ordered us to deploy for a battle that became known as 'Bloody Gully.' "

HQ Co had settled into Folleville Farm, which was located midway between Houesville and St-Côme-du-Mont. "After Capt Shettle stood me down for the day I had a light breakfast of D-bars and took off my pack tray," recalls Ed Shames. "I then found a comfortable spot in the corner of the kitchen and got some long overdue sleep."

On June 9 the battalion's new commander, Bob Harwick, arrived at the farm with new orders. In the shake-up that followed, Shettle became executive officer and temporary commander of HQ Co. Bobbie Rommel and his gun team were ordered to set up their weapon in a ditch on the western side of the RN13 facing a large field. "After we got settled," recalls Rommel, "I decided to have a look around. On the far side of the field I found a dead German lying face down near a hedge. As I started to turn the body over I saw a stick grenade hidden beneath. At the same moment an American column came marching down the road – helmets just visible above the hedge. That was it, I was spooked and hurried back to my guys."

Meanwhile, Shettle had ordered Ben Hiner to lead a small patrol into St-Côme-du-Mont. Hiner's task was to locate American dead and collect scattered equipment. As the patrol moved west along the Rue Mary, which was strewn with all manner of debris, it began to rain. At the stone cross (La Croix) the patrol turned north into the Chemin des Campagnes.

This sunken dirt track was 1,400 yards long and cut directly across high ground to the west of the town. Hiding in the area was the enemy tank that had fired on St-Côme-du-Mont the previous day. Luckily for Hiner this was as far as the patrol was supposed to go. Several dead soldiers were in a field to the right and three bodies lay close together on the crest of a gently rising slope. Graves Registration had already attached identification labels to the men and Hiner read out their names: "S/Sgt Paul Simrell, 1st Sgt Jim Shirley, and T/5 Bill Atlee. All three were good friends," remembers Hiner. "Graves Registration had collected the bodies and left them in a spot where they wouldn't be forgotten." Further checks revealed that the men's personal effects had been removed and as all seemed in order Hiner returned to Folleville Farm. He reported his findings to Capt Shettle and recalls that, "Shettle asked me if I wanted to take over Paul Simrell's job. I said I'd be honored and he promoted me on the spot to S1 Chief Clerk."

That night, whilst patrolling the perimeter, Bobbie Rommel saw a shape in the gloom:

> Twice I challenged what appeared to be a man lying on the grass verge of the RN13. I fired a couple of shots from my carbine and then went to investigate. All I found was a pile of gravel about a foot high... oops! After a while we began to tell when dead Germans were nearby. Many times, as the wind changed direction, one of us would say, "Smells like a dead Kraut somewhere around here." The German corpses smelt different, I can't explain why, but we were rarely wrong.

Saturday June 10 turned out to be a quiet day at Folleville Farm and whilst Ed Shames was sleeping Ben Hiner decided to take a look around. At the rear of the building was a large courtyard enclosed on both sides by stable blocks that were being used by the enlisted men. "It was the northernmost block that caught my attention," remembers Hiner. "There must have been at least 200 brightly painted oval metal plaques fixed high up on the wall." These plaques were awards won by the farm's owner, Msr de Folleville, who was known throughout the region for his champion bulls. A few moments later 2nd Lt John Williams came strolling across the courtyard toward Hiner with Pfc Otto Dworsky (H Co), who was holding a captured German pistol. "Would it be OK if 'Chick' [Dworsky's nickname] went inside the farmhouse to clean my Luger?" Williams asked. "That's no problem, sir, just leave the kid with me and I'll see that he's OK," replied Hiner.

A little while later Williams returned to the farmhouse and dismissed Dworsky, who handed him the pistol as he left. Ed Shames had been asleep in the room and was woken by the noise. Williams was admiring his newly oiled weapon and started fooling around. Ben Hiner was also in the room and recalls:

Eddy and I began laughing and sharing a joke with Williams. We were standing about 3ft from the officer when he produced a clip from his pocket and loaded the gun... we both stopped and looked at each other. In the blink of an eye he pulled back on the slide and let it drop with his finger on the trigger! The gun went off and I was hit in the abdomen. For a second or two we stood in stunned silence unable to comprehend what had happened. As I staggered across the kitchen Eddy helped me up onto the table and tried to stop the bleeding. He then shouted at Williams, "You stupid son of a bitch," before sending Elwood Kendall back into St-Côme to fetch Doc Ryan!

Ed Shames recounts:

While we were waiting I held Ben's head and stroked his hair. I told him to stay calm and not to panic as help was on its way. Then a jeep pulled up outside – it was Doc Ryan. After stabilizing Ben the doctor ordered Williams (who was still in a daze) and myself to load him onto the jeep. I watched from the kitchen doorway as they left and wondered just what had possessed Williams to do such a damn fool thing.

Initially Hiner was sent to a newly established field hospital at Boutteville and then to a larger hospital near Utah beach. He was there for 21 days and underwent a successful operation before being evacuated to England.

On June 9 Stedman, Lujan, Rosdahl, Fishel, and Madona arrived at the Beaumont Farm bivouac area. Stedman noticed 1st Lt Nye hiding in a foxhole and shouting orders to soldiers who were out in the open. Stedman remembers:

> I wondered how anybody could do such a cowardly thing in front of his men. He was the only officer around, so we handed him the covering note given to us by Col Sink explaining that we'd been fighting with the 82nd. Nye flicked through the letter and burst out laughing. We couldn't understand his sarcastic attitude. Sneering, he looked up and accused us of being malingerers who'd avoided the objective. Still ranting, he screwed up the letter and then sent us to find Jim Shuler and Pvt Jerry O'Christie from 2 Ptn's 60mm mortar squad. Thank God Nye was nothing to do with my platoon and it was only on occasions like this that I had to take orders from him.

A few days later Stedman learned that his own platoon leader, 1st Lt Andy Anderson, wanted to question his group about what they had been doing between June 6 and 8. "I knew that Nye had taken great pleasure in misleading Anderson and that it would take some doing to get him back on side."

Stedman soon realized that 3 Ptn was desperately under strength. Shuler was now acting as 60mm sergeant and was glad to have people like Stedman and Lujan around. I Co was missing all its 60mm squad leaders. Two had been captured – Bob Nash (2 Ptn) and Jim Layfield (3 Ptn) – while Sgt Bev Manlove had drowned when chalk no. 24 crashed into the sea. Word had just begun to filter through about the tragic loss of the two I Co aircraft – for in addition to the fate of chalk no. 24, chalk no. 15, carrying 1st Lt Gerry Howard and the entire communications team, had crashed near Magneville.

That same day Pfc Bill Weber and Pvt Johnnie Edwards arrived at Beaumont Farm, much to the amazement of their friends, and wanted to recommend Pvt George McMillan for a posthumous bravery award for saving their lives on June 7. Due to a last minute change of plan the pair had not jumped, as originally intended, with the pathfinders on D-Day. The following morning McMillan turned up alive and well and the recommendation of an award was forgotten!

At around 0830hrs on the 9th, Col Sink issued an order that each company should organize a patrol, even though the battalion was now officially in reserve. The three officers nominated to lead the patrols were 2nd Lt Linton Barling (G Co), 2nd Lt Clark Heggeness (H Co), and 1st Lt Jim Nye (I Co). Curiously, Nye failed to join his patrol, which consisted of Bill Galbraith, Bill Weber, George McMillan, Johnnie Edwards, and Jim Brown. George McMillan's arrival meant that 2nd Squad now had five men in its ranks, making it I Co's most complete squad. Their orders were to check for enemy activity and to question anybody they came across (reports had been received that Germans were in the area posing as American soldiers), and they headed out to where the I Co pathfinder security team had landed on the 6th. Jim Brown had a vested interest, as he desperately wanted to find out what had happened to his twin brother Jack.

"We came across a dead German sniper," recalls Bill Galbraith. "I took his rifle, which had its stock blown off, and fixed it up later for use as my own personal weapon." The men knew they were searching the right area when they found Jack Brown's gas mask case. Shortly afterwards they discovered George Kenfield's body – he had a bullet hole between his eyes. Most of the corpses had been looted and were surrounded by scattered items of clothing and equipment. Although Kenfield was not generally popular, his loss was a terrible waste of a young life. They recorded the body's location and continued their mission until a shot rang out. At that exact same moment Bill Weber bent down and ducked under a fence; had he not done so the bullet would have struck him square in the head. At that point the men decided the area was far too exposed and returned to base.

Many of the fields in the area had well-sited machine gun positions dug along the hedge lines and one in particular sticks in Bill Galbraith's mind:

> I came around a corner and saw a German pointing a machine gun at me. I thought for sure I was going to die but the German was dead. I went up to the body and kicked it; as it fell the corpse kept its same alert position. Much later, when I stopped to think about what I'd done it really bothered me – he deserved better than that! Later a Frenchman gave us a bottle of wine. We didn't know whether to trust him or not as there wasn't much of this stuff around. For all we knew it could've been poisoned.

When the patrol returned to Beaumont Farm, they noticed Nye hanging around and decided to play a little game. They knew if he saw the wine bottle he would take it from them, so they passed it around and pretended to drink. Sure enough Nye came over, snatched the bottle from them, and consumed about half of its contents. "Ten minutes passed and he was still on his feet," recalls Galbraith, "He was showing no signs of sickness so we reckoned that the rest was safe to drink!"

G and I companies (around 40 men in total) left Angoville at around 2000hrs and headed for new locations. I Co went to Le Vivier Château at Houesville and G Co was sent half a mile further west to an area near the Cherbourg–Carentan railway line at Le Boujamet. The men had only gone a few hundred yards when they were forced to take cover as a couple of Me109 fighters flew low overhead.

Le Vivier Château

Mme Blanchard and her elderly grandmother owned the beautiful 18th-century house known as Le Vivier Château. Like most large properties in the region, it had been occupied by the Germans and used as a headquarters. When I Co arrived they discovered that the officers had been quartered upstairs in elegantly decorated bedrooms. The senior NCOs had slept downstairs in bunk beds with the remainder of the unit in outbuildings surrounding the château.

On arrival Lt Nye ordered 2nd Squad to check for booby traps. Galbraith recalls:

> We knew full well that our officers would take all the best rooms as quickly as we could clear them, so we saved the master bedroom until last hoping to secure it for ourselves. We couldn't believe the size of the bed! Jim Brown took a running jump shouting "Room clear!" and landed slap bang in the middle followed closely by the rest of us. We all squashed together hoping to settle down for the night. Nobody seemed to bother us and we thought that we'd got away with it. However, our hopes were dashed when Nye stuck his head around the door and ordered us into the courtyard.

Nye then gave the five men duties that he wanted undertaken that night. He instructed Galbraith and McMillan to patrol the grounds whilst Weber, Brown, and Edwards were ordered to guard the house. During the night, while Galbraith and McMillan were patrolling the long oval perimeter drive that ran from the château to the RN13, they heard voices. "We issued a challenge," recalls Galbraith. "Just as the safeties were clicked off, a hushed voice said, 'Don't shoot. We're Americans.' Several men emerged from the bushes. It turned out that they were from the 82nd Airborne on another patrol." This was the beginning of a link-up that 506th Regimental HQ had been waiting for.

As dawn broke and the pair returned to the château, they passed a ten-wheeled truck parked in the courtyard. Galbraith was intrigued and took a look in the back, "I was shocked to find dead American paratroopers stacked up like driftwood." Horrified, he jumped down, cursing the Graves Registration team – he could not understand why they had not parked it out of sight.

They entered the house and went upstairs looking for Nye, as Galbraith recalls: "I wasn't surprised to find him in the master bedroom. After we reported the 82nd incident we were stood down and went to the kitchen to look for something to eat." They found Mme Blanchard in the room and asked if she had a frying pan they could use to cook eggs. Unfortunately she could not understand their request and they ended up eating K-rations!

As each day passed, and as men continued to drift in, I Co's numbers steadily grew. However, its overall strength was still well below par. Johnny Houk arrived during the evening of the 11th. He had been fighting near St-Côme-du-Mont with G Co pathfinder Pfc Wilbur Croteau (who was killed a few days later). Lenny Goodgal and Ray Crouch turned up at roughly the same time after fighting for five days with the Rangers at Pointe du Hoc. "I gave my letter from Col Rudder to lieutenants Anderson and Kiley," recalls Goodgal:

> They thought we were making the whole story up, and laughed sarcastically saying, "We need a volunteer for a very dangerous mission." "I'll go any place you go," I snapped back, and walked away, dismayed by their attitude. Of course Nye thought it was very funny, but we knew what we had done and how hard it had been for the pair of us – I shall never forget the scene from Pointe du Hoc on D + 2 of a sea of ships looking like foam on the water.

There was growing concern as to the whereabouts of the enemy tank that was still at large somewhere on high ground northwest of St-Côme-du-Mont. On the 12th, Johnny Houk and George McMillan were sent out to see if they could find it (they had been chosen because, following their earlier encounters, both had a good understanding of the area). They moved south along the Chemin des Campagnes but found nothing of significance, and on reaching the end of the track at La Croix turned and headed back. McMillan remembers:

> The land to the left of the road fell steeply down hill but to the right it was level enough for cultivated fields. Suddenly, as we were looking across the field to our right, the German tank fired once, started its engine and took off. The shell exploded about 40 yards away on the downhill slope. Houk fell on his back. I rushed over, took off his helmet, and saw a large hole in the side of his skull from ear to eyebrow. He was dead and it was

a shocking sight! I replaced his helmet and pulled his jump jacket over his head to cover up the mess.

McMillan rushed back to Le Vivier where he reported the incident and recalls, "Later that day we brought in seven bodies that included corpses from both sides, but Johnny Houk was given special treatment." Harold Stedman was involved in similar events and remembers, "Some of us were put on burial detail and picked up dead from both sides. We placed their personal things like dog tags, wallets, rings, and pictures into bags. Many had been there for quite some time so it was a terrible mess."

∞11∞

"Still an American paratrooper"
POWs and counterattacks

T/5 John Gibson

On June 9, after a three-day journey covering nearly 56 miles, John Gibson arrived at the evacuation hospital in Mortain. Gibson recalls:

Previously a Catholic schoolhouse, the place was called Abbaye Blanche. I was told that I'd be working with another airborne medic and Mike Weiden appeared in a doorway. I couldn't believe my eyes and ran over, throwing my arms around him and crying in disbelief. After we had both calmed down, Mike told me he'd been there for a couple of days and had arrived with wounded from St-Côme-du-Mont. A room on the second floor had been set aside for wounded prisoners and we were working under a German medical officer who Mike called "the commandant." He was about 50 years old and handled workloads that would have pushed younger men to their limits. He had a large scar across his face inflicted whilst fencing without head protection [an extreme version of the sport practiced by many Germans and Prussians]. He treated all patients from both sides equally — an attitude that I later learned was not shared by all of his colleagues. A Spanish family lived and worked at the hospital assisted by two local girls. The husband seemed to be a decent man but his family would have nothing to do with me even though I spoke Spanish.

Two urgent cases dealt with by the German doctor were S/Sgt Zol Rosenfield and Pvt Richard Johnn (both G Co), who had been amongst

FROM TOP TO BOTTOM:

This reconnaissance photograph, dated June 12, 1944, shows both the foot and road bridges after the Allies had bombed them on June 7. In the center of the picture is a large crater caused by one of the 500lb bombs. On the far right is a temporary pontoon bridge built by the 238th Combat Engineer Battalion to replace the damaged crossings. (Crown Copyright 1944/MOD, reproduced with permission of the Controller of Her Majesty's Stationery Office – special thanks to the Air Photo Archive at Keele University, Staffordshire)

This picture was taken on June 17 in the Place de la République, St-Côme-du-Mont. It shows a wagon left behind by the retreating Germans, who were still very reliant on horse-drawn vehicles. (Signal Corps via French archive)

FROM TOP TO BOTTOM:

The people of St-Côme-du-Mont spent June 8 in these stables at Lemarchand Farm, well away from the dangers of the shelling. Directly behind the stable block is the old RN13 highway.

On June 8, 1944, around 400 German soldiers withdrew from St-Côme-du-Mont and made their way along the Paris–Cherbourg railway line toward Carentan. The following morning, the Germans destroyed the railway bridge over the river Madeleine. This picture, looking northwest toward St-Côme-du-Mont, was taken several weeks later and shows the damaged bridge. (NARA via John Klein)

An immediately postwar aerial photograph of St-Côme-du-Mont looking north. The route used by the villagers to escape the intense shelling of June 8 took them 800 yards north of the settlement, along the RN13, toward Folleville Farm (seen here top right). (John Gibson)

Following his capture on D-Night 1st Lt Alex Bobuck (left), with help from Dr Stanley Morgan, convinced the Germans he was a member of 3rd Bn's medical detachment. He stayed to help the medics in St-Côme-du-Mont until the village was liberated on June 8. This picture was taken later that afternoon and shows Bobuck reporting for duty at the regimental CP in Angoville. The man on the right is another escapee, 2nd Lt Shrable Williams from Regimental HQ. (John Reeder via Michel De Trez Collection)

Col Bob Sink pictured in the doorway of the Cousin family's farmhouse at Angoville. Sink used the farm as a command post between June 7 and 11. (John Reeder via Mark Bando)

This photograph, taken on February 16, 1946, shows members of St-Côme-du-Mont's town council, including a number of the French civilians mentioned in the narrative. L to R: Msr Judels, Msr Sébire, Mme Clot, Rev Couillard, Robert Judels, Msr Mildrogues, Msr Manquest, Gustave Laurence (Mayor), Msr Sans Refus, Pierre Mauger, Cécile Judels, Msr Le Tual, Msr Dufour, Maurice Hébert, Msr Leprelle, and Théophile Fortin. (Picture and information via Nicole Laurence and Michel Léonard)

FROM TOP TO BOTTOM:

The damage to Carentan railway station caused by shelling from the USS *Texas* on June 8.

The rear courtyard at Folleville Farm. Most of the enlisted men slept in stables on either side of farmhouse, although Ed Shames and Ben Hiner's quarters were in the house with the officers. During the war the stable wall on the right was covered with over two hundred oval metal plaques won by Msr de Folleville, who bred championship bulls.

1st Lt John Reeder (506th regimental communications officer) pictured around June 10 near Col Sink's command post at Angoville. The dead soldier is from the German Fallschirmjäger-Regiment 6 and was killed by naval shelling on June 6/7. (John Reeder)

Sgt Ralph Bennett (front right kneeling) posing with H Co comrades in the Le Ferage bivouac area at St-Côme-du-Mont on June 9. Rear L to R: Sgt Frank Padisak (1 Ptn), Pfc John Purdie (1 Ptn), Sgt Phil Parker (2 Ptn), Pfc Bill Briggs (1 Ptn), unidentified, Pvt Jim Moore (3 Ptn), Cpl Lou Vecchi (1 Ptn), Pvt Bob Wyss (3 Ptn), Pfc Sam "Dud" Hefner (3 Ptn), and 1st Sgt Gordon Bolles. Front kneeling L to R: Cpl Jay Barr (3 Ptn), unidentified, Pvt Richard Wilcox (3 Ptn), Pfc Don Zahn (1 Ptn), Pfc Glenn Sweigart, Pfc Godfrey "Jon" Hanson (1 Ptn), Pfc Spencer Philips (3 Ptn), and Sgt Ralph Bennett (3 Ptn). (Fred Bahlau via Mark Bando)

Le Boujamet Farm, Houesville – G Co bivouac area, June 10–12, 1944. Sgt Harvey Jewett and his 1 Ptn colleagues pose with local farmer Maxime Mousqueron and the Lecheminant children. Rear standing L to R: Pfc Harry Buxton, Pfc Stan Clever, Pfc Eldon Gingerich, Maxime, and Harvey. Front L to R: Paulette, Léon, Jeannine, Michel, and Marcel. (Harvey Jewett via Mark Bando; French information courtesy Mme Paulette Menilgrante (née Lecheminant) and Michel Léonard)

FROM TOP TO BOTTOM:

Le Boujamet Farm, Houesville – G Co bivouac area, June 10–12, 1944. Pfc Eldon Gingerich and Pfc Harry Buxton pose with their .30cal machine gun. In the background is Pvt Stan Clever. (Harvey Jewett via Mark Bando)

Looking northwest along the RN13 toward Houesville. The men in the jeep, members of 1st Lt John Reeder's regimental communication team, are en route to Col Sink's newly established forward command post near Carentan. The building in the background is Folleville Farm, 3rd Bn's command post. (John Reeder via Mark Bando)

A view looking northeast toward Houesville along Route des Fardelles (known as Chemin des Campagnes in 1944). This ancient track skirts the western edge of St-Côme-du-Mont. The German army used it on June 7 when withdrawing from Houesville. On June 12 George McMillan and Johnny Houk were on patrol in the track when a shell fired from a tank hidden in the field on the right killed Houk.

A list of casualties kept secretly by Cpl John Gibson during his imprisonment at the German evacuation hospital at Mortain. It reads:

Talford Wynne – KIA France, FALSE [annotation added on return to UK]*, Girlfriend Rosland Sewell, 270 9th St, N. E. Atlanta.*

Charles K Louis [actually spelt Lewis] *– I received ID, died June 6th in a German hospital near the front in France 1944.*

Pvt Law – Last seen in hospital and not at all well – was shot in chest.

Henry Loebe – shot twice in R lung and once in the abdomen near edge. Evacuated from Mortain hospital about June 11th '44 – Para Eng.

Stanley H Job – T/5 36650874, died in France. Mother Joanna Maresch, wife to be – Miss Dora L. Parenitie 2222 W23rd Pl Chicago (8) and Mother's address 2458 S. California Ave, he passed away 19th July 19, 1944, at 4am in a hospital at Mortain, France. Buried at 8pm 20th July. Placed among French soldiers who were buried in 1940.

James William Kennedy – Templeton, Pa, died July 21st AM in Mortain, France. Mother – Mrs Frank Kennedy, Templeton Pa? Info was in wallet. On litter under person was a pay book with two receipts and the following name – Pvt John B. Bukewski, ASN 32959416, APO 15328 Wife – Mrs Jeanette Bukewski, Wilmington, Del?? (John Gibson)

"Bloody Gully" as it looks today. The picture was taken at its southern end in an area occupied by I Co during June of 1944.

People of Carentan hang out the Stars and Stripes in the Place de la République to celebrate the town's liberation. (Imperial War Museum)

This monument at La Croix de Méautis is inscribed "CREDO 13TH JUIN 1944" (a prayer for June 13). The memorial is located at the southern end of "Bloody Gully" and was erected shortly after the war by local farmer Msr Baudouin. The Capet Cross, as it has become known, is a memorial to all those who lost their lives in this area during June 1944.

the wounded evacuated from St-Côme-du-Mont on D-Day. Johnn's leg was in bad shape and had to be amputated.

On the 10th two prisoners were brought in with severe gunshot wounds. One was an airborne engineer called Henry Loebe, who had been shot twice in the right lung and once in the abdomen, and the other was Pvt Law. Both were in a critical condition and needed immediate specialist care. An ambulance arrived the following day and moved a number of the patients including Rosenfield, Johnn, and the two new arrivals. "I stayed behind but Mike Weiden and one of our orderlies traveled with the wounded to Stalag 221," remembers Gibson. "Johnn was lying on a stretcher in the hallway and the French girls wished him luck and kissed him on the cheek. As he was leaving Henry Loebe grabbed my arm and said, 'If I ever get out of this alive, I'll owe my life to you buddy... see you later,' and waved goodbye."

Two weeks after Weiden's departure for Rennes, the number of patients at Mortain had risen to 42. They varied in rank from colonel to private and came from various Allied divisions. The American orderly working with Gibson treated the wounded with indifference and left much of the patient care to John. Gibson remembers:

Although I was a prisoner it did not alter the fact that I was still an American paratrooper. I cherished my role and was always presentable. Once a week a French girl working at the hospital took my uniform home where she washed and pressed it. One person who objected to this was the heavily built German head chef who ran the kitchen. Sly and disagreeable, he hated all Americans and went out of his way to make life difficult for me. However, his English-speaking assistant, who had worked as a butler in New York before the war, was the total opposite, but could not protect me from the daily harassment dished out by his boss.

One day a wounded soldier arrived and as soon as I'd got him to the ward he told me he had a grenade hidden under his clothing. He also said that he had a large quantity of money that he'd taken from a payroll truck. At first I thought he was hallucinating but it turned out to be true. All the notes were French francs and we weren't sure if they were legal tender. I managed to persuade him to give me the grenade and I hid it in my room. My orderly had suddenly decided to take an interest in what was happening and was surprised when the wounded GI offered to split the stolen money with us. I kept my notes in a money belt, which I never took off, that I'd made from an old jacket.

Beds and stretchers were in short supply and some of the wounded were lying on straw that had been spread on the floor. Despite the shortage of space, the German commandant allowed Gibson and his orderly to keep their own private room and seemed unaware that Weiden's bed was still there and unoccupied. However, it was not long before an inquisitive German medic discovered the spare bed and made the two Americans share their room with an injured German who was unconscious.

Gibson treated the soldier's injuries and after a while he began to regain consciousness and started to look around the room. He recalls:

> The patient began to focus on me. I could see a look of shock on his face when he realized I was wearing an American uniform. He began to shout and swear deliriously before pushing me aside and staggering out of the room. I followed him into the corridor and watched him lurch from side to side as he disappeared down the passageway.

Summer arrived with a vengeance and the heat encouraged flies. Bandages and medicines were in short supply, but the resulting maggots did the medics a favor by helping to clean festering wounds.

By the beginning of July the Allies had total air superiority. Most of the French rail network had been damaged or destroyed, and the Germans were only able to move safely by night. Ambulances were continually arriving at Mortain but, despite the fact that they were all clearly marked with red crosses, some had been strafed by Allied aircraft and Gibson was often dragged outside to look at the damaged vehicles. Despite these problems he still managed to make friends with one or two of the ambulance crews. He recalls:

Argus, who spoke fluent English, would always look for me when he arrived. Another guy was a Russian but he was unlike the men I'd encountered earlier in Normandy. He would often talk to me while his ambulance was being unloaded. We would discuss politics and I asked what he thought Joseph Stalin would do with men like him when the war was over. He knew it wouldn't be good and thought there was little hope of him ever finding his wife and five children. I also encountered some Poles who told me they'd volunteered from prison camps with the promise of new uniforms, good food, good pay, and an assurance that they would never have to fight for Germany.

As the tide of war turned in the Allies' favor, the attitudes of some German soldiers began to harden and Gibson felt more vulnerable than ever. One morning he heard a screeching of tires outside. Looking down into the courtyard from his bedroom window he saw a high-ranking immaculately dressed German officer getting out of a two-seat black convertible. The officer looked up and on seeing Gibson's American uniform flew into a rage. He then began shouting and paced furiously back and forth shaking his fist at the bewildered medic. Gibson moved away from the window just as the officer stormed into the building via the kitchen. Fearful for his safety, he grabbed the grenade he had hidden earlier and waited. Half an hour went by and nothing happened. Then, much to his relief, he saw the officer drive away.

Incidents like this started to occur more regularly as German soldiers, en route to the front, stopped for food at the hospital kitchen. The head chef often sent soldiers up to the second floor, where they shouted at Gibson and stared at the Allied wounded, stirring up a lot of anger. John knew exactly what the chef was trying to do and recalls, "Hitler's propaganda machine spread rumors that American airborne soldiers were ex-convicts and murderers. I think that's why human feces was thrown at American prisoners as they were marched through Paris."

Between July 19 and 21 two Americans died in the hospital. These were the first deaths Gibson had to deal with and he recalls:

Just before dark on July 18, T/5 Stanley Job arrived from the front. We carried him up the four flights of stairs to the ward where he crawled onto a cot. Early the next morning he began foaming at the mouth. We tried to help but nothing could be done to save him. The town's priest administered the last rites just before he died. Afterwards I went through Job's pockets and found letters from his fiancée and mother. The commandant gave me permission to bury him in the town's cemetery and the priest made the arrangements. Stanley Job was buried on July 20, 1944, amongst French soldiers killed in 1940.

The next day we lost another guy – James William Kennedy. I found an old scrap of paper and made a note of the names of the men who'd passed away and hid it in my money belt. I eventually handed everything over to US intelligence in London in the hope that the bodies would be recovered and receive a proper military burial.

On July 27, Allied troops broke out from Normandy and the front line moved closer to Mortain. Gen George Patton's 3rd Army began to threaten the town and the Germans decided to evacuate the hospital. Under the cover of darkness, Gibson and the wounded were driven nearly 47 miles to Stalag 221 at Rennes, where they were reunited with Mike Weiden.

The prison hospital was heavily guarded and ringed with barbed wire. Weiden was at his wits' end trying to cope with all the problems facing him. The conditions within the hospital were deplorable. The Germans were no longer able to supply the hospital and food was scarce. The only medical supplies left were crepe bandages and an antiseptic tincture called Mercurochrome. There was no gauze, tape, aspirin, sulfa powder, or proper sanitation – it was a "hell hole." Gibson was shocked by the condition of some of the wounded. He had thought Mortain was bad, but this was far worse.

I asked Mike Weiden how Henry Loebe was doing and was saddened to learn that he'd died soon after arriving at Rennes. Mike gave me the job of looking after 14 seriously wounded in a room on the main floor. One of the first men I recognized was Zol Rosenfield who looked like a skeleton, as did most of the wounded. If someone needed clean gauze then we had to boil out the pus and scabs before we could reuse the dressings. There seemed to be a lot of people milling around but only a few were actually doing anything. I asked for extra help but none was forthcoming, so I carried on the best I could.

As the Allies closed in on the city of Rennes, so the hospital came under heavy shellfire. Plaster was falling from the ceilings and Gibson told all the patients to get under their beds. An American got permission from the Germans to go outside in an attempt to stop the shelling. He tied a white bed sheet to a broom handle and walked out into the street waving the makeshift flag. It was a very brave thing to do, and had precisely the right result as no other shells were targeted on the building.

It wasn't long before the few remaining Germans took off, leaving two Polish soldiers to guard us. I had only been at Rennes for a week but it seemed much longer. As soon as the Germans left, the Polish soldiers unloaded their rifles and handed them over to us. On August 4 Gen Patton's 3rd Army liberated Rennes, which was an incredible day full of joy and happiness.

Next began the task of evacuating the hospital's 574 American, British, and Canadian patients to Britain. The process took three days and 3rd Army threw every resource it had at the problem, helping to make the evacuation run smoothly.

Gibson and Weiden were told that they were going to be reassigned to another outfit in France and both asked if they could return to 3rd Bn 506th. Unfortunately their request was denied and a couple of days later they were sent to a marshaling area in Cherbourg and were split up.

After experiencing a couple of weeks of very wet weather, and seemingly no nearer returning to Britain, Gibson was becoming impatient with his predicament:

Everything I possessed was wet through. It was miserable, I had a terrible dose of flu, couldn't bear the situation any longer and threatened to climb the fence and go AWOL. The officer in charge took a dim view of this and threatened to have me arrested if I persisted with my insubordination! I reminded him that they had made no attempt to repatriate me and it was now mid-August. A huge argument ensued and the officer stormed off. I thought that I'd blown it but the guy came back around 4pm and told me to stay put, not to do anything stupid and be ready the following morning to move out. Before dawn the next day he returned with a jeep and took me to a small airfield. There I was loaded into a Piper Cub belonging to a one-star general and then flown to London. On arrival I was told to report to the US intelligence service for a debriefing. When I handed over my casualty list I was delighted to discover that Talford Wynne was alive and well!

Gibson had thought that Wynne had been killed on D-Day. There was another surprise in store for him. The French francs he had been given at Mortain were legal tender and worth $266, almost three months' wages!

Pvt Ray Calandrella

The Hôtellerie Notre-Dame at Troisgots (Starvation Hill) had become overcrowded, and plans were being drawn up to move some of the prisoners west to Brittany. "I had only been there for a few days before they sent some of us to Rennes by truck," remembers "Doc" Dwyer. Several of his colleagues, including Marty Clark, Joe Mielcarek, and Clarence Kelley, stayed behind. It would be three months before he saw any of them again.

The Germans had turned an old French garrison in Rennes into a prison and called it Stalag 221. Ray Calandrella arrived there sometime around June 10 or 11 and was made to work in the prison hospital, which was a mile or so from the main camp. Initially conditions were good, but after six weeks medical supplies began to run out and the health of the patients deteriorated as a result. Calandrella recalls:

Part of the prison was home to some French Moroccan POWs who'd been captured in 1940. We found out later that they had led a fairly normal life – the Germans even let them go into town! We were separated from the Moroccans by a high fence but this didn't stop them throwing shoes to people like me who had nothing to wear on their feet. We were kept at the prison for about a month. Several of us started to dig a tunnel and we asked an officer from the 82nd if he'd like to join us. He refused, saying there might be reprisal killings for escaped POWs. We all felt he was using this as an excuse not to put himself at risk.

The tunnel was never finished. On July 5 all the healthy prisoners (700 in total) were bundled into "forty and eight" boxcars. (This was a term originating from World War I that was used to describe railway wagons that could carry either 40 men or eight horses). They then began an epic 23-day rail journey to a transit camp 326 miles east at Châlons-sur-Marne in the Champagne region of France.

Although every available rail network was utilized, delays were inevitable. The tracks were in continual need of repair due to the damage received from Allied bombing. Many people saw these "hold ups" as a chance to escape. For Doc Dwyer and Joe Gorenc, the opportunity finally came on July 20, deep in the French interior in the Indre-et-Loire region.

The two men jumped from their train near the town of Loches (28 miles south of Tours) and swam the river Loire to make their escape, as Doc Dwyer recalls. "We hooked up and fought with the FFI [Forces Françaises de l'Intérieur or Maquis] for a couple of weeks before making it back to American lines. We were taken for interrogation to Paris, which was still very unstable as the city had only just been liberated. Once the US intelligence service had finished with us we were flown to London and arrived back in Ramsbury just in time to start preparing for Holland."

Meanwhile, back on the train SS guards were brought in to carry out spot checks and make head counts. "They didn't mess about and the escapes soon stopped for genuine fear of reprisals," recalls Ray Calandrella. "We were always hungry, sometimes going two or three days without eating, and when we did get fed it was just barley soup or bread."

The men arrived at Châlons (62 miles east of Paris) on July 28 and within a couple of weeks Ray Calandrella had started to plan his escape, as he describes:

> The POW block had been an old four-storey French cavalry barracks with a large walled courtyard. We occupied the lower half of the building and security was a little slack at times. I found I could usually move around the upper floors without challenge. These were unused and acted mainly as a store for spare beds and mattresses. On one of my covert trips I noticed a loft hatch on the top floor. Because the ceilings were so high the Germans had not considered this as a possible means of escape. I thought that if I could get up into the roof then I might be able to hide, but I couldn't do it alone.

When a second group of prisoners arrived from Paris, Calandrella noticed Jack Brown amongst them. Ray never mentioned his plan to Jack because he had already selected another soldier as his accomplice. Ray had got to know Elmer Draver (29th Infantry Division) during the long train journey to Châlons. He remembers:

> Elmer was from Chicago. He was tall (6ft 4in), a non-smoker, and seemed the perfect partner. We saved our meager rations and acquired some extra blankets. Early one morning around the third week we slipped up to the fourth floor before roll call. Turning one of the old bed frames on end, I held it steady as Elmer used it to climb up into the roof. I tied our supplies onto a rope fashioned from knotted blankets and Elmer hauled them up and shut the hatch.
>
> I went back to bed and after reveille turned out into the courtyard as usual for roll call. When the Germans discovered that Draver was missing they immediately organized a search party and selected prisoners to bolster their teams. Although I was not chosen I took my chance and fell out with the other guys. I ran straight to the top floor and stood by a window near the loft. Someone came rushing up the stairs and into the room. "It's clear," I told him, "there's nothing to be found, I've just checked." Following him downstairs, I rejoined the parade where reports confirmed the barracks were empty.

The Germans came to the natural conclusion that Draver had escaped and dismissed the parade.

Two days later (August 23), Ray returned to the fourth floor, where Draver hauled him up into the loft. A small gap in the roof allowed the two fugitives a limited view of the courtyard where they could see the prisoners preparing for roll call. Calandrella recounts:

There was a lot of shouting and I knew that I'd been marked as missing. Although the Germans searched the building, they still failed to figure out where we had gone. The search was dropped and we soon found out why. Much to our surprise that same afternoon the prisoners were paraded again. We looked down in disbelief as they were marched out of the front gate and disappeared down the road. Later we learned that they were being moved to Germany because the Allies were almost on our doorstep.

A day or so later a couple of German tanks arrived and parked in the courtyard. There was a platoon of soldiers with them but they never entered the building. We remained hidden for nearly a week, and on our last day a shell hit the roof and exploded in a brilliant flash. Luckily, we were not hurt. That night we climbed down and hid under mattresses on the third floor. Early the next morning we returned to the loft and found the roof had been hit again by another shell, which exploded exactly where we would have been sleeping! As we were examining the damage church bells began ringing. Looking down into the courtyard we noticed the Germans had gone. Scrambling over to the other side of the roof we saw a column of Allied vehicles from the 4th Armored Division coming down the road... it was Tuesday August 29.

The Germans had left the gates wide open and the French were gathering in the courtyard. We came down from the loft and ran outside. It didn't seem to matter to the locals that we were bearded, unwashed and lousy. They proceeded to hug and kiss us like crazy and we were swept away on a tide of emotion. Some of the 4th Division's MPs saw what was going on and came to our rescue. After a brief interrogation we were moved to a field hospital at Orleans, where we got cleaned up and issued new uniforms.

On September 1, Calandrella and Draver were flown back to England to the very place where Ray had started his mission almost three months earlier – USAAF Station 463, Exeter. This was now the location of Field Hospital 101. Calandrella remembers:

> The following day I was passing the wards on my way to the PX, when one of the orderlies shouted, "Hey Mac, someone in here wants to see you!" "You must be mistaken," I replied, but the medic wouldn't take no for an answer and ushered me inside the tent. I couldn't believe my eyes, for lying on a bed was Zolman Rosenfield. Zol had been here for nearly a month and had started to regain a lot of the weight that he'd lost. A couple of weeks later Elmer Draver took the ZI [Zone of the Interior] option, which meant he had a guaranteed ticket home.
>
> I was sent to Eisenhower's HQ in London for a formal debrief but wasn't sure exactly where to go. So I just wandered around until I found myself outside his office door. A passing officer asked what I was doing and then whisked me away to be interviewed. Once the interview had finished a sergeant took me to a railway station and sent me to the 10th Replacement Depot near Nottingham. I was there for nearly a week and met up with a guy called Ernie Jackson who was being posted to the 3rd Bn as a replacement.

Around September 19 he eventually returned to Camp Ramsbury, where he met 2nd Lt John Williams.

Most of the battalion had been deployed to Holland, leaving Williams and a few others behind as rear echelon. The camp was officially closed and Calandrella was given quarters near Hungerford. He recalls:

> Things had clearly changed since Normandy. There were two 15-year-old girls living in the block. Before taking my seven-day furlough I spoke with Williams about the girls and they were gone by the time I returned.
>
> When I eventually rejoined the unit in Holland I immediately told Jim Brown that his brother was alive and most likely somewhere in Germany.

Sadly, Jim never lived long enough to see Jack, as he was killed on January 13, 1945, during I Co's entry into the village of Foy, Belgium.

Pvt David Morgan

For those that remained behind at Starvation Hill, it was a different story. Dave Morgan had been held at the camp for nearly two weeks and during this period Jack Brown had managed to escape by going over the wall. However, by the middle of June the remaining prisoners had been moved to Alençon. Morgan recalls:

> The journey took three or four days. Every time we passed through a French village the people tried to give us bread but the guards wouldn't allow us to take it. One night the Germans gave us four rotting ox heads that were turning green and stank. We buried them and went hungry.
>
> When we arrived at Alençon the first person I saw was Jack Brown; he'd been recaptured. The Germans had taken his boots and replaced them with wooden shoes. The prison camp was an old coal warehouse run by a British NCO who was ramrod straight: the kind you see in the movies. He would wake us in the morning and make everyone stand formation. The Englishman wasn't there for very long before the Germans moved him on. After he went everything seemed to fall apart. Some of us were made to sweep the streets while Jack Brown, Bill Harrington (I Co), and myself worked in the local hospital.

During early August the prisoners were moved to Paris and about 80 of them were forced to march through the streets of the city. Luckily Dave Morgan, Bill Harrington, and Jack Brown were spared the humiliation but men like Joe Beyrle, Jim Sheeran, and Bernie Rainwater were not so fortunate. Afterwards the prisoners were herded into "forty and eight" boxcars. Their destination was Châlons-sur-Marne.

Most of the travel was by night and there were numerous stops. On one occasion the train halted beside a beetroot patch. "The men who chose to eat the crop were shitting red for days, much to the amusement of the Germans," remembers Morgan.

As already mentioned, I Co's Pfc Jimmy Sheeran from New Jersey was amongst the group. He had been captured on D-Day along with Cpl John Simson, who had been shot in the hand and had to have his forearm amputated. Sheeran could speak fluent French and as the train passed Château Thierry, Sheeran, Pvt Bernie Rainwater, and several other men jumped. Jim and Bernie made it to the town where Jim's father had met his mother during World War I. He then successfully located his family, who hid the pair until the town was liberated.

The remainder of the prisoners arrived at Châlons around August 15. On the 23rd they were moved again, this time to Germany, where most remained for the duration of the war.

Carentan/Méautis and the German counterattack June 12–13

On Sunday June 11, the German Fallschirmjäger-Regiment 6 withdrew from Carentan and took up new positions southwest of the town, but it was far from beaten. The troops had been joined by the newly arrived 17.SS-Panzergrenadier-Division "Götz von Berlichingen" and were planning to break through the American lines and recapture St-Côme-du-Mont, thus driving a wedge between Carentan and Ste-Mère-Église and forcing the 101st Airborne back to the beaches.

The following day, 101st Divisional HQ ordered Col Sink to set up defensive positions west of Carentan, and he moved 1st and 2nd battalions into that area. At around 1400hrs a German counterattack began, and 1st Bn 506th ran into heavy mortar fire near the tiny hamlet of Douville (now called Donville). The intense shelling cut them off from 2nd Bn, who were on their right, and also opened up a large gap on their southern flank. Luckily the attack was successfully repulsed. Shortly after this incident Sink decided to go on the offensive and brought in 3rd Bn 506th from reserve in readiness for a regimental attack, which was planned for 0500hrs the following day.

By early evening 3rd Bn had been relieved by 2nd Bn 502nd and its 200 remaining men gathered in St-Côme-du-Mont's main square. "As we were waiting for transport I felt a tap on my shoulder," recalls Ed

Shames. "It was Joe Madona. 'Happy birthday,' he said, 'How are things? I'm sure glad you made it, buddy boy.' 'Thanks for the sentiment, Shorty, but my 22nd isn't until tomorrow.' 'I know that,' he laughed, 'but I doubt we'll be around then... so happy birthday.' We were still joking as the vehicles arrived to take us into Carentan."

Ralph Bennett approached one of the vehicles and asked its driver where he could find spare ammunition. "He said there wasn't any," remembers Bennett, "and then started bitching about how heavy the .45cal clips were for his Thompson submachine gun! I was down to my last 15 rounds and about to go into battle! 'If it's such a problem I'll take some from you,' I said, trying not to sound too desperate. The idiot gave me two clips and thanked me for helping him out! At that moment I would have given anything for a few extra rounds!"

At 2300hrs the battalion was dropped off near the northern outskirts of Carentan (which was still burning, following 24 hours of relentless bombardment) and continued its journey by foot. The men had been trained to freeze when the enemy fired flares into the sky, but because of the urgency of the situation the battalion was ordered to keep moving, and it pressed on toward the front line through dense smoke that was drifting across the town. "The men were bunching," remembers Bill Galbraith. "A circling German aircraft saw us silhouetted against the flames and dropped several bombs. I don't think anyone was hit but it scared us and we cleared the street."

The battalion was told to wait in a field close to Col Sink's command post. The men were still desperately short of ammunition and were angered to learn that there would be no resupply. "We only had two 60mm mortar rounds," recalls Ralph Bennett, "I sent my riflemen away to scrounge for what they could, but all returned empty handed." Bill Galbraith had 750 rounds for his machine gun while Jim McCann had just one rocket for his bazooka.

Meanwhile, Col Sink had ordered his company commanders to report to his command post. "At around 2330hrs Capt Shettle told Gordon Bolles and myself to attend a briefing," recalls Ed Shames. Also present were commanders from the 501st PIR plus the 65th and

397th Artillery regiments (who would have observers attached to each 506th battalion). Intelligence sources had discovered that the 17.SS-Panzergrenadier-Division had deployed two regiments (six battalions) plus tanks from the 6.Panzer-Division in the area. Allied tanks from the 2nd Armored Division were being offloaded at the beachhead but were not expected to arrive until early the following morning (the 13th). However, nine M5 light tanks (from D Co 70th Tank Battalion) each armed with a 37mm cannon were present and had been attached to the regiment. Following an artillery barrage, which was intended to neutralize enemy positions, the attack was to begin at first light. "The battalion didn't seem to know what to do with me at this point," remembers Ed Shames. "Someone, perhaps Capt Harwick, decided I should be paired up with a radio operator and attached to H Co. My orders were to keep Battalion and Regiment appraised of the situation on our right-hand flank." The briefing broke up at around 0200hrs and a number of men, including most of 3rd Bn's company commanders, set off to establish contact with 1st Bn and make plans for the attack. G Co's commander, 1st Lt Joe Doughty, recalls:

> It was dark and misty as we walked down the road [RN803, now D223] toward where we thought 1st Bn 506th might be located. A motorcycle dispatch rider appeared out of the mist and rode slowly past me, heading toward Carentan. We stopped the man and asked how far ahead 1st Bn was. As he jumped off his machine we were amazed to discover that he was a German. We decided to abort the mission and return to Carentan with our prisoner – we never did find those 1st Bn positions.

When all the company commanders had returned, it was decided that moving across country would be far safer than using the road. "1st Lt Kiley briefed us on our order of 'march' and objectives," recalls Bill Galbraith, "He told us that 2nd Bn would be on our right flank and the 501st beyond a road to our left."

"Orders came down the line to move out in company order and advance to contact," remembers Ralph Bennett. The rifle companies moved forward in columns echeloned to the right, and G Co headed the advance. The "start line" was about 1,400 yards away on high ground east of a sunken drover's road that would soon become known as "Bloody Gully." "Leading the advance was a huge responsibility that I didn't feel totally comfortable with," remembers Joe Doughty.

The gully was 1¼ miles long and on average 15ft wide and 9ft deep. It was lined on each side by high hedges and stretched northeastward from La Croix de Méautis in the south to the Carteret–Carentan railway line. The RN803 road dissected the gully at about its midway point. All that remains today (2008) is an 875-yard section between La Croix de Méautis and the D223, which was 3rd Bn's area of operations on June 13, 1944. The northern part (held by 2nd Bn 506th) was destroyed when American units constructed the Carentan ring road (D971) in July 1944. To this day it is still called "the American road."

"As dawn broke we followed a hedgerow and moved into fields on our right," recalls Bobbie Rommel. "Within minutes my legs were soaked with heavy dew from the long grass." Several platoons lost contact with each other after encountering the thick hedgerows, and a number of squads were late getting to the start line. Among those was G Co's 1 Ptn, commanded by 2nd Lt Tom Kennedy. "I goofed up and lost touch with my company and the rest of the battalion. By the time we got to the gully, the battle was already well under way."

West of the gully the land rises to a height of about 80ft, and this feature gave the enemy a tactical advantage over the 506th. The 3rd Bn's area was, and still is, divided into three fields surrounded by thick hedgerows. For the purpose of this book we have numbered them 1 through to 3, with the battalion's left or southern flank being field number 3 (see map on page 226).

To escape the fighting in Carentan, many civilians had moved out into the countryside. Nearly 100 people had taken refuge at La Maison Neuve and a further 59 at Baudouin Farm. Now the civilians found themselves caught up in another battle as the Germans began commandeering some of the larger houses.

The enemy's plan was to advance on its left flank along the Carteret–Carentan railway line and then break through the American positions and head for the northern outskirts of Carentan. Artillery and assault gun batteries supported the attack. The troops of the Fallschirmjäger-Regiment 6 and 17.SS-Panzergrenadier-Division were well trained and highly disciplined, unlike some of the enemy soldiers the 101st Airborne Division had encountered previously.

~ 12 ~

"I ain't dead yet"

The battle of Bloody Gully,
June 13, 1944

By first light, Cpl Bobbie Rommel and his gun team were in position on high ground 220 yards west of the gully. Their orders were to provide covering fire for the battalion and they set up their machine gun beside a hedge that bordered the RN803. "One of the guys thought he saw movement in the hedge up ahead of us," remembers Rommel. "We fired a short burst and a figure jumped down onto the road and took off." Moments later M5 light reconnaissance tanks from the 70th Tank Battalion arrived (in support of 2nd Bn 506th) and mistook Rommel's group for the enemy, as he recalls. "The tanks were moving along the road and we could see their turrets above the hedge. The lead tank fired its heavy machine gun and a couple of the guys behind me were hit. I then moved everybody into the cover of a nearby hollow. To make matters worse, we were also being targeted by some of our guys in the gully. Then we heard the whistle of our own incoming artillery."

Because of the shortage of ammunition, the opening barrage did not last too long. About 12 rounds landed short of the gully, showering the battalion with dirt, branches, and leaves. Unfortunately Rommel's team was in an exposed position. "As the shells exploded behind us I watched a piece of shrapnel come tumbling toward me," he recalls. "The red hot chunk of metal bounced off my hand without leaving a mark!" Pvt Darvin Lee and Pfc John Hermansky were not so lucky. A small fragment of shrapnel hit Lee in the corner of his left eye while another larger piece smashed through Hermansky's helmet and into his temple. Rommel and his men then made their way to the relative safety of the gully, carrying their wounded with them. "Sgt 'Chuck' Easter managed to get a stretcher from the medics," recalls Rommel, "and we carried one of the more seriously wounded guys down the road to the aid station."

G and I companies had been deployed on the battalion's left flank in fields 2 and 3. However, Bill Galbraith and Jim Brown had been assigned to H Co, whose orders were to attack along the right flank in field 1. Three of the M5 tanks remained and moved along the road, giving H Co support. 1st Lt Dick Meason and his HQ group had orders to move forward independently on the left side of the same field.

1st Lt Ken Christianson was leading the main H Co attack. Ed Shames and his radio operator followed him out of the gully and started

3rd Bn 506th at Bloody Gully, June 13, 1944

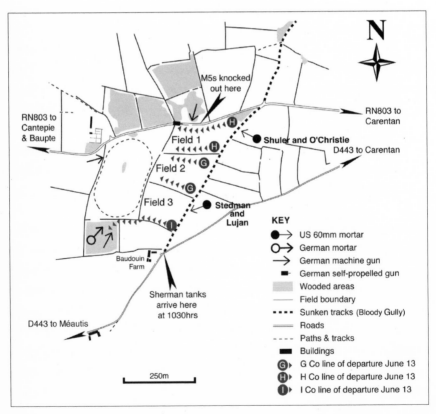

moving along a hedgerow. "I looked over the road to the field on my right where F Co should have been and realized they weren't there. They were supposed to be protecting 2nd Bn's left flank and I just thought they were late getting into position."

Field 1 sloped upward, and as H Co's scouts reached its crest the enemy opened up with a ferocious mortar and artillery barrage that continued, on and off, for the best part of 2 hours. The men split up and dropped to the ground. Bill Galbraith was separated from Jim Brown. "Jim managed to drag our gun and tripod into a hedgerow up ahead," he remembers. "A machine gun was trained to fire through a gate opening just in front of me, and had us all pinned down." The gun had been set up on the northern side of the road and its murderous fire split H Co in two, preventing all forward movement.

Ed Shames recalls:

> Over to my left Lonnie Gavrock was hit by machine gun fire and fell to the ground, [Gavrock was from I Co but had been temporarily attached to H Co as a scout]. He'd been hit in the chest and was unconscious by the time I reached him. The bullet had left an enormous exit hole in his back. I thought he was dying and called for a medic. I then made my way back to the hedge line and as I did so the same machine gun began to target me. Peering through the hedge I looked to see if F Co had arrived, but nobody was there – 2nd Bn's left flank was totally exposed.

After encountering a number of German self-propelled guns (SPGs), F Co had been forced to withdraw, jeopardizing 2nd Bn's advance.

Ralph Bennett was about 25 yards from the western boundary of the field and recollects, "The rest of my guys were back down the hedgerow on the eastern side of the gate through which the German machine gun was firing." Bullets then began flying diagonally across the field into Dick Meason's group. They immediately returned fire but soon realized they were endangering Christianson's men and stopped. Ralph Bennett recalls:

Ken Christianson, Clark Heggeness, "Mac" McCullough, and Leo Lecuyer all made it into the hedgerow ahead of me. I could see Christianson urgently motioning me to join him. I was wondering what to do next when an enemy machine gun opened up on them. At that precise moment a German SPG came lumbering along the road from Douville and stopped directly opposite me. The chassis took up the whole width of the road and it was the first time I'd seen a gun of this size close up!

The German vehicle was a Stug Sturmgeschütz 40 armed with a powerful 75mm gun. Heading toward the SPG, but unaware of its presence due to a bend in the road, were the three M5 tanks supporting H Co's advance. Ed Shames remembers:

> As the tanks came up beside me, I rose to my feet and trotted alongside, using them as a shield from the German machine gun fire. I was trying to locate F Co and had been shadowing the tanks for about 20 seconds. Suddenly a couple of 75mm rounds went through the lead vehicle and into the tank directly behind it. The shots had been fired at point blank range and the lightly armored M5s didn't stand a chance. The explosions were terrific and a blast of searing heat threw me to the ground, scorching my face and eyebrows. The third tank started backing out and as it did so I picked myself up and ran. My clothes were smoldering and my ears ringing but other than that I was OK. As I made my way back to where I'd left my radio operator I thought about what "Shorty" Madona had said back in St-Côme... and realized I'd been very lucky.

The muzzle blast from the German SPG was terrific and it shook Ralph Bennett to the core. "Cautiously the SPG reversed away from the action," remembers Ralph. "Then I spotted a Kraut machine gun team trying to set up in a hedge across the road to my right. I could see that together with the other gun they were going to try and bracket us with interlocking fire." Bill Galbraith was watching the same activity through a small hole in the hedge and recalls:

The Germans stopped firing and sent a couple of guys forward to where the tanks were burning in an attempt to outflank us. I could see another group of Germans gathering and fired my sniper rifle, hitting one of them. I tried to squeeze off another shot but the trigger wouldn't work. In all the excitement I'd forgotten that the rifle was bolt action and I hadn't reloaded. Machine-gun fire started pouring across the road and I tried to throw a grenade over the hedge toward it. Unfortunately my arm got caught up in an equipment strap and the grenade fell to the ground. It rolled a few yards in front of me before exploding – luckily nobody got hurt.

Shortly afterwards, Ed Shames dashed past Galbraith and got straight on the radio to Battalion.

I told them that there was nobody on the right flank. The response was, "Are you sure? This is serious – you'd better speak to Regiment." After a nailbiting few moments I got through and Maj Hannah answered. "We've got a problem," I said, "There's no one on our right flank – repeat NO ONE." Hannah was astonished and replied, "Are you kidding me... who in the hell did you say you were?" Once I'd explained, Hannah told me to sit tight and wait for Col Sink to call. Within 10 seconds my phone rang, "Sink here... Shames, do you know what the hell you are talking about?" "Yes, sir," I replied. He then said, "Get your ass back to my forward CP [command post] and give me a situation report – NOW."

The Kraut machine gun started up again at an increased rate of fire. The noise was overwhelming. I slapped the radio guy on the shoulder and shouted in his ear, "Don't go away, stay here." I forced my way through the hedge and dropped down onto the road. Smoke was pouring from the knocked-out tanks and I thought I was safe from the machine gun. I was wrong and stepped directly into its line of fire. The asphalt seemed to come alive as bullets peppered the surface. I started to run, zigzagging my way out of the killing zone and sprinted down the road to Col Sink's CP. The first thing the colonel said was, "Shames, do you know what the hell you are talking about, boy?" I couldn't believe it. "Yes, sir," I replied.

Sink responded "Show me on the map." Col Charlie Chase, the regimental XO, looked on as I began to point out the problem areas, doing my best to convince both men that the situation on 2nd Bn's left flank was desperate. "We are wide open and taking extremely heavy fire from the northern side of the road, sir," I said. "Are you sure?" Sink responded. "Yes, sir," I replied again. Finally Sink said "OK, Charlie, get up there with Shames and give a full situation report."

The pair quickly set off and ran back along the RN803. Ed continues:

I told Chase how dangerous this was but he ignored me. On the way he kept saying, "Where's Harwick, where's Harwick?" Of course I didn't know but it made me think that there was more to this mission than just a situation report on the right flank. Much to my surprise my radio operator was still waiting in the same place that I'd left him. He was very scared and became quite emotional when he saw us. Col Chase got straight on the radio to Sink and said, "Shames is right, there's nobody on the right flank. Get any unit you can up here quickly to fill the gap." He then went back down the hedge line and disappeared into the gully.

Without doubt Ed Shames's quick thinking had changed the outcome of the battle. About an hour or so later (roughly 1030hrs) Sink had placed 2nd Bn 502nd in the gap on 3rd Bn's right flank and ordered in antitank guns and air support.

Earlier that morning, in Carentan, BrigGen Maurice Rose (2nd Armored Division's commander) and Gen Taylor had worked out a plan of attack using Rose's tanks and airborne infantry reserves. Starting at 1400hrs this new force, supported by heavy artillery, was sent in to relieve the 506th.

Meanwhile the German machine gun on the northern side of the road in field 1 briefly stopped firing. Bill Galbraith broke cover and dashed forward toward the hedge where Jim Brown had set up their gun. As he slammed into the ground, he noticed two wounded men to his right and quickly discovered they were Ken Christianson and Leo Lecuyer. Galbraith recalls:

> Both had been shot by the other enemy machine gun some 250 yards away. As Jim Brown engaged the enemy gun I moved along the hedge to see if I could help the wounded. Christianson had been hit in the shoulder and Lecuyer was in very bad shape. I was applying a field dressing when a bullet hit Lecuyer's body, tearing him out of my arms and killing him. I then turned my attention to Lt Christianson and doctored him up. As he crawled away I prayed that he'd make it back to our medical aid station in one piece. Before he left I took his .45cal automatic as I knew he wouldn't be needing it where he was going.

Then, a small group of soldiers from 1st Bn approached Galbraith and Brown from the right flank. Galbraith continues:

> Jim Brown opened fire thinking they were Krauts in American uniforms trying to come through our position. We were expecting the enemy from this direction – not our own troops. Thankfully the burst went wide. We learned that they had been stuck in a kind of No Man's Land and during a lull in the firing pulled back. As they left, one of them turned around and shouted, "You damned near killed us back there, you sons of bitches!"

The struggle to advance had been just as difficult for G Co in field 2, as Jimmy Martin recalls:

> Due to a lack of ammunition we didn't deploy our 60mm mortars. Before moving forward we were ordered to fix bayonets and had just started to bridge the slope of the field when the intense shelling started. Most of 2 Ptn was in the center of the field but quickly dispersed to the hedges on either side. Shrapnel was flying everywhere and I was next to Pfc Owen Magie when he was killed. Sgt Austin was caught in the face and Pvt Vernon Mull was badly wounded and died the following day.

Machine-gun fire from an enemy gun that was causing problems in field 1 was passing through the hedgerow on G Co's right. Its bullets were slowed by the hedge's dense earth bank, thus saving Pfc Jimmy Hollen from more serious injury, as he was hit four times during one burst. "An officer from another unit [perhaps an artillery observer] gave the order to pull back and shouted 'every man for himself,'" remembers Martin. "Although Floyd Gardner had been hit in the arm he was furious when I told him what the officer had said. We fell back into the gully under terrific artillery fire, with mortar shells air-bursting in the trees above us."

Some of the enemy fire was coming from an apple orchard on the left flank just beyond field 3. This was 440 yards southwest of where Capt Shettle had set up his position in the gully. Shettle sent an artillery observer up onto high ground to the east to direct fire onto the enemy positions. The barrage failed to materialize and the company had to deploy its two 60mm mortars instead. Harold Stedman recalls:

> We did not have enough ammunition to support the counterattack. Frank Lujan and I scrounged as many 60mm shells as we could from the people around us, but it still wasn't enough. S/Sgt Jerry Beam pointed out our target on a map. Jimmy Shuler and Jerry O'Christie had the other tube and were ordered to take out the machine gun in the H Co area. We were deployed a short distance behind the gully where the ground was higher and devoid of overhanging branches.

Stedman set up next to a hedgerow behind the company position while Shuler moved further north behind field 1. Both teams were now roughly in line with their respective targets. "I used the tube without its base plate and managed to put ten rounds into the orchard," recalls Stedman. "I guess we came close enough to keep them quiet for a while." The four mortar men returned to the gully and joined the rest of I Co, which had also been forced back.

Capt Shettle was working with John Kiley (I Co's commander) and they both felt that the German positions in fields on the left flank beyond the front line needed to be dealt with. Shettle ordered a number of men from G Co, led by 2nd Lt Barling, to attempt a counterattack by joining forces with I Co. The small group arrived in the gully at about the same time as Stedman returned with his mortar men, and by 0745hrs they were ready to go.

Rosdahl and Fishel were ordered forward with their machine gun to provide covering fire. No more was heard from them and Capt Shettle sent Lenny Goodgal to find out where they were. Goodgal recounts:

I went up to a hedge [200 yards west of the gully] and began to follow a ditch that ran alongside it to my left. I then caught a glimpse of someone ahead of me. As we were getting small-arms fire from our front I assumed he was a Kraut and shouted "Come out – *raus mit hein*" [probably meant to be "raus mit Hände hoch," – "come out with your hands up"] but got no response. Panicking, I fired a burst from my Thompson submachine gun before realizing it was 1st Sgt Gordon Bolles, who was with a couple of other H Co men. ["Pop" Bolles had been scouting southwest along the hedge line toward the orchard]. Clutching his side, Bolles screamed back at me, "Watch it, there's a sniper up there." I was horrified at what I'd done and ignored his warning. In a state of panic I pulled up his shirt to check the wound and could not believe my eyes. By some miracle the bullets had only grazed the side of his body. Snapping back to reality I said, "Where's that sniper?" Bolles pointed to some trees; I fired a couple of rounds and then took off looking for Rosdahl and Fishel. I eventually found them and explained that Shettle wanted to know why they weren't giving supporting fire. They told me they couldn't see anyone firing and had decided to wait and see what would happen. I could not argue with their decision and started back to the gully. During my return a piece of shrapnel hit me in my left knee, making walking difficult. After reporting to Shettle and Kiley I was ordered to join our medic, Bill Kidder, who was taking wounded back to the aid station. On our arrival one of the medics said, "Where are all the wounded men coming from?" I replied "Up in that bloody gully." I always wondered if this was where the name came from! Kidder said his goodbyes and returned to the line.

As a result of I Co's mortar bombardment, the Germans in the orchard area stopped firing and readied themselves for an American counterattack. This lulled Shettle into thinking that the enemy had been successfully knocked out.

The counterattack, comprising some 50 men, started around 0900hrs. As they entered the orchard I Co came under heavy fire from a concealed enemy machine gun. "I didn't actually see any German soldiers in the orchard but they could sure see us," recalls Stedman. Then Sgt Shuler told Stedman, Lujan, and O'Christie to follow him, as they were going to knock out the gun. "We hadn't moved more than 20 yards when German mortar shells began to airburst in the tops of the densely planted trees," remembers Stedman. "We were showered with branches and leaves. This didn't seem to bother Jim Shuler but it put the fear of God into us. We eventually managed to pull him back into the cover of a hedgerow. It was only afterwards we learned that he was nearly deaf and couldn't hear the mortar shells coming in!"

Kiley was desperately trying to find a way to neutralize the enemy fire. 2nd Lt Santarsiero, 2nd Lt Barling, and one other man from G Co tried to circle around the gun. Barling dropped out when a burst of fire shot off his canteen. The overwhelming mortar barrage forced Kiley to withdraw his men and as they began to pull back Santarsiero was hit in the thigh.

By 1030hrs several Sherman tanks from 2nd Armored arrived via the dirt road east of the gully. They attacked a German command post at Les Six Chemins (500 yards southwest of Baudouin Farm), losing one tank and vital time. I Co was pleased to see them and watched as the Shermans' 75mm rounds slammed into the western side of the orchard, temporarily breaking the enemy's grip. This was the opportunity Kiley needed to withdraw his men, and the tanks eventually forced the Germans to pull out.

I Co made its way back along a hedgerow 200 yards west of the gully. There they ran into the group of soldiers from 1st Bn that Jim Brown had shot at earlier in the day. Santarsiero recognized 1st Lt Eugene Knott from C Co and briefly spoke to him. At that precise moment a burst of machine-gun fire cut through the hedge. Knott was killed instantly and Pvt Bob Penner (who was with Santarsiero) was hit in the face. By 1130hrs most of I Co had scrambled back to the gully. Harold Stedman remembers the scene. "Everywhere you looked there were wounded men lying about. I helped a couple of guys who had leg wounds – it was an unbelievable sight."

Much later, Dr Barney Ryan and S/Sgt William Roots, the medical supply sergeant, arrived in the gully with Bill Kidder to assess the situation and decide which cases should be evacuated directly by jeep. Ryan remembers:

> Walking up the sunken track I saw Don Austin lying on his back. His head was covered in blood from the shrapnel wound to his eye. Turning to Roots, I said, "There's another dead one, Sergeant," and with that Austin spat back, "I ain't dead yet, now get me the hell out of here." We jumped back in surprise and then put him on the next available jeep to Carentan. He survived the ordeal but lost his eye. After the attack had broken [1130hrs] there were so many casualties that the gully was full of wounded. I never before or afterwards saw such a concentration of casualties or witnessed such a head-to-head tank battle as this.

As 2nd Lt Tom Kennedy's platoon arrived at the gully, the men found G Co, which was in field 2, in disarray. Tom remembers:

> Joe Doughty told me to resupply 1st Lt Meason (in field 1) with bazooka rockets. I ordered Pvt Alfred Summerfield, one of my platoon runners, to help me. We could see Meason positioned in the hedge up ahead, and set off cradling the rockets. Crawling toward us looking very pale was Ken Christianson, who was trying to support his arm. Using a path that ran beside the hedgerow we continued forward, but came under intense German artillery fire. During the barrage Summerfield was hit and I had to abandon the mission. His arm was hanging by a small thread of skin and he was losing a lot of blood. When the enemy fire subsided, I took Summerfield to some medics who'd set up an aid station in a road ditch near the gully.

By 0730hrs, 3rd Bn's right flank was in danger of crumbling and attack had been turned into defense. Later, Col Chase was to sack Bob Harwick for his part in these events, clearly believing that he had been negligent in the way he commanded the situation. However, despite what Chase may have thought, his sacking of Harwick was considered by many to have been a very harsh decision. With the exception of Ed Shames, radio contact was virtually nonexistent. Precious time and vital information was being lost, as Ralph Bennett recalls:

> I ordered T/5 Harvey Holcomb to get on the "net" and give a situation report to "Kidnap blue" (Harwick's call sign), but the handy talky was unserviceable. I had no choice but to send a runner back through all the machine-gun fire to try and let the boss know how desperate the situation was. At around 0830hrs several 60mm rounds were fired from the east of the gully, so I guess my message was received and understood. The shells landed in woods across the road to my right and the enemy machine gun temporarily stopped firing. This gave me an opportunity to get back to Pfc "Dud" Hefner, who had our 60mm mortar, and knock out the machine gun. I told the men around me what I was going to do and dashed to where Hefner was sheltering. "What the hell we gonna do, Bennett?" Dud shouted. I told him to get the mortar legs locked into place. There were only two rounds so we had to make them count.

The German machine gun was only 20 yards away so the mortar tube had to be elevated into a near vertical position, which was a very dangerous maneuver. They fired both shells and the German gun was silenced.

Bennett's quick thinking allowed most of H Co to escape and regroup. Bennett remembers:

> Although the Germans had moved back, there was still an enormous amount of enemy activity over to our right. It was clear that we couldn't stay where we were and pulled back. We passed the knocked-out tanks and made for the nearest cover, which was the gully.

Platoon sergeant "Mac" McCullough crawled past me on his stomach shouting, "I'm hit, I'm hit." He had a bullet wound in the top of his foot. I watched a soldier grab his arm and help him into the gully. We all said it was a "chicken shit" kind of wound that was probably self-inflicted, as most of the German ammo flying around was at head height. Hefner and I then came across a man lying face down on the ground. We each took a suspender (webbing) strap and began dragging him along. After about 20 exhausting yards we stopped to see what we could do for him.

As Bennett turned the casualty over both men stepped back in horror when they saw his face. "At first glance it looked like some of it was missing," recalls Bennett. "Congealed blood covered his features giving him a grotesque, horrific look. Hefner put three fingers on the man's jugular and said, 'There's nothing we can do, absolutely nothing... I think he's dead!'" Leaving the soldier they made their way to the gully. German artillery was exploding behind them as Bennett began regrouping his men. "There was nobody in authority to tell us what to do [as the rest of the battalion was fighting a rearguard action in fields to the south]. We waited next to the aid post for a couple of hours before helping ourselves to a nearby box of grenades."

The grenades had arrived a little earlier in the day courtesy of Bob Webb, HQ Co's supply sergeant, who had been ordered to fetch them from Carentan by Capt Harwick. Harwick was impressed with the way the resupply mission had been carried out, and recommended Webb for the Silver Star. However, it was not uncommon in situations such as this for bravery awards to be downgraded by higher authority, and this was almost certainly what happened in Webb's case, as he ended up with a Bronze Star.

Initially, there were insufficient stretchers available to evacuate the wounded, and the company medics had to improvise using ladders and blankets scrounged from nearby farms. After a while a number of jeeps turned up, as Ralph Bennett recalls. "We watched as some jeeps arrived. Each was rigged to carry two wounded men. They backed off the road near our position and one by one took the casualties away."

Eventually S/Sgt Jerry Beam (I Co) found Bennett, told him the battalion was being withdrawn and that he should do the same. Before Bennett had time to move, he saw remnants of the battalion walking along the gully toward him. "We joined them," he recalls, "and then marched off along the RN803 toward Carentan."

1st Lt Nye sent a runner to Galbraith and Brown who were still on the far (western) side of field 1 with remnants of H Co. Galbraith remembers:

We were told to shift over and rejoin I Co who were gathering behind a hedgerow in the next field [field 2]. Jim and I set up a defensive position halfway along the hedgerow to give covering fire. By the time we got into position, 20 or so men from I Co were making their way toward us. Nye sent Jim Brown to help Pvt Bob Penner, who lay wounded in the next field. Using the field's slope for cover Jim just walked out to Penner like he was on a Sunday stroll. There was a lot of ordnance whistling about at hedgerow height and the enemy was putting down a walking blanket barrage. It made moving about very difficult. A mortar shell exploded in the trees above me, and the shrapnel pockmarked the barrel of my machine gun! I was then told we were pulling out and headed back toward the gully.

As Galbraith approached the gully (1130hrs), he noticed someone drop down behind him. Leaving his machine gun he threw his prized sniper rifle over his shoulder and went back to see what he could do for the wounded man. Pfc Sam Porter (H Co) had been hit in the throat. Galbraith was acutely aware of the danger he was in but knew that he was safe from enemy fire so as long as he did not stand up. Porter was in a serious condition but by some miracle was still breathing. Dragging the casualty down the slope, Galbraith eventually found a safe spot and attempted to pick the man up, as he recalls: "I just couldn't lift him and ran down into the gully looking for assistance. Clambering over a wire fence I found Sgt Ernie Mann and Pfc Johnny Edwards who'd both fallen back with the rest of the company." Galbraith left his sniper rifle propped against a large tree and together with his two colleagues ran back into the field to fetch Porter. Galbraith continues:

> The kid seemed so heavy we thought he was dead [in fact Porter survived his ordeal and was evacuated to the United States] but we got him back into the gully and laid him down on the bank. I had to go back out and get the machine gun that I'd left behind. I didn't want to but Lt Nye told me that I was to cover the withdrawal from this part of the gully. I had to do it by myself because Jim Brown was nowhere to be seen.

Before recovering the machine gun Galbraith went to fetch his sniper rifle but it had gone. "Someone must have taken it as they'd left the gully," he recalls angrily. "That rifle was a great weapon and I really wanted to keep it."

Galbraith eventually set up his machine gun on high ground toward the southern end of the gully near Baudoin house. There, together with Rosdahl and Fishel, he covered the withdrawal. Most of the firing had died down by this stage and except for occasional small-arms fire it was comparatively quiet. The 506th Regiment had been ordered to hold its current position, but men were still pulling back. Several Sherman tanks arrived via the D443 road east of the gully and this helped relieve the pressure.

Galbraith, Rosdahl, and Fishel followed the battalion as it withdrew, covering each other as they made their way into the gully. Galbraith could not work out why the battalion was withdrawing. He recalls:

> I'm damn sure that we weren't beaten. However a rumor did go around that the 501st had asked for artillery support and pulled back – maybe that's why? I think the Krauts had just about had a belly full of us, in our sector at least, and had quit. We covered the withdrawal without firing a single shot, which was very fortunate because we didn't really have enough ammunition. At around 1500hrs we got back to where the battalion had set up a new defense line. Shortly after that 1st Bn 502nd

came up with tank support and relieved us. As we regrouped I remember hearing the tanks firing at the enemy machine gun positions. Jim Brown returned and jointly we set up our gun in a roadside ditch. We then watched men from the 502nd, together with the tanks from 2nd Armored, move past and the soldiers taunted us, saying we weren't man enough to finish the job. We'd been hard at it for nearly 11 hours and I was utterly exhausted – they had no idea what we'd been through.

"It wasn't one of our better days," concludes Joe Doughty. "I was left to command a company that was minus one platoon leader and a first sergeant. We were later told that we were going to make a counterattack that afternoon, which could have got pretty ugly had 2nd Armored not come to our rescue."

A tank recovery outfit was busy moving the M5 tanks that had been knocked out earlier by the German SPG. As the battalion filed past the recovery team stopped work. "I heard somebody shouting 'is that Slim... Slim McCann?'" remembers Jim McCann. "I looked across the road and couldn't believe my eyes when I saw Joe Uboski, who had lived next door to me back in Pennsylvania. I got permission to fall out and went over to talk to him."

The battalion marched on and was directed to a field 550 yards east of the gully. "As we began to assemble, a lone Sherman tank appeared on the horizon," remembers Ralph Bennett. "It must have mistaken the recovery team for the enemy and fired four rounds before realizing its mistake. Several of us took cover in a nearby orchard. Fortunately nobody was injured."

The battalion now formed part of the divisional reserve, and had begun digging in on the western edge of Carentan. Col Sink set up his regimental command post in the town's courthouse (previously a German headquarters) near the settlement's port area. That evening he ordered Ed Shames to meet him there. Ed recalls:

I just knew Sink was going to commission me. I arrived at the courthouse and reported to Sink, who said "Stand easy, Shames, your conduct today was superb and I have spoken to Division about making you an officer. You're the regiment's first battlefield commission – congratulations. You will have to wait until we get back to England before the paperwork can be officially sorted out. I'll put the word around about your promotion and why we've given it to you. I will expect people to treat you as an officer despite the fact that you're still wearing your old rank."

Before leaving I told Sink that I'd seen Lonnie Gavrock killed in action earlier that morning, and he made a note of it.

Leaving the courthouse, I felt over the moon but was neither "fish nor fowl." Later that evening 1st Lt Jim Morton, G Co's XO, told me that he had just been offered command of HQ Co, as Capt Shettle was being transferred to 2nd Bn. All this would become official in a week or so. Morton said he'd heard about my promotion but wanted me to become his first sergeant – just until we returned to England. I was pleased to accept Jim Morton's offer. J. P. Shirley (the former first sergeant) had been a good friend and I was devastated when I heard about his death on D-Day. He was an A1 guy and I was proud to follow in his footsteps.

After the battle the battalion was sent to an area just east of the gully. There, together with 1st Bn 401st, they provided security for a Sherman tank unit, as snipers hidden nearby were causing them problems. They also used this short period to clean themselves up and undertake administrative duties. "2 Ptn was in the best shape and had maybe 15 or 16 men," recalls Bill Galbraith. "I don't think that there were more than 28 of us left in I Co after Bloody Gully."

At 2300hrs the 506th withdrew to Carentan and became part of the divisional reserve. "As we moved out the guys began shouting, 'Galbraith, there's a guy with your rifle.' They'd spotted a lieutenant from another outfit and sure enough he had my gun. 'Excuse me, that's my gun, sir,' I said. 'Well, it's mine now, son,' he sarcastically replied. I didn't argue and carried on walking. Later I spoke to Capt Shettle about it and he told me, 'If you see the gun again, let me know and I'll make sure you get it back.'"

During this period, groups of Frenchmen were sent out on to the battlefield to collect bodies and, incredibly, a number of German soldiers tried to get into the town dressed as civilians. "That night everyone was exhausted," recalls Bob Webb. "I flopped down and rested my head on the guy next to me. I must have gone to sleep in a second. Later, someone punched me and said, 'Get up, we're ready to go.' I nudged the guy I was lying on and he felt funny. He was a dead German and there was no telling how long he'd been there. When you're tired I guess it doesn't matter where you lay your head!"

The following morning (June 14) the 502nd and 3rd Bn 327th pushed southwestward from Carentan, mopping up German resistance as they went. By 1600hrs the 502nd had successfully linked up with the 82nd Airborne at Baupte, removing any possible enemy threat to the 506th's western flank. Meanwhile, back in Carentan, soldiers from the regiment were lining up for haircuts in the town's reopened barbers' shops!

From a 101st Airborne Division perspective, the battle of Bloody Gully was one of the most important and decisive engagements of its entire Normandy campaign. Many airborne veterans have said that the German artillery they encountered that day was the most intense they experienced throughout the entire war!

Capt Harwick was not the only officer from the 506th to lose his job, as Capt Mulvey was relieved of his command of F Co for allowing his men to break during the initial assault.

When the division's wounded arrived in Britain from Normandy, they were sent to 188 and 292 general hospitals in Britain. Those who made a full recovery returned to duty via the 10th Replacement Depot near Nottingham in the north of England. It was felt by many in the battalion that returning veterans should never have been sent to this depot, as the treatment they received was nothing less than shameful. One of the depot's main tasks was to prepare newly arrived troops from the United States for the harsh realities of war. Unfortunately, the training went well beyond acceptable boundaries. Lenny Goodgal recalls, "The 'repple depple' was run by a man called Col Killian. He was forced to quit after the mistreatment and abuse came to light." By September 1944, when Ray Calandrella arrived at the depot, conditions had improved noticeably.

After leaving hospital, Gordon Bolles was sent back to Ramsbury, where he started to get the camp ready for the battalion's return. When they arrived Bolles discovered that in his absence Fred Bahlau had been promoted to H Co's first sergeant. It was an embarrassing situation that meant the company now had two first sergeants; however, it was eventually resolved about a month later when Bahlau was transferred to HQ Co.

~ 13 ~

"Things are pretty calm right now"

Operations on the Main Line of Resistance

Bassin à Flot – June 15–22

On June 15, the battalion passed through Carentan en route to a bivouac area near the Bassin à Flot section of the Carentan–Douve canal. Bobbie Rommel recalls:

> I was struggling along loaded like a pack mule and was the very last man in our column. As we crossed the twisted railway tracks on the southern side of town, I spotted Col Sink waiting impatiently in his jeep. He put his hand up and ordered me to stop. I thought he was going to tell me something important but his driver just put his foot down and accelerated across the road in front of me. I stood there wondering why they couldn't have waited another second for me to pass.

Sink was heading for a medal awards ceremony in the center of town where, together with colonels Michaelis, Johnson, and Harper, he received his Silver Star. The medals were presented by Gen Maxwell Taylor, the commanding officer of the 101st Airborne Division.

As the battalion passed the burnt-out shell of Carentan's milk factory, Harold Stedman noticed some familiar items in the debris: "I picked up some Carnation labels and put them in my pack. I'd worked for the Carnation Milk Company back home and I wanted to send them to my folks. My old boss got a big kick out of it when Dad showed them to him."

On reaching the bivouac area the men started to relax, as they were expecting to return to England within a week or so. Evaporated milk from cans "liberated" from the Carnation factory was added to their ration pack's dry cereal, which made a welcome change. Champagne was also freely available! However, the battalion still had a number of jobs to do, which included establishing listening posts approximately half a mile to the front and guarding the bridge at St-Hilaire-Petitville. The bridge was not strong enough to carry tanks and needed to be replaced by a Bailey bridge. Construction began the following day with the arrival of the 207th Combat Engineers from Omaha Beach (part of Gen Courtney Hodges's 1st Army).

To supplement their rations, about six cows were slaughtered and when the owner found out he complained! The man responsible for the slaughter was Bob Webb:

> Capt Harwick had ordered me to supply the men with fresh meat and I set about the task with my pistol. After killing the animal I found that if I tied its hind legs to a big two-wheel farm cart, and with some men acting as a counterbalance, I could raise the carcass for butchering. Tom Simms had been a butcher before the war and did all the preparation. We cooked them in a big iron pot and the hot stews really hit the spot, but we could have done with more salt!

Owing to the hot weather, decaying bodies, which still littered the area, were starting to smell. "I got hold of three guys and commandeered a horse and wagon," recalls Bob Webb. "I'd been ordered by Capt Harwick to organize a clean-up operation. We found 13 bodies in the river, including two Americans. Dead animals were also removed and dumped in a pit and burned. Afterwards we all went down to the canal and washed our clothes and ourselves, but the smell lingered for days."

Cpl Bobbie Rommel and his machine-gun team were ordered to guard the swing bridge spanning the Bassin à Flot. The gun was set up facing southeast at Quai Lepelletier close to the customs house building. As there was little happening, Bobbie decided to scout around:

> I came across an open fronted wooden boat shed and went inside. On a shelf was a German stick grenade and I thought it might be booby trapped. I decided to try and set it off remotely and attached a length of rigging line to the porcelain bead on the fused pull cord. I then wedged the grenade behind a large lump of concrete and gave it a sharp tug. Five seconds later... boom! When I got back to the guys I was feeling very pleased with myself. However, after hearing the blast they were worried that something had happened to me.

On June 15, after fighting with the 3rd Bn 502nd for nearly two weeks, Walter "Luke" Lukasavage arrived in the 3rd Bn's bivouac area. He had taken part in the bayonet charge led by Col Cole during the attack on Carentan (June 10), where his I Co colleague Harry Westerberg had been seriously wounded. Lukasavage was glad to see some familiar 3rd Ptn faces, especially Harold Stedman's.

Although small patrols were sent out on a regular basis to the railway yard in Carentan, most of the men were kept occupied with outpost duty. One night Bill Galbraith was returning from duty with Cpl "Shorty" Gilbertson when they heard a noise. "We issued a challenge, something started to run, and we emptied our guns at whatever it was. When we got in, Lt Nye wanted to know what the hell we'd been shooting at. Tragically it turned out to be a mare and her colt."

Any hopes the battalion might have had for an early return to England were shattered when the 501st called for assistance. For more than three days, between June 13 and 16, the regiment had been fighting in and around the town of Méautis but had been beaten back and was expecting a German counterattack. Twenty-seven of the town's residents had been killed by artillery and machine-gun fire and the remainder had fled. Thirty-six properties were totally destroyed, and it was mid-August before the locals were able to return and begin the job of rebuilding their shattered homes.

On June 16–17 3rd Bn (less I Co, which arrived a few days later) joined the 501st along a newly established Main Line of Resistance (MLR) that was about half a mile northeast of Méautis. Under cover of darkness the battalion boarded a number of trucks driven by black American soldiers. Bobbie Rommel had found a German rifle and about 50 wooden-tipped bullets and gave the whole lot to one of the drivers, as he recalls: "I learned that the heads were manufactured in wood for close quarter fighting. Unlike the regular copper-headed bullets, these would lose momentum more quickly and pose less of a risk to friendly troops. I didn't want to take the rifle into a combat area for fear that if I was caught carrying it, the Krauts would execute me on the spot. So I left it in the back of the lorry with the ammo and told the driver he could keep it."

On arrival at the MLR, HQ and G companies were assigned to the 501st's 1st Bn whilst H Co joined 2nd Bn. Patrols were sent out almost immediately but without much success, and failed to penetrate any further than the established Outpost Line of Resistance (OPLR).

MLR, Méautis, June 17–27

The 101st Airborne Division was deployed along a 4½-mile stretch of the front line between Baupte in the northwest and Auverville in the southeast, and was ordered to hold the line until relieved by the 83rd Infantry Division.

A shallow waterlogged valley lay between the town of Méautis and the American MLR. To the south, 3rd Bn could see several knocked-out Sherman tanks in a field just off the Périers road between le Calvaire and Mare Palu. They had been destroyed by German 88mm antitank guns, which caused the battalion all manner of problems during the following two weeks. "From our position we could see most of the ground to our left, which was the direction we were expecting the 83rd Infantry to come from," recalls Tom Kennedy. "The 83rd was a National Guard unit on its first combat mission, and big delays getting its troops and supplies ashore meant they were late getting to us."

On June 19, Maj Oliver Horton (former 506th regimental S2) took command of 3rd Bn from Bob Harwick, who resumed his original position as H Co's commander. Although the men viewed Horton as a fairly capable officer, they soon discovered that he lacked many of Col Wolverton's qualities.

Two days later, satisfied that everything was under control, Col Sink moved his Regimental HQ to a large farmhouse called Le Sapin, which was nearly 2 miles southwest of Carentan, and this region became the 506th's area of operations from June 15–26. Le Sapin was owned by Msr Jean Sanson and was located on the Périers road (RN171, now D971) northeast of the crossroads at La Fourchette. It had previously been the German 17.SS-Panzergrenadier-Division's command post. On June 14 it was attacked by an American armored unit and was abandoned by the Germans, who left the civilians inside to their own fate. The American tanks moved up the long drive toward the house and opened fire, damaging the building. One of the French civilians courageously stopped the attack by standing in front of the tanks waving a white bedsheet.

After a short spell on the OPLR, 3rd Bn was ready to take over the MLR's southern flank from the 501st. The section was about half a mile long and ran southeastward from the Périers road to the village of St-Quentin.

The following day (June 22), H Co went to nearby Auverville where it spent four days in reserve (during this period 1 Ptn was sent to Cherbourg with 1st Bn 506th to guard German prisoners). At about the same time I Co arrived from Bassin à Flot. It took up positions on the west flank near La Lande Godard beside elements of the 502nd, and two machine-gun squads from HQ Co were added to its strength. Galbraith and Brown found a gap in a hedge where they set up their machine-gun position, which was a couple of hundred yards northwest of the other gun manned by Rosdahl and Fishel. Midway between the two guns, and about 50 yards behind them, Sgt Shuler had deployed his four-man 60mm mortar team.

Galbraith and Brown were unhappy with their ammunition. "When we fired our gun during daylight we always gave away our position," recalls Galbraith. "This was because our ammunition smoked like a diesel truck. The Germans usually responded by carpeting us with mortars. For this reason we removed all the tracers from our belts of ammo. This was 2 Ptn's policy – I don't know what the other gunners did."

Cleanliness is always a problem for the men serving on the front line, as Tom Kennedy recalls:

The only way to keep clean was to take a whore's bath, which meant washing directly out of your steel helmet. However, there was always plenty to eat. Grazing in a pasture behind our position were several cows and we all fancied steak for dinner. Being a city boy I didn't know much about slaughtering animals and thought it would be easy. Using my .45cal automatic I shot one of them right between the eyes. The animal just mooed and strolled away – I couldn't believe it! To everyone's amusement I started chasing the cow around the field and after firing three more rounds it fell over! Some of our country boys told us they knew a thing or two about butchering and carved up the fresh meat, which was still quivering! It continued to quiver as we cooked and ate it – I wouldn't recommend that to anyone. Nobody realized that the meat should have been hung for at least a day before being eaten!

Since June 17 the battalion's medical detachment had been working from a house near La Desillerie and had little to do, as casualties (mainly caused by landmines or random shellfire) had been mercifully light. However, Barney Ryan remembers one incident that broke the boredom. "A supply truck got lost and went straight through the MLR into No Man's Land. When the driver realized his mistake he abandoned the vehicle. That night we went out to see what it contained, and the first box we opened was full of whisky bottles! We had to leave the rest of the cargo (mainly medical supplies) as it became too dangerous for us to stay and the truck was still sitting there when we pulled out."

For the first time since entering combat, the men received V-mail letters from home and were anxious to reply. Using captured German ink Bob Webb wrote a letter to his parents in which he said:

Received your first V-mail letter since "D" day today. It was swell to get such a swell letter at such a time. Things are pretty calm right now. These Huns do make us stay pretty close to our foxholes but hell we make them get in theirs and keep digging (China bound) ha ha. I could have sent you a wire but I didn't want to, because that's what I've been trying my damndest to keep you from getting ever since "D" day... catch? Got Muriel's D-Day letter today, gee whiz! I can't wait much longer on this darn war. I've had all I want already. She's really wonderful, I feel awful lucky to have her to come home to (I hope it's soon now).

Love you... Bob.

On the evening of June 20, staff sergeants Harry Clawson and Fred Bahlau from H Co, plus nine other men from the 101st (including the divisional artillery commander BrigGen Anthony McAuliffe), were presented Silver Stars by generals Middleton and Taylor at the Place de la République in Carentan. This was followed by a presentation of flowers by local children. Fred Bahlau's citation reads:

> On the 6th June 1944, about two and a half miles east of Carentan, France, Staff Sergeant Bahlau displayed outstanding courage as a volunteer of a group assaulting enemy-held positions. Crossing a 283ft bridge in the face of strong enemy machine-gun and small-arms fire, Staff Sergeant Bahlau and his group forced the enemy to temporarily withdraw. This enabled his own force to reorganize against enemy counterattack. His conduct was in accordance with the highest standards of military service.

"One of the children only had nine flowers and ran into a nearby flower shop to get some more," recalls Bahlau. "When the kid returned she gave me a flower and then threw her arms around me and gave me a big kiss."

Three days later a third Silver Star ceremony took place in Carentan, and H Co (still in reserve) was sent along by Col Sink to represent 3rd Bn. The men arrived by truck and the ceremony began at about midday in the Place de la République.

Ralph Bennett and his squad were standing behind the men receiving their awards. "Suddenly, just as the ceremony was ending, a green signal flare burst overhead. This was followed by a German barrage, which quickly cleared the streets of the civilians who'd gathered to watch the proceedings. The heavy shellfire rained down onto the town and many soldiers and civilians took shelter under the arches of the old cattle market in the square." At least six civilians were killed during the shelling, including Danielle Laisney, one of the children who had taken part in the flower presentation on the 20th. She was just four years old.

Meanwhile, back on the MLR, I Co was watching six German Me109s attack an Allied L-5 spotter plane. Seconds earlier the fighters had flown low over 3rd Bn's area. Harold Stedman remembers:

> It had rained in the night and we were all wet through. The sun came out so I stripped to the waist and hung my clothes over a bush to dry out. I had just laid my head back to rest when suddenly Me109s came right over the top of us. They came in so quickly that they couldn't get their guns on us, but they shot that spotter plane down in No Man's Land. One of the guys in our company went out to see if he could help but the pilot was dead.

Because they were so low Bobbie Rommel mistook them for friendly planes and waved at one of the pilots, who waved back!

During this period Division issued an order to each battalion stating that it wanted at least one German captured for intelligence purposes every day. On June 24, 2nd Lt Tom Kennedy was ordered to form a night patrol with the sole purpose of capturing Germans. Kennedy chose Sgt Flint Brown as the patrol's senior NCO and the crossroads at Le Calvaire (about 1,650 yards southwest of their position) as the target area. At dusk Kennedy set off in a jeep for his initial reconnaissance, as he recalls: "I received the assignment on short order and was lent a jeep to save time. We went out looking for the 501 OPLR to tell them we'd be coming through at dusk, but took a wrong track and as we were reversing out hit a land mine."

Pfc Albert St Jean was driving the jeep with Tom Kennedy and Flint Brown sitting in the back. When the vehicle hit the mine Brown was blown out and knocked unconscious. When he came to he found Tom Kennedy in bad shape, as the jeep's engine had landed on his head. St Jean had been thrown clear and was in a fairly stable condition.

Flint tried in vain to lift the engine off Kennedy. Then several men, including Col Sink, arrived at the scene and the engine was lifted clear. The three wounded men were quickly evacuated to Dr Kent's regimental aid station at Le Sapin. Tom Kennedy was continually drifting in and out of consciousness and recalls:

I looked up and asked Col Sink if I was going to make it. He replied, "Kennedy, this is a direct order... get well son!" Flint Brown was covered in blood and most of it was mine. Some while later he was awarded a Purple Heart. To this day he still maintains that he won the medal with my blood! [Flint died in 2007]. Of course this would never have happened if the 83rd Infantry hadn't taken so long to arrive! The next thing I remember was waking up in a tent on a stretcher, throwing up blood and feeling very thirsty. They evacuated me to England by C-47 from an airstrip behind Omaha Beach. The first hospital was very near the coast – I think it was the 10th Station hospital. A day or so after my arrival they cleared the place of all Allied casualties and turned it over for German wounded. From there I was taken to the 158th US hospital in Salisbury. 2nd Lt Eugene Dance took command of 1 Ptn until the battalion returned to Ramsbury. He was then transferred to 2nd Bn.

Elements of the 83rd Infantry Division began to arrive in the Méautis region on June 26 and went straight to a holding area near Le Sapin. 1st Lt John Reeder (506th regimental communications officer) was astonished to discover that he knew one of the division's regimental commanders, as he recalls: "He was my company commander in Washington and kick-started my career by sending me to OCS [Officer Candidate School]. The 83rd was playing softball in a field opposite our

CP. Suddenly some mortar rounds came thumping in and I can still see them scattering – it was their first experience under fire."

Later that day Bill Galbraith decided to liven things up by injecting a little humor into the daily routine. Lt Nye had instructed Galbraith to make up a range card with written instructions for a gun crew from the 83rd Infantry who were about to take over his position:

I didn't really want to do it and wrote FINAL FIRE – DON'T GIVE A DAMN, RANGE TO GERMAN POSITION – TOO DAMN FAR AWAY and such. Nye wasn't at all pleased and threatened to bust me back to private, but it kept me amused.

A little while later, as the 83rd was marching up behind the MLR, I heard a few shots and Jim Brown, who had been manning our listening post, appeared. Somebody always shot at us either going to or coming back from that damned post. I told him what had happened with Nye and we started to laugh. We were still rolling around with tears in our eyes when we heard... "That's about enough of that," booming from behind us. It was 1st Lt Kiley with Col Chase and a captain from the company that was about to relieve us. The officers didn't seem to appreciate our childish antics but before they could take it further, 88s started whistling in. The shells were skipping off the ground in front of us and exploding in the hedgerows behind our position. The three officers jumped into our foxhole and jostled around for cover – it was like a scene from a Marx Brothers film. It was a miracle that none of us got hit, but I'm not so sure about the men from the 83rd who were on the road behind us. I think they got it pretty bad.

Our company HQ was a two-storey building near the road; when the 83rd relieved us at dawn on the 27th they thought the CP looked kind of exposed and vulnerable. Lt Kiley was standing with the 83rd's officers and I heard him say, "Hell no, once in a while they throw something at us but it's never a problem." No sooner had the words left his mouth than a couple of shells crashed in and blew the top floor clean off. It was the funniest thing we'd seen in a long while – you should've seen their faces!

Just before we pulled out, Nye told me to take a lieutenant from the 83rd and some of his guys over to our OP and show them where the listening post was. I really think he was trying to get me killed because of my "goofing off" earlier that morning. I told the officer not to bother, as he was never going to be out there after dark and besides the place was 4ft deep in water. Nye went crazy and told me I had to do what he asked. Amazingly our large group wasn't shot at once either on the way out or on the way back!

"The machine-gun platoon was one of the last groups to leave," recalls Bobbie Rommel. "As we withdrew we came under intense accurate artillery fire, which skimmed through the grass all around us. One of the boys had the muzzle of his rifle squashed flat by the blast from one of those shells."

On June 27 the 506th pulled out and joined the rest of the 101st Airborne Division at St-Sauveur-le-Vicomte, 19 miles south of Cherbourg. It was the first time since leaving England that the entire division had been able to assemble in one place, and it was held there for three days before moving 15 miles north to a tactical bivouac area near the village of Tollevast.

Tollevast

In order to create a defensive ring around Cherbourg, the tiny hamlet of Tollevast, in common with other settlements in the area, had been fortified by the Germans. When the 101st arrived, it found many abandoned pillboxes. Gen Taylor chose to stand on top of one of these structures and delivered a speech in which he said, "You hit the ground running toward the enemy. You have proved the German soldier is no superman – you have beaten him on his own ground and you can beat him on any ground." Despite these fine words the 101st had lost many good men during the liberation of Normandy. The division in total had suffered around 4,000 casualties, with 3rd Bn 506th experiencing the highest percentage. Out of the 575 officers and men who jumped, 93 were killed and about 75 taken prisoner.

With losses running at 50 percent among the officer grade, it was left to senior NCOs to tell the staff intelligence officers everything they could remember about the battles they had fought. The questioning was conducted in a rigorous manner, as Ralph Bennett recalls: "We were interviewed in great depth and soon began to resent the patronizing attitude these people showed toward us."

Although the battalion was in a relatively safe area, danger was never too far away. Four soldiers were killed when a truck carrying captured German mines exploded. Some people blamed the regimental S2, Capt Leach (who had ordered the explosives to be collected for training purposes), for the tragic event. Bill Galbraith remembers another incident:

> Jerry O'Christie and I were exploring a couple of bunkers when we came across a store full of stick grenades. We carefully removed the detonation cords from each grenade and set off the fuses like mini-fireworks. We had accumulated a pile of "handles and heads" when a guy from another outfit came over and asked where they had all come from. We pointed to the place and as we were walking away there was a loud explosion. We rushed back to the bunker to find that he'd lost both hands and had also been blinded by the blast. We set about applying tourniquets and after flagging down a jeep we went looking for an aid station. On the way he got the sight back in one eye but it all seemed so needless.

The men spent a lot of time at Tollevast cleaning and reconstructing equipment in preparation for their return to England. Also they attended lectures and critiques, where every aspect of the 101st's contribution to the invasion was covered. During one of these sessions a lieutenant from another unit was describing German sniper techniques. As the lesson progressed he held up a captured rifle, drawing attention to its unusual modifications. Pvt Stan Fadden (I Co) recognized the weapon and spoke up when he realized it was the gun Bill Galbraith lost at Bloody Gully. Although Galbraith could not see clearly from where he was sitting, he remembers the officer's response. "He told Stan in a very abrupt manner that he was clearly mistaken and that he had personally killed the Kraut who owned the rifle."

Afterwards Galbraith went to see I Co's new commander, Capt Anderson, who understood the history of the situation. "His response was positive," recalls Bill. "An interview was arranged with the young lieutenant (whose name was Danny) and his company commander." Danny stuck to his story and was then ordered to strip the rifle. He was unable to complete the task and Galbraith was asked to step forward and take over:

> I told everybody there was a particular cut underneath the stock that was only visible when the weapon was dismembered. Because Danny had lied in a way unbefitting of an officer, his commander took a dim view of things. We classed this incident as a victory for the enlisted man and nicknamed Danny "the sniper killer"! I later discovered there was a restriction on contraband weapons, but Andy Anderson stepped in and allowed me to take the rifle back to England.

A couple of days before the regiment left for England, Ralph Bennett was given two days' guard duty, known as Charge of Quarters (CQ). Bennett recalls:

> On my last night of CQ, a French civilian came running up the road into the guardroom. The man was shouting and pointing toward some nearby buildings. Realizing that there was a genuine problem, the sergeant of the guard ordered me to go with a duty corporal and see what was going on. The excited Frenchman led us to a house and warily we went upstairs. I could hear the screams of a young woman in the latter stages of labor. Putting down my Tommy gun, I grabbed her hand. The husband started shouting "Madame, Madame, Madame," and forced me to look down at his wife's fully dilated vagina! I panicked when I saw the baby's head appearing and shouted at my colleague, "For Christ's sake, she's about to give birth, go fetch one of our doctors." The woman continued to push and with one last painful contraction I found myself holding a beautiful baby boy. When the midwife eventually arrived she took one look at me

A view of the first Silver Star Ceremony held in the center of Carentan on June 15. (SC photo via James Bigley)

The Place de la République, June 14. A group of 101st Airborne Engineers and local children sit at the foot of the town's World War I War Memorial. Danielle Laisney (third left), Sylviane LeFevre (fifth left), and Jean LePoitevin (seventh left) were invited to take part in three Silver Star Ceremonies held in the town. Tragically, on June 23, four-year-old Danielle Laisney was killed and Jean LePoitevin injured when the ceremony was shelled by German artillery. (NARA via John Klein; information via Jim Bigley)

On June 15 Gen Maxwell Taylor, commanding officer of the 101st Airborne Division, presented medals at the Silver Star Ceremony and is pictured shaking hands with Col Robert Sink (506th PIR). Throughout June a further 22 Silver Stars were awarded, many going to enlisted men. (SC photo courtesy Margaret Swenson-Sink via Paul Woodage)

FROM TOP TO BOTTOM:

After the ceremony local children were invited to present the officers with bouquets of flowers. Sylviane LeFevre, who lived in the square, is handing her bouquet to Col Howard Johnson, watched by, L to R, LtCol "Mike" Michaelis, Col "Bud" Harper, and Col Robert Sink. (SC photo and French information courtesy James Bigley)

Capt Tilden S. McGee, 506th Anglican chaplain, conducting a church parade in the Place de la République on Sunday June 18. (NARA via John Klein)

This Bailey bridge (built by 207th Combat Engineer Battalion on June 16/17) still spans the river Taute and is as good as the day it was erected. Nearly 1,000 bridges of this type were constructed in Normandy and this rare survivor is near the northeastern end of the Bassin à Flot canal at St-Hilaire-Petitville.

FROM TOP TO BOTTOM:

This farmhouse at Le Sapin was a former command post of the German 17.SS-Panzergrenadier-Division. Between June 21 and 27, 1944, it became Col Sink's final Normandy combat command post. (John Reeder via Mark Bando)

This picture was taken in July 1944 shortly before the 101st Airborne Division returned to England. 1st Lt Gene Brown (regimental S2) is standing on a German bunker addressing the regiment and is flanked by colonels Sink and Chase. (John Reeder via Michel DeTrez Collection)

On June 15 at 1600hrs the 101st Airborne Division was officially attached to the US VIII Corps. Five days later Gen Troy Middleton, VIII Corps Commander, presented Silver Stars to 11 men from the 101st, including H Co's Fred Bahlau and Harry Clawson. Before the presentation, Gen Taylor (front of podium) addressed the crowd in both English and French. Behind him are local dignitaries and senior American officers including Middleton (fifth from left). Among the medal winners facing the podium are BrigGen Anthony McAuliffe (101st divisional artillery commander), LtCol Julian Ewell (3rd Bn 501st), S/Sgt Harry Clawson, and S/Sgt Fred Bahlau (H Co). (SC photo and information courtesy James Bigley)

FROM TOP TO BOTTOM:

This picture was taken around July 12 at Utah Beach where the division was awaiting the arrival of LSTs (Landing Ship Tank) to take them back to England. Col Chase (center left – holding cigarette) is talking to Capt Leach (regimental S2). (John Reeder)

Members of the 101st Airborne Division disembarking from an LST at a slipway in Southampton, England. (John Klein)

A Distinguished Service Cross award ceremony was held on July 10 at Tollevast near Cherbourg and this picture shows the commander of the US 1st Army, LtGen Omar N. Bradley, pinning a DSC to the chest of Gen Maxwell D. Taylor. (SC)

A band plays as elements of the 101st Airborne Division march through Southampton toward the town's railway station. (John Gibson)

During October 2007 Ed Shames visited Marlborough's Town Hall for the first time since the war's end. On July 15, 1944, the place was decked out with colored parachutes and reverberated to the sound of music and the noise of several hundred paratroopers. As a mark of respect the band stopped playing so that the men could observe a minute's silence in memory of those who had fallen in Normandy.

When in London, newly commissioned 2nd Lt Ed Shames had this picture taken for his girlfriend Ida, who was waiting for him back home in Norfolk, Virginia. (Ed Shames)

FROM TOP TO BOTTOM:

Ed Shames and his friend George Retan stopped on this bridge to assist a young woman in distress. Sadly, 2nd Lt George Retan (inset) was killed during the first day of Operation *Market Garden* in September 1944.

On August 9, 1944, Tom Kennedy married Sheila Thompson in Salisbury, Wiltshire, where he was recovering from wounds received in Normandy (note his walking stick and leg plaster). On their wedding night Col Sink let the happy couple use his personal living quarters at Littlecote House. L to R: Tom Kennedy, Oohna (Sheila's sister), Mrs Thompson, the lady who owned the bed-and-breakfast, with some of Sheila's family, and, on the far right, Sheila Thompson and her father. (Tom Kennedy)

This picture was taken in the graveyard of St Peter's church, Marlborough, probably at the time of the enlisted men's party. Slightly worse for wear are from left, Pvt Earl Widmen, Pvt Harold Stedman, and Pfc Walter "Luke" Lukasavage, all 3 Ptn I Co Normandy survivors. (Harold Stedman)

At 11am on Sunday August 27, 1944, to honor men of the 506th PIR killed in Normandy, a memorial service was held in the grounds of Littlecote Park. The main photograph shows Chaplain Tildon McGee (with Sink and Taylor to his right) giving an address entitled "Our heroic dead." Earlier there had been an organ prelude by Pvt Jack Hayden followed by the hymn "O rest in the Lord" sung by Sgt Donald Harms. Both Hayden and Harms are standing on the far right of the rostrum. Afterwards Capt Salve Matheson (visible between Taylor and Sink) had the unenviable task of reading out a roster of the regiment's 414 dead and missing – to those listening the roster seemed endless. The laying of flowers and a rifle salute concluded the main proceedings, and the inset picture shows the Honor Guard at attention while nine-year-old Patricia Owen lays a bouquet of flowers. (John Reeder via Michel De Trez Collection).

This photograph was taken in October 1945 shortly after Marty Clark (left) and George "Doc" Dwyer had been discharged from the US Army. "We left Fort Benning on October 14 and drove across the country to my home in California," recalls Dwyer. (Bob Webb Jr)

The 3rd Bn reunion held in the Muelbach Hotel, Kansas City, Missouri on Friday June 7, 1946. On the eve of D-Day, during his speech at Exeter, Col Wolverton had suggested that "a year from today a reunion should take place in the center of the USA at Kansas City," although this did not happen until 1946. The reunion's high spot was a memorial service for all the 3rd Bn men who had lost their lives during the war. L to R: (1) Ed Austin (I Co), (2) Forest Troxel (HQ Co), (3) Bob Nash (I Co POW), (4) Ed Shames (Co HQ S3), (5) Oscar Saxvik (G Co), (6) Jim Morrow (HQ Co), (7) Billy Bowen (G Co), (8) Jim Martin (G Co), (9) Vince Michael (G Co), (10) Cecil Hutt (G Co POW), (11) Edward "EE" Lee (HQ Co), (12) George Rosie (HQ Co POW), (13) John Gibson (Med Det POW), (14) Walt Lukasavage (I Co), (15) Charles "Chick" Stewart (HQ Co), (16) Ray Calandrella (HQ Co POW), (17) John Allison (HQ Co), (18) Fred Bahlau (H Co), (19) Audrey Lewallen (HQ Co), (20) Ivan Glancy (HQ Co), (21) Jim Bradley (HQ Co), (22) Miss Helen Briggs (American Red Cross), (23) Mrs Kathleen Wolverton, (24) Sam "Dud" Hefner (H Co), (25) Harold Johnson (I Co), (26) Daniel Seasock (G Co), (27) Robert Harwick (H Co), (28) Dominic Mazzalorso (H Co). (Bob Webb Jr)

Shortly after the war Maxwell Taylor presented Kathleen Wolverton, on behalf of her late husband, with the Legion of Merit. This is awarded for exceptionally outstanding conduct in the performance of meritorious service to the United States. Kathleen Wolverton and her baby son Lachlan (Lock) eventually settled in Charlotte, North Carolina, where she married Fred "Andy" Anderson who had served as a captain in I Co. (SC photo via Mark Bando)

and burst out laughing. I was covered in blood and as I handed her the baby the doctor turned up.

The following morning (July 10) a Distinguished Service Cross (DSC) ceremony took place at the camp. In total 25 people received medals from 1st Army Commander Lt Gen Omar N. Bradley, including four from 3rd Bn 506 – Chaplain John Maloney, 2nd Lt Charles Santarsiero, Cpl George Montilio, and Pfc Andy Sosnak. Because of wounds he had received on June 13, Santarsiero was not present at the ceremony. Many felt that there were other equally deserving candidates who, for whatever reason, had been overlooked.

The ceremony was followed by another presentation, albeit unofficial, where Col Sink gave each battalion of the 506th a barrel of finest quality French cognac "liberated" from Cherbourg. Afterwards the men climbed aboard a convoy of trucks waiting to take them to Utah Beach. Ralph Bennett remembers:

We were still gossiping about the baby when an MP came over and asked if there was a Sgt Bennett present. "He's here," the men shouted, and I clambered to the back of the truck, poking my head over the tailgate. I was surprised to see the Frenchman I'd met the previous evening with the MP. "He wants to call his son after you... what's your Christian name?" Stunned, I stuttered, "Ralph, my name's Ralph." As we drove away I waved frantically with tears streaming down my face until both men were out of view.

Utah Beach

"As we marched toward the embarkation area we passed a column of soldiers coming up from the beach," recalls Bill Galbraith. "Someone spotted Pfc Charles 'Chuck' Abeyta (I Co). Chuck never made the jump because he was in the stockade when we were mobilized for the invasion. We all shouted, "Hello and good luck," and that was the last we ever saw of him." Between July 10 and 13, 101st Airborne Division was gradually shipped back to Southampton aboard a number of tank landing craft.

While they were waiting to leave, and in between endless supplies of coffee and donuts served up by the American Red Cross, Bobbie Rommel and members of his machine-gun platoon decided to check out the beach and found a German minefield. "The area was clearly visible during daylight," remembers Rommel. "The sand was piled on top of each wooden shoe mine. Someone had the crazy idea of removing the explosive and taking it back to England!"

All the landing craft had seen action during the invasion and some showed signs of battle damage, as Bobbie Rommel recounts. "On our LST you could see where a bomb had dropped right through the middle and been patched up. The living quarters ran down both sides of the ship and seemed like luxury to us. We showered, ate, and slept beneath white sheets – it was wonderful." Joe Doughty was even luckier. "The naval embarkation officer who met me and the rest of G Co turned out to be a high school friend of mine. He allowed me to use his own quarters, which really were a cut above the rest."

"There was a lot of talk on the way home about what had happened to our friends and colleagues," remembers Ralph Bennett. "Most of the guys were still very jumpy and any noise got everybody's full attention."

During the crossing, on board Barney Ryan's ship, things started to get a little out of hand, as he recalls:

> The men had been in combat for nearly five weeks, living in foxholes and existing on K-rations with little chance of getting clean. The LST was comparative luxury and men started raiding the refrigerators, looking for the kind of food that they had not had in weeks. Our LST commander threatened to court martial the next person who was caught stealing supplies. One of our officers countered by threatening to throw the "son of a bitch" overboard. The second-in-command of our ship, Louis Auchinchloss, managed to settle the situation down. Later as we stood on the deck talking, he said that he thought his commander was being too rigid and inflexible considering what our men had gone through.

∾ 14 ∾

"Go on, Yank, have a drink"
Return to Ramsbury

Much publicity had surrounded the 101st's actions in France, and local people greeted the division's return with enthusiasm. Robert Webb remembers 3rd Bn returning to Ramsbury in a fleet of buses and that the whole village appeared to turn out to greet them.

In the days that followed, the battalion was restructured and a number of changes made to its table of organization. For example, John Kiley transferred to HQ Co (to lead the S3) and took Bill Galbraith with him as his assistant. H Co still had two first sergeants and this awkward situation was eventually resolved when Fred Bahlau moved to HQ Co and filled the vacancy left by Ed Shames's promotion.

To celebrate the battalion's return from Normandy, two parties had been hastily organized and took place on consecutive evenings in Marlborough Town Hall. The first, for all officers from the regiment, was on Friday July 14, with the following evening reserved exclusively for enlisted men from 3rd Bn. Fueled by the barrel of cognac brought back from Cherbourg, the latter soon spiraled out of control. At that time John Mundy was an 11-year-old schoolboy living in the High Street directly opposite the town hall, and recalls:

> The upper floor of the hall was decked with many parachutes of all colors
> – the parachutes created a false ceiling. The Americans had lost many
> soldiers in France and came back with lots of wine and calvados. At age
> 11, I had never seen so many totally drunk men – I remember how the
> guards at the side door of the Town Hall would try to prop the "pie-
> eyed" soldiers upright against a brick pillar in the wall while waiting for

the next US police jeep to arrive. The police all had white helmets and were called "snowdrops." There was no violence, although the snowdrops were not gentle in "stacking" the soldiers in their jeeps. I am sure I should have been asleep, but my bedroom overlooked the dance hall and it was all too fascinating. I seem to remember that there were a few windows broken that night, but the townspeople let the Americans know that after their experiences in France they should not worry about a few broken panes of glass.

Ed Shames helped organize the event and recalls the clean-up operation:

Some kind of church service was planned for the following day. The hall was in a filthy state with half-empty glasses and bottles lying everywhere. I was trying to figure out where to start when the vicar arrived and asked if he could use the stage. As I pulled back the curtains his face changed from a smile to one of total shock, for there hidden behind the drapes were about a dozen semi-conscious, semi-naked men and women! I shrugged my shoulders and started to laugh, but he was definitely not amused and stormed off in a huff!

After receiving a sizeable amount of back pay, the regiment was given seven days' leave and set off to places all around the United Kingdom. However, because they were waiting to receive their commissions, Ed Shames, M/Sgt Lloyd Wills (Regiment), and S/Sgt George Retan (I Co) had to stay behind. Ed recounts:

We were ordered to report every day to Sink's adjutant, Capt Max Petroff, at Littlecote House. Every time we turned up he told us the same thing, that Gen Bradley (who was going to preside over the ceremony) was still busy in France and we should come back tomorrow. On the morning of the 21st, Petroff gave us a small interim wage payment and told us to take the weekend off. As we had nothing better to do, George Retan and I decided to visit the NAAFI at Ramsbury Airfield.

The two men had been friends since their early days at Toccoa, and were deep in conversation as they crossed the bridge over the River Kennet that led to the airfield. Ed recalls:

> We passed a young girl who was leaning over the rail sobbing her heart out. We hadn't gone far before my conscience got the better of me. "She looks pretty upset, doesn't she?" I remarked to George. "Let's go back and see what's wrong." I asked her if she was OK. Through floods of tears she told us that she had just gone to see her fiancé up on the airfield and found out that he'd been killed.
>
> She was devastated and wanted to go home to her parents. "Where do they live?" we asked. "That's the problem," she replied, "My mum and dad live in Llanelli, South Wales, and I don't have the money to get there." Retan and I looked at each other, shrugged, wished her luck and carried on. "Awhh, we gotta do something, George," I said as we were walking away, "Come on… let's take her home." He agreed and we took her to Hungerford railway station, bought three tickets and escorted her to Wales! Her family appreciated everything we had done for her and offered us a room for the night, but we declined. On advice from the girl's father we headed to the Gower coast, booked into a bed-and-breakfast and spent the rest of the weekend exploring the Mumble hills.

Sixteen-year-old Monica Trim received the terrible news of her fiancé Pfc Martin Collins's death whilst roller-skating with friends in Swindon. She remembers:

> Five or six of the boys from 2 Ptn came over and asked me to sit down by the side of the rink. When they broke the news of Martin's death I went to pieces. I couldn't imagine life without him and at that moment just wanted my mother. When I got home I was in a terrible state and threw my arms around her. I could barely get the words out to tell her what had happened. As she comforted me I began to calm down, and her demeanor changed. I will never forget what she said: "Monica, you have got to forget about this boy and get on with your life – he's gone and you are too young

to let this destroy you." Throughout the intervening years I have come to realize that she was right, but I could never bring myself to forget that wonderful American boy who made such a great impact on me.

A few days later Monica learned more about the circumstances surrounding Martin's death from some of his colleagues: "They thought that he had been shot between the eyes from the second floor of a house by a female sniper on D-Day." Could this possibly be the same incident witnessed by Bob Webb at the lock near St-Hilaire-Petitville? (See page 177).

Meanwhile, the rest of the battalion was making the most of its well-earned leave. Bobbie Rommel recalls:

> I went to London with Harold Stedman, Luke Lukasavage and a couple of other guys. We ended up at this cheap hotel near where all the buzz bombs were falling. I picked up this gorgeous girl and took her out to dinner. Afterwards we went back to my room and spent the night. The following evening I got split up from the boys and decided to get my pants pressed at the USO [United Services Organization] club at Rainbow Corner. Sitting there in my shorts I waited (back pay in hand) with a few other guys. One of these men followed me outside. I turned around thinking he was going to rob me but it was worse than that – the bastard was trying to proposition me!

Jim Morton and Barney Ryan were staying at the Regents Park Hotel in the more upmarket part of the city. Barney recalls:

> This didn't stop us from getting into trouble. One night we were out partying with Col Robert Strayer (2nd Bn 506th) and Maj John Stopka (executive officer of 3rd Bn 502nd) when two Air Corps colonels came over and ordered us to "Keep the noise down." Strayer told them to take off their eagles [metal rank badges worn on caps and collars] and step outside, but Stopka managed to calm the situation before things went any further. The officers decided to leave, and as they walked out one of them

turned and said "Don't think you've heard the last of this, we'll be reporting all of you for disorderly conduct."

Elsewhere in the city things got even more out of hand when Linton Barling became involved in an altercation with John Williams over the shooting of Ben Hiner. Williams was a giant of a man but it did not deter the diminutive Barling from seeking retribution. After nearly two hours of bristling argument he attacked Williams with a hail of blows, breaking his jaw, nose, and several ribs. The injuries were so severe that Williams was unable to make the Holland jump and had to remain in England with the rear echelon.

Although both incidents were reported to Col Sink, Ryan and Morton managed to escape punishment. However, the charges against Barling were far more serious. Luckily several "witnesses" came forward and spoke up on his behalf, telling Sink that Williams had received his injuries whilst trying to break up a fight involving Barling and several Air Force men. Believing the incident to be no more than high spirits, Sink chose not to press charges.

Not everybody went to London. Ralph Bennett headed for Windsor with Chuck Richards, George Montilio, and Mike Eliuk, where he met the girl of his dreams, Miss June Earl from Slough. "There was one small problem... June was already dating Chuck, but it didn't last long," recalls Ralph. "When they split up, I jumped in feet first and asked June out on a date, which changed my life forever. Although we married in 1945, I had to return home without her. It was almost a year before we saw each other again, but my God it was worth the wait."

A similar thing happened to Bill Galbraith in Edinburgh, where he met his future wife Anna Nertney:

We all went to this dance and I got talking to Anna. She agreed to look after my jump jacket while I went to the bathroom. Although there was no drinking allowed in the dance hall, I quickly discovered where most of it was being consumed. Every time I went to the toilet people were saying "Go on, Yank, have a drink," so I kept going back for more!

Toward the end of the evening Anna began to wonder what was wrong with me. As we were leaving she asked if I wanted to spend the night at her house in Shotts (which was only a short train ride away). Of course I leapt at the chance and waved goodbye to the boys. However, it wasn't what I thought it was going to be and I spent the night bunking in with Anna's older brother Owen. The family invited me to stay for the week and we traveled back into Edinburgh every day to meet up with the guys.

I bumped into a sergeant who was a gunner on a B-17 bomber. He promised a ride back to England on his plane when my seven days' leave was up. I knew it could affect my train connections so I called Ramsbury and informed them of my intentions. I was told that if I was late getting back I'd be in big trouble.

Eventually the time came to go home. I waited all day at the airfield for the plane to take off and missed all my train connections. Eventually the pilot turned up and the sergeant asked him if I could fly back with them. The pilot said, "Sure, he can – if he has a 'chute." Of course this was a British airfield and you couldn't borrow anything from the Brits. So I ended up having to catch a train, was very late getting back to Ramsbury and was busted back to private by Capt Kiley as punishment.

Incredibly, despite the terrible injuries Tom Kennedy sustained in Normandy he also managed to tie the knot. Joe Doughty had made a special trip to London to chaperone Tom's fiancée Sheila and her sister to Salisbury, where Tom was in the hospital recuperating. "It wasn't an easy job getting them out of the city," recalls Joe, "mainly due to restrictions imposed because of the flying bombs. We eventually arrived at Parliament Piece, Ramsbury, where we were joined by 'whispering' Cliff Carrier, who was to be Tom's best man." Tom recalls:

I married Sheila at the Catholic church in Salisbury on August 9, 1944. At the time I was on crutches, my front teeth were missing, my jaws were wired together and I weighed just one hundred and seven pounds. Oh yes, I was cross-eyed as well – Sheila was a brave girl to marry me. I was released from hospital in December 1944. Sadly our marriage never worked out and we were divorced in 1950.

Eventually a day was selected for Ed Shames and his two colleagues to receive their long-awaited battlefield commissions. Gen Bradley was just too busy to make the trip to Littlecote, so Col Sink stepped in and the men were presented with their rank bars in the great hall. Ed recalls:

It wasn't quite the grandiose occasion that Regiment had hoped for. But we were pleasantly surprised when each of us was given $500 with which to purchase new uniforms. I managed to cut a deal with one of the military tailors in London and returned to Aldbourne with money in my pocket!

When I got back, Col Strayer told me to go get some lunch at the second battalion officers' mess in the village. The place was packed and the only available seat was next to Jim Nye. I don't know what he was doing there but he made it clear that he didn't want me sitting anywhere near him. I had nothing but contempt for this man and was now in a position to say so to his face. "You don't recognize me, do you?" I remarked. He just ignored me and carried on eating. I got angry and told him he was a worthless son of a bitch who was not a leader but a bully and a damned yellow one at that! The place fell into total silence and everybody looked on as he stormed out of the room. I felt better for what I'd said but secretly wished "Shorty" Madona and the other boys from I Co had been there to hear it.

The incident caused a few problems with Col Strayer, but Ed soon put the matter behind him and started to prepare for the seven days' leave he was still owed. He remembers:

I went to London with George Retan who was now with 1st Bn. As our tube train pulled into Piccadilly Circus underground station and the doors began to open, I could hardly believe my eyes. There, waiting on the platform to board, was Lonnie Gavrock who looked like he'd just come back from vacation! I immediately grabbed hold of his jacket and dragged him off to the toilets, mumbling, "You're dead, you're dead, I was right there... Christ almighty, you're dead." George walked in behind me and said, "What the hell is going on?" Still in a state of shock I began to explain what had happened at Bloody Gully.

Lifting up Lonnie's uniform, we could see his wound had healed beautifully. He told us that the speed of his evacuation had contributed to his survival and he was once again on the active duty roster for I Co. I looked at George and just shook my head in utter amazement.

On his return to Aldbourne, Ed soon realized that Strayer had not forgotten about the Nye incident and was determined to make life as difficult as possible for him. "Strayer found out that I'd been going to Ramsbury when I was off duty to visit 'Shorty' Madona," Ed recalls. "It shouldn't have been a problem but Strayer chose to make it one. He fined me $50 for fraternizing with an enlisted man, and I never forgot or forgave him for that."

By the later part of August 1944, John Gibson had made it back to the familiar surroundings of Ramsbury and it felt good to be amongst friends again. "I soon learned that Herman Bonitz and Ralph Daudt had been killed," he recalls. "Nobody knew what had happened to me and consequently all my things had been divided up [all clothing and personal items not needed for the invasion had been stored at the camp. Unfortunately, those who returned during August and September found that many of their possessions had been looted]. Most of my stuff was returned except my 240lb set of training weights. The Air Force up on the hill stole those and I never saw them again."

At 11am on Sunday August 27, a memorial service took place in the grounds of Littlecote Park to honor the men of the 506th PIR killed in Normandy. An organ prelude and a hymn were followed by an address by Chaplain Tildon McGee, with the title "Our heroic dead." There followed a seemingly endless reading of the roster of the regiment's 414 dead and missing, and the ceremony ended with the laying of flowers and a rifle salute. Nine-year-old Patricia Owen was chosen to lay the flowers. Now Pat Howard, she has vivid memories of the occasion:

My grandmother, Anne Scott West, was working for Sir Ernest Wills as an interim chef. I lived in Uxbridge, Middlesex, with my parents and older brothers, Trevor and Malcolm. On June 22, 1944, our house was badly damaged by a German V1 flying bomb and shortly afterwards Sir Ernest invited us to stay on the estate. We made our new home in one of the old gardeners' cottages and soon became friendly with the "Yanks" when they came back from Normandy. On the morning of the ceremony my brothers and I were playing near the cottage when we heard music coming from the field in front of the manor house. Of course we went over to investigate and were stopped along the way by a young lieutenant carrying a bunch of flowers. He said, "You are just the person we need to carry this bouquet during the ceremony." I refused at first but Trevor and Malcolm convinced me to go along with the idea. The officer took my hand and led us to the reviewing stand, where he asked how the flowers were to be placed. Leaving my brothers behind, we walked around the edge of the field to where the US flag and the regimental colors were positioned. Pointing toward the stand, the same man told me, "When I tell you to go, you are to walk real slow to the middle of the troopers, lay the flowers, then turn and walk slowly back to me." After laying the bouquet and turning as instructed, I was completely unaware that the men were about to fire a salute! I nearly jumped out of my skin when the shots rang out but somehow managed to control the urge to run. It was a day that I shall never forget.

As the weeks passed, more escapees began to drift in. Marty Clark, Joe Mielcarek, Bernie Rainwater, Jim Sheeran, Joe Gorenc, and Doc Dwyer arrived during the early part of September. Joe Gorenc was particularly pleased to reach Ramsbury. About a week before the battalion left the village for the marshaling area, he had got lucky and won $2,000 in a card game. Because of time constraints and cash postal restrictions, he was unable to send his winnings home and was reluctant to take the money into battle. He asked Ed Shames to hide the cash in his room at Hills Stores. Ed did as his friend asked and made sure the money was safe and well hidden. On his return, the first thing Joe Gorenc wanted to do was find Ed Shames and retrieve his cash. Luckily for him Ed still had the money and recalls, "Joe was overjoyed and somewhat relieved that it was all there – something in my mind always told me he would make it back!" Following the war, Joe used the money to start up his own business, but sadly was killed in an industrial accident in 1956.

After leaving hospital, Hank DiCarlo was stunned when the doctors told him he was medically unfit.

I was classed as "ZI" and sent to a "repple depple" [replacement depot] just south of Bristol to await my shipment orders to the USA. One night, during the first week of September, several of us who were in the same predicament broke into the records office. We stole our medical documents and then went AWOL, determined to return to our original units.

When I eventually arrived in Ramsbury the place was empty. The division had been alerted for a jump at the Falaise Gap. The next day when the guys came back to camp we had an emotional reunion and I was saddened to learn of those who'd been killed – Franklin Cato, Martin Collins, Sam Plyer, Ignacy Pobieglo, Howard Porter, Robert Repine, Fred Neill, Leo Lecuyer, and Secundino Alvarez.

I was ordered to see Capt Morgan at the dispensary. He looked at my medical records and gave me a thorough physical examination. Morgan then sealed his recommendations into an envelope and told me to take it to 1st Sgt Bolles. On the way I opened and read the note that said I was to be kept off jump status until further notice! I was absolutely furious and burnt it. "Pop" Bolles, now fully recovered from the wounds he'd received at Bloody Gully, was on duty in the orderly room. He seemed genuinely pleased to see me as I handed him my files. After reading the contents he looked at me and said, "Anything else?" I replied, "No, that's it, sir." "Pop" gave a hint of a smile and said, "OK, go up to the barracks, and welcome back." Then there was a slight pause before he said, "Oh, by the way, we are on standby for another mission. I think it might be Holland."

Epilogue

On September 17, 1944, the 101st Airborne Division parachuted into Holland as part of Operation *Market Garden*. After the liberation of Eindhoven, the regiment was sent north toward Arnhem. 3rd Bn 506th played a pivotal role when a major German attack was thwarted near Opheusden on October 5.

When Field Marshal von Runstedt began his counterattack into the Ardennes Forest, Belgium on December 16, 1944, the 101st, unprepared and underequipped, was rushed to the town of Bastogne. Completely surrounded and with the onset of the worst winter in 50 years, frostbite and hunger became an additional enemy.

By April 1945, with victory in Europe fast approaching, the 506th was sent into the heart of Nazi Germany to capture the Alpine village of Berchtesgaden. Together with the rest of the 101st Airborne Division, the regiment's time in Europe ended on November 30, 1945, when the division was disbanded and its men sent home.

On Friday June 7, 1946, a 3rd Battalion reunion was held at the Muelbach Hotel, Kansas City, Missouri. About 50 veterans from all corners of the United States attended the event, which was organized by Helen Briggs and Kathleen Wolverton.

Several years later, the 506th, minus 3rd Bn (which became the 10th Infantry Battalion), was reactivated and saw action in Vietnam. The 506th is currently on deployment in Iraq and Afghanistan, forming part of the 4th Brigade Combat Team, 101st Airborne Division.

Bibliography

Listed below are works that we have consulted during our research. To their authors we offer our sincere thanks.

Books and papers

Balkoski, Joseph, *Beyond the Beachhead*, Stackpole Books (1999)

Bando, Mark A., *The 101st Airborne at Normandy*, MBI (1994)

Bando, Mark A., *101st Airborne: The Screaming Eagles at Normandy*, MBI (2001)

Burgett, Donald R., *As Eagles Screamed*, Bantam Books (1979)

Day, Roger, *Ramsbury at War*, privately published (2004)

De Trez, Michel, *American Warriors*, D-Day Publishing (1994)

DiCarlo, Hank and Westphal, Alan, *Currahee Scrapbook*, 506 PIR (1945)

Hoyt, Edwin P., *The Invasion Before Normandy*, Robert Hale (1985)

Killblane, Richard and McNiece, Jake, *The Filthy Thirteen*, Casemate (2003)

Koskimaki, George, *D-Day With the Screaming Eagles*, 101st Airborne Division Association (1970)

Laurence, Nicole and Léonard, Michel, *Saint-Côme-du-Mont Témoins d'hier*, Eurocibles (2005)

Marshall, S. L. A., *Night Drop*, Atlantic Monthly Press (1962)

Mehosky, Ivan Paul, *The Story of a Soldier*, Rutledge Books, Inc. (2001)

Nekrassoff, Philippe R., and Eric Brissard, *Magneville Ce Jour Là*, Park Printing, (2000)

Pöppel, Martin, *Heaven & Hell – The War Diary of a German Paratrooper*, Spellmount (2000)

Ramsey, Winston G. (ed.), *D-Day Then and Now*, volumes 1 and 2, Battle of Britain Prints International Ltd (1995)

Rapport, Leonard and Northwood, Arthur Jr, *Rendezvous with Destiny*, Infantry Journal Press (1948)

Ross, Donald C., *He Beat the Odds – WW2 Autobiography*, self-published (2004)

Taylor, Thomas H., *The Simple Sounds of Freedom*, Random House (2002)

Webb, Robert, *Freedom Found*, self-published (2000)

Reports and personal letters

Headquarters 3rd Bn 506th PIR Combat Report for Neptune (1944), *Utah Beach to Cherbourg June 6–27, 1944*, The Historical Division (US Army World War II)

Headquarters VII Corps Exercise *Tiger* Reports, US National Archives

Medical History of Normandy Campaign, 506th PIR Medical Detachment (1944)

Operation *Neptune* – 506th PIR Regimental Journals May 28, 1944 – June 27, 1944 (1944)

Participation of 101st Airborne Divisioni in Exercise *Tiger* (1944), US National Archives

Personal letter of Adrian Saint, c/o Michel Léonard

Personal letters of Gustave and Louise Laurence (to Cecile Judels, 1946), c/o Nicole Laurence

Index